Thanks for your partnership

This book is for you,
compliments of

The

THE BATTLE IS THE LORD'S

Waging Victorious
Spiritual Warfare

THE BATTLE IS THE LORD'S

TONY EVANS

MOODY PRESS
CHICAGO

© 1998 by
ANTHONY T. EVANS

All Scripture quotations, unless indicated, are taken from the *New American Standard Bible,* © 1960, 1962, 1963, 1968, 1971, 1972, 1973, 1975, and 1977 by The Lockman Foundation, and are used by permission.

Scripture quotations marked KJV are taken from the King James Version.

Scripture quotations marked NEB are taken from the *New English Bible* © 1961, 1970 by the Delegates of the Oxford University Press and the Syndics of the Cambridge University Press. Used by permission.

ISBN: 0-8024-3924-1

1 3 5 7 9 10 8 6 4 2

Printed in the United States of America

This book is gratefully dedicated
to
the faculties and staffs of
Carver Bible College
and
Dallas Theological Seminary
for giving me the resources
to wage spiritual warfare and help others do the same

CONTENTS

WITH GRATITUDE

I want to thank the people who helped to make this book possible. They include Greg Thornton, Bill Thrasher, Cheryl Dunlop, and all the staff at Moody Press. And for this, our tenth book together, I want to thank my editor and close friend, Philip Rawley.

INTRODUCTION

There was once a boxer who was being pummeled in the ring by his opponent. Blow after blow by his adversary left him with a bloody nose, swollen eyes, and an enormous amount of pain.

The battered boxer's trainer, trying to encourage his man between rounds, kept telling him, "You're doing great, Fred. That bum is barely touching you."

To which the boxer responded, "Then you better keep your eye on that referee, because somebody is killing me!"

No amount of smooth talk could camouflage the reality of the bloody battle in which this fighter was engaged. Psychologically correct talk and personal encouragement could not mask the pain he was suffering.

In the same way, you and I are engaged in a real battle, one of cosmic proportions. We know we are facing a real opponent because this world bears the bloody, painful scars of this conflict: war among nations, shattered lives, broken homes, suicide, rape, abuse, and immorality of every imaginable kind.

Although it is easy for preachers to tell God's people, "Greater is He who is in you than he who is in the world," and "We are more than conquerors through Christ," these statements often seem to fly in the face of life's day-to-day realities. Myriads of believers are troubled by questions such as, "If God is so strong, why am I so weak?" and "If He gives us victory, why am I losing so many battles?"

It is because we are in a real battle with a real enemy, and because God's people are often frustrated when it comes to waging successful spiritual warfare, that I have written *The Battle Is the Lord's*. This book is my humble attempt to address the subject of spiritual warfare in a comprehensive way. I have sought to confront the issue head-on, dealing with controversial aspects of this subject along the way.

I am certain that in some places my perspective will be different from what you are used to reading. That's why I have put forth so much effort to defend my views biblically.

My thesis in this book is quite simple. Everything visible and physical is the result of something invisible and spiritual. Therefore, only by addressing the invisible, spiritual cause can we fix what is wrong with our visible, physical lives.

The implications of this thesis are tremendous. It means, for instance, that many of the things we are doing to fix our broken and bruised lives are misplaced activities of the flesh which do not properly address the spiritual cause of our problems.

This thesis also suggests that Satan's greatest achievement is not necessarily in the problems he has caused. It is, rather, in the perspective he has duped us into believing —namely, that what we see, hear, taste, touch, and smell is the real deal. But what we detect with our senses is merely the outworking on earth of unseen spiritual activity and conflict in heaven. To miss this is to miss dealing with what is really wrong.

My hope and prayer is that by the time you finish this book, you will have a greater awareness of and sensitivity to the battle we are engaged in with the enemy of our souls. And even more importantly, that you will come to realize and use the spiritual resources our great God has given us to defeat Satan.

It is also my hope that this book will save you some money, because you'll stop spending so much of your money seeking merely physical solutions to spiritual problems. I hope to save you some time too, by starting with the spiritual realm instead of spending all your time on man-made solutions.

Finally, my ultimate goal is to help you see that this battle in which you and I are engaged is first and foremost the Lord's battle, not ours. Only when we see this will we be able to wage victorious spiritual warfare. So let's get started. It's time to go to war!

PART ONE

YOUR AGENDA

1

THE NATURE OF THE BATTLE

Remember that old newsreel that shows President Franklin Roosevelt addressing Congress the day after the Japanese attack on Pearl Harbor in December of 1941?

Calling it "a day that will live in infamy," the president declared that in reality, America was already at war. Roosevelt just needed a declaration of Congress to make it official.

I am not the president, but I have a declaration to make. You and I are at war! In fact, we are engaged right now in the mother of all battles. No war in history can compare with the battle you and I are fighting. It can be either the cause of your greatest joy as a Christian, or of your deepest pain.

The war I am talking about is the spiritual warfare that you became a part of the day you trusted the Lord Jesus Christ as your personal Savior.

This war affects every area of your life. There is no

way you can avoid the conflict. There is no bunker or foxhole you can crawl into that will shield you from the effects of this cosmic battle between the forces of God and the forces of Satan.

A lot of Christians don't even know they're at war. But others can see the results of the battle in their lives, because they have become casualties of spiritual warfare. Some Christians are emotional casualties of spiritual warfare. They are discouraged, depressed, downtrodden, and defeated. Others are marital and family casualties. Divorce, conflict, and abuse are some of the battle scars these believers bear.

Still others have been morally wounded in the battle. They cannot control their passions, or else they make poor moral choices. For some Christians, the wounds have been inflicted on their finances. It's not just a matter of how they use their credit cards. They are losing the financial battle because they are losing the spiritual battle.

I could list more casualties, but you get the idea. Since we are all at war, and since there is so much at stake both here on earth and in eternity, we'd better find out what spiritual warfare is about and how to fight the battle successfully. That's what I want to help you do in this book.

THE ESSENCE OF THE BATTLE

Let me begin by stating the obvious. The essence of the war we are talking about is spiritual.

The reason I need to state this is not so obvious. Because this warfare is first and foremost spiritual and not physical, the degree to which you and I will be successful is the degree to which we are prepared to understand and fight this battle on a spiritual level.

A Definition

Perhaps a definition will help. Spiritual warfare is that conflict being waged in the invisible, spiritual realm that is being manifest in the visible, physical realm.

In other words, spiritual warfare is a battle between invisible, angelic forces that affects you and me. The cause of the war is something you and I can't see. But the effects are very visible in the kinds of problems I mentioned above and in the day-to-day stuff you and I face all the time.

It's hard enough to fight an enemy you can see. It's much harder to fight someone you can't see. In his classic statement on spiritual warfare, Paul wrote: "Our struggle is not against flesh and blood, but against the rulers, against the powers, against the world forces of this darkness, against the spiritual forces of wickedness in the heavenly places" (Ephesians 6:12).

This verse identifies the enemy, Satan and his demons. We'll develop all of this as we go along, but the point I want you to see here is that we make a grand mistake if we think people are the real enemy.

People can be bad, no doubt. But as bad as people can be, they are merely conduits for this greater battle. Satan has been successful in getting us to fight people rather than fighting that which is causing people to be the way they are.

All of us have tried to change people who are not doing right. What we need to understand is that what happens through people, including you and me, has its roots in something much larger. This fact does not excuse the wrong things people do. They are still responsible. But it helps us focus on the real enemy. Let me set down a foundational principle for spiritual warfare: Everything we see in the visible, physical realm is caused, provoked, or at least influenced by something in the invisible, spiritual realm. Your five senses are not the limit of reality.

Daniel 4:26–32 states that heaven rules over all the affairs of earth. So until we address the spiritual causes of a problem, we will never fix the physical effects of that problem.

Not only are your physical senses very limited, but they are often of little help in spiritual warfare. This means that if you are going to wage successful spiritual battle, you need a "sixth sense"—a keen awareness of the spiritual realm. This awareness begins with your worldview.

Two Worldviews

Your worldview is simply the lens through which you perceive reality. It has to do with the presuppositions that determine what you believe and the way you look at life.

There are really only two categories of worldviews. One is a natural or materialistic worldview, what people today call the scientific worldview. This view says that man by his reason can figure out how the world works. People who hold this view seek life's answers in the natural realm. If you can put it in a test tube, examine it under a microscope, or explain it through natural processes, that's all you need.

The naturalistic view is not sufficient because it is limited to the physical realm. Therefore, it doesn't answer the ultimate questions: who you are, where you came from, why you are here. It doesn't answer the question of the first cause, how this universe got started.

The naturalistic worldview also doesn't explain things like why teenagers are killing each other and why the moral standards of mankind are being eroded. This view does not address the invisible part of human beings, the soul and spirit.

This worldview has quite naturally led to agnosticism and atheism. That is, you don't need God as long as you have test tubes, microscopes, and telescopes. The tragedy is that many Christians live as though they hold this view, although they would never admit it. But we are talking about the way people think and behave, not what they say.

I can say loudly, "I believe in God!" But if I don't live as if I believe in God, then people can rightly challenge whether I really do. I just know the right theological terms to use to make everybody else think I believe in God. A person's worldview is demonstrated by his feet, not just his tongue. In other words, his walk has to match his talk.

The second category of worldviews is the spiritual worldview, which says there is a realm outside of the physical. We have to recognize that there are competing spiritual worldviews, just as there are many variations of the naturalistic worldview.

A spiritual worldview is very popular right now, but unfortunately it is often not a biblically based, theistic view that believes in the one true God.

Instead, it is a man-centered view that believes in any form of spirituality that seems to pay off. This is the world of horoscopes, palm readers, and all sorts of New Age teaching. When people pick up their newspapers and turn to their horoscope for the day, they're looking for something outside of this world that will guide their lives and their decision making.

Obviously, this is not the worldview of the Bible. It is possible to have a spiritual worldview that is plugged into the wrong spirit. Your worldview affects your approach to spiritual warfare because it colors the way you see the nonmaterial world—and it determines whether you even believe in a spiritual realm.

In order to understand spiritual warfare, we have to address it through the lens of the spirit, with the help of the Holy Spirit. The worldview of this book is, of course, a spiritual one that assumes the power of the Holy Spirit and the rest of the Godhead. Although we will be spending a lot of time on the role of angels (good and evil) in the spiritual battle, ultimately we are dealing with God.

THE IMPACT OF THE BATTLE

Even though the battle we are talking about is spiritual in nature, it has very definite effects in the visible, physical realm. You know you're in a battle when you get shot and start bleeding. We are seeing the "bleeding," the result, of spiritual warfare in at least four areas of life today.

Personal Impact

Many believers are seeing the wounds of spiritual warfare in their personal lives. This doesn't mean these people are doing something really bad. It could be that they have a problem such as uncontrolled anger.

Our emotions can give the devil an entry into our lives. To see the relationship between your emotions and spiritual warfare, look at several familiar verses in Ephesians: "Therefore, laying aside falsehood, speak truth, each one of you, with his neighbor, for we are members of one another. Be angry, and yet do not sin; do not let the sun go down on your anger, and do not give the devil an opportunity" (4:25–27).

Please notice that failing to control anger grants the devil an opportunity to get a foothold in your life. Then he can use it as a base of operations to launch more spiritual attacks against you.

Many Christians are suffering today because of anger that was not resolved yesterday—and anger is just one of an assortment of human emotions. If Satan can seize our emotions, he can destroy our ability to function by crippling us emotionally or leading us into all manner of destructive and addictive behavior.

We could multiply these examples, but suffice it to say that the personal effect of spiritual warfare is great.

Family Impact

Many believers are also feeling the effects of spiritual warfare in their families. The devil messed up the first family in the Garden of Eden, and we have been dealing with the effects of Adam's and Eve's sin ever since.

Let me give you a specific example of family relationships and spiritual warfare. Paul wrote to husbands and wives in 1 Corinthians 7:5, "Stop depriving one another, except by agreement for a time that you may devote yourselves to prayer, and come together again lest Satan tempt you because of your lack of self-control."

Paul is saying that when a husband and wife don't have a fulfilling sexual relationship, the devil sees that lack as an opportunity to come in and bring about moral destruction in the family. So this thing of spiritual warfare gets right down to the nitty-gritty aspects of everyday life.

Church Impact

Spiritual warfare also has an impact on church life. Paul told Timothy to watch out for "doctrines of demons" that will infiltrate the church (1 Timothy 4:1). The church is being undermined in many places today by teachers who purport to teach the Bible, but are teaching doctrines from hell.

Anyone can quote the Bible. But we need to be like the Bereans, who checked out what Paul and Silas were teaching them to see whether their teachings agreed with the Scriptures (see Acts 17:11). Some people will say amen to things that aren't in the Bible, simply because the person saying them is using the Bible. But the devil will use, or misuse, the Scriptures when it is to his advantage to do so.

Cultural Impact

Finally, spiritual warfare affects the life of a nation, the culture in which we live.

According to passages like Daniel 10, entire nations are influenced by the invisible battle in the angelic realm. Satan is called "the prince of the power of the air" with good reason (Ephesians 2:2).

In other words, you and I are breathing this stuff. It's in every compartment of life. There is no place we can go to escape the effect of spiritual warfare. We need to learn how to fight. Our ability to deal with the spiritual realm will determine whether we win or lose in the physical realm.

Satan's job is to get us to ignore the spiritual realm or give it low value (or look at it inappropriately and worship spiritual beings other than God). If he can divert us from the spiritual realm, he can divert us from finding spiritual solutions.

THE LOCATION OF THE BATTLE

Where in the universe is this great battle called spiritual warfare being fought? Paul tells us it is "in the heavenly places" (Ephesians 6:12), which means the spiritual realm.

The Heavenly Places

In the Bible, the word *heaven* describes three levels of existence (see 2 Corinthians 12:2). The first heaven is the atmosphere that surrounds the earth, the environment in which we live.

The second heaven is what we commonly refer to as outer space, the stellar heavens where the stars and planets exist. This is also a realm in which angels operate, because in the Bible angels are often called stars (Job 38:7).

When you see the stars at night, they should remind you of spiritual beings called angels and the reality of the warfare we are engaged in. I'll have more to say on this in the next chapter.

The third heaven is the throne room of God, the place we normally think of when we hear the word *heaven*. It is about this heaven that the Bible has the most to say. In fact, the third heaven is a very busy place because it is the control center of the universe.

In the book of Ephesians alone, we find numerous references to heavenly places in addition to the reference in 6:12. I want to review these with you, because understanding how to tap into the heavenly places is crucial to waging victorious spiritual warfare.

Ephesians 1:3 says, "Blessed be the God and Father of our Lord Jesus Christ, who has blessed us with every spiritual blessing in the heavenly places in Christ." This verse tells us that God resides in the heavenly places, and so do *all* of our spiritual blessings.

This is important because if you are engaged in a spiritual battle and need help to win, the help you need is with God the Father, who is in the heavenly places. But if you don't know how to get to heavenly places, you won't know how to get to the heavenly help you need to win the battle in earthly places.

You may say, "I'm facing Satan here on earth." Yes, but your blessings are in heaven. So unless you learn how to open your arsenal of spiritual weapons in the heavenly places so you can use them down here, you'll be a casualty of the war.

According to Ephesians 1:20, when God the Father raised Jesus Christ from the dead, He seated His Son "at His right hand in the heavenly places." Not only are the Father and your blessings in heavenly places, Jesus Christ is there too. So if you need Christ's help in earthly places, you'd better know where He is hanging out and how to take a trip there to obtain His help in your warfare.

But it gets even better. God also "raised us up with [Christ], and seated us with Him in the heavenly places" (Ephesians 2:6). Do you get the picture here? You and I as believers are also in heavenly places.

You may say, "Wait a minute, I'm here on earth. I'm in a physical place." But that's the problem. If you only see where you are physically and never understand where you're supposed to be spiritually, you'll never be able to win in spiritual warfare.

Paul is saying that when you accepted Christ, you were transported to another sphere. Even though your body is limited to earth, your spirit that should be controlling your body is operating in a wholly different realm.

Too many Christians don't understand that. The most real part of our existence is what happens in our spiritual lives, not what happens in our bodies. We are residents of heaven, in our spirits now and someday in our bodies too. Once you understand how the heavenly sphere operates, you can begin changing what happens on earth.

What else is in heavenly places? Spiritual rulers and authorities are there, according to Ephesians 3:10. These are angels. This is important from the standpoint of spiritual warfare, because it takes an angel to beat an angel. Remember, Satan and his demons are also "in the heavenly places" (6:12).

See, if your problem originates in the heavenly places, you need a solution that originates in the heavenly places. Most of us have very little consciousness of angels because they're not part of our physical world. But we need to understand that the angels of God and the demons of hell are the "foot soldiers" in the cosmic battle between God and Satan.

When you hear believers say they are being attacked by the devil, they probably mean they are being harassed by his foot soldiers. Satan is a limited being. He is not everywhere present, all-knowing, or all-powerful.

Satan is not God, but he has a whole host of evil angels called demons he can use for spiritual attacks. Anything that hell can bring against you is the result of satanic activity in the same realm in which God operates, called heavenly places.

You and I are no match for the power and deceptiveness of Satan and his army. We need the power of God to neutralize Satan's attacks against us.

If you need divine help but don't have a "heavenly places" mind-set, you won't know how to get the help you need at the time you need it. Since Ephesians says that everything related to our warfare is in the spiritual realm, we need to know how to reach into the heavenly places for help. That's where the action is.

The good news is, you can take a trip to the spiritual realm any time you feel like it—because spiritually, you're already there. You are seated with Christ in heavenly places.

A Spiritual "Capitol Hill"

In Washington, D.C., sits Capitol Hill, where Congress makes decisions about how our country will be run. What is decided there will affect you no matter where you live.

On Capitol Hill two parties are vying for power and control. These two parties have competing philosophies, and the party that is in control sets the basic direction for the country.

"The heavenly places" refers to the Capitol Hill of the universe. It is where decisions are made that affect our lives. There are two opposing parties, the kingdom of God and the kingdom of Satan, each seeking to promote its agenda.

Our party, headed by Jesus Christ, occupies the spiritual "White House," and He has veto power. Satan's party, however, seeks to undermine, sabotage, and destroy those who have aligned themselves with Jesus Christ. At the same time, Satan seeks to keep the members of his party from switching their allegiance to Christ.

Deciding Who Is in Charge

We can be thankful that God has established His throne in heavenly places, because a war is on out there, pitting His kingdom against the kingdom of darkness. The kingdom of darkness has its own king, Satan, and he wants to be in charge of the universe.

When it comes to the universe, there is no question that the kingdom of God and His King, Jesus Christ, are firmly in charge. And Jesus' eternal victory is already assured. But God has allowed us to choose in our individual lives who will be in charge.

Some people have decided for Satan, and they will spend eternity with him in hell. Those of us who have decided for Christ will live eternally with Him. But while we're here on earth, we still need to decide for Christ each day in terms of our spiritual warfare.

That's important because it is possible for children of God's kingdom to live as if they belong to the devil. That's sort of like Republicans or Democrats who look and talk like loyal members of their party, but when they go behind that little curtain in the voting booth, they secretly vote for the other party. And it's the vote that counts, not the look or the talk.

Sometimes, Christians fail to vote for the kingdom of light. The result is that the effect of the kingdom of darkness comes upon them, even though they're part of the kingdom of light.

One evening my wife, Lois, and I were having dinner in the home of one of the associate pastors at our church in Dallas. This pastor is from Nigeria, and the dinner included foods and spices from Africa.

Lois and I wanted to know where we could get these items, so our hosts told us about a store in Dallas that specializes in foods and spices from different cultures, especially Africa and the Caribbean.

In other words, I could go to that store and find a little bit of Africa. Or I could find a little bit of the Caribbean in the food items on the store's shelves. All I had to do to enjoy African or Caribbean cuisine was make my purchase.

That's what God has done. He has stocked earth with heaven, so all you and I have to do to enjoy the benefits of heaven is shop at the right store.

The reason so many believers are messed up is that they have been shopping at the wrong store, picking up goods that don't belong to the kingdom of God. They are shopping in the devil's kingdom and wondering, *Why am I so spiritually weak all the time? Why am I always so defeated in spiritual warfare?*

The devil is smart. He knows how to make the merchandise on his store shelves look inviting. He knows how to make you want to pick up his stuff and buy it, because it looks good. But it's not good for you. It will make you spiritually weak and sick.

THE ENEMY IN THE BATTLE

Revelation 12 depicts a day when the invisible warfare in the heavenly places will break out in a very visible form.

We will consider this passage in more detail later, so I just want to note right now that verse 7 shows us the enemy in this conflict called spiritual warfare: "And there was war in heaven, Michael and his angels waging war with the dragon. And the dragon and his angels waged war."

The archangel Michael and the holy angels are fighting Satan and the angels who rebelled with him. The battle is angelic, but they are fighting over the earth.

So the war in heaven directly affects what is happening on earth. We are in the midst of an angelic conflict, a satanic rebellion, in which Satan is seeking to bring this whole world under his domain. That means when you were born into the kingdom of God, you were born into a war.

You may not want to be born into a war, but you have been. It's like the children who are born in Israel. The moment they come out of their mothers' wombs, they are part of an age-old conflict. Surrounding them are people who consider themselves Israel's enemies, and the battle is on for the land that is claimed both by the Israelis and the Arabs.

The Enemy's Goal

We are surrounded by our spiritual enemy, but the battle is not for land or anything physical. This cosmic battle is for *glory*. The issue is, who is going to get the glory in this universe? Who is going to be worshiped?

Satan said to God, "You cannot have all the glory in creation. I want some of the glory for myself."

God's response was, "My glory I will not give to another" (Isaiah 48:11).

Satan said, "You are going to share glory with me. Let's go to war."

The battle is for glory, for the throne of creation. Praise God the outcome has never been in doubt, but the battle goes on every day in our personal, family, church, and community lives as to who will get the glory by what we do.

That's why Paul told us, "Whatever you do, do all to the glory of God" (1 Corinthians 10:31; see Colossians 3:23). This is the essence of the battle.

The Enemy's Strategy

What is Satan's battle strategy in spiritual warfare? The Bible gives us his basic plan.

The fact that Satan has a plan is very clear. Ephesians 6:11 speaks of Satan's "schemes," and Paul said, "We are not ignorant of his schemes" (2 Corinthians 2:11).

Further on in 2 Corinthians, Paul outlined the schemes of the devil. Speaking to this carnal church, the apostle wrote, "I am afraid, lest as the serpent deceived

Eve by his craftiness, your minds should be led astray from the simplicity and purity of devotion to Christ" (11:3).

Satan's battle strategy is simple. He is out to deceive us, to trick us into buying his lies and temptations. He's been at his plan for countless years, and he's good at it. Paul even said that Satan can disguise himself as an "angel of light" (2 Corinthians 11:14).

Satan has a lot of different schemes to draw on, one of them being the use of false and deceptive teachers, as the passage above speaks about. We'll get into these schemes in future chapters, but this is the bottom line of Satan's strategy: He wants you to think he is right; he wants you to follow him and not God. And not only is Satan good at what he does, he can give you a good time while he is deceiving you.

STRENGTH FOR THE BATTLE

Since I don't know where you are in your Christian life, I don't know where you stand in relation to the reality of spiritual warfare.

You may be one of those believers who didn't realize the Christian life is a war. If so, this chapter, and this book, will be a real eye-opener for you. Or you may be a Christian who knows there's a war on, and you have been feeling the effects of your battle scars. You may have been experiencing defeat at the hands of Satan.

Paul said in Colossians 1:13–15 that everyone who comes to Jesus Christ for salvation is delivered from the domain of the devil. When you received the Lord Jesus as your Savior, God set you free.

You may be wondering, *If God set me free, why am I still in bondage to the devil in my daily life? If I'm on the winning side, why am I losing so often?*

There can be a number of answers to that question, but many believers are suffering defeat in spiritual warfare because they are trying to fight Satan in their own strength.

Our Source of Strength

I have news for you. Satan isn't afraid of you at all! He's not afraid of me either. But he cannot stand up against God for even a second.

That is why Paul wrote, "Be strong in the Lord, and in the strength of His might. Put on the full armor of God, that you may be able to stand firm against the schemes of the devil" (Ephesians 6:10–11). It is when God fights the battle for you, not when *you* fight the battle for you, that you win against the evil one.

Lack of victory in the spiritual battle reflects a lack of understanding of our divine resources. Every Christian has problems, but it's the inability to move beyond the problem, the inability to get past the failure, that keeps us in spiritual defeat. Victory is found in dependence on God, so Satan's plan is to detach us from dependency on God.

Time to Fight

No matter where you are in your Christian walk right now, it is not too late to put on the armor of God, pick up your God-given weapons, and join the battle. It's time that we learn to wage victorious spiritual warfare using divinely provided weapons. Only then will we experience the thrill of victory rather than the agony of defeat.

Let me tell you the benefits of being a soldier. When a nation is at war, the government's first priority is to feed and clothe its soldiers, not its civilians. Soldiers who give themselves to fight can do so knowing that the government they are fighting for is committed to putting clothes on their backs, food in their stomachs, and ammunition in their weapons. Paul asked, "Who at any time serves as a soldier at his own expense?" (1 Corinthians 9:7). Answer: no one. When you enlist in God's army, He picks up the tab.

Our problem today is that we have too many Christian civilians and not enough Christian soldiers. Some of us simply want to jump into a soldier's uniform when we run into a problem, rather than understanding we *are* soldiers who are supposed to be in uniform at all times because we are in a war.

You can take a major step toward victory right now by praying something like this: "Lord, I am facing Satan in these areas of my life [name the areas]. These are the areas where Satan is attacking me and where I am being defeated in my personal life, family life, church life, and life in this culture. I can't beat Satan on my own, so I am going to stand against him in Your name and Your strength, using the resources You have provided."

Remember, the devil isn't afraid of us. Trying to stand against him in our strength is like me telling the heavyweight boxing champion, "I rebuke you in the name of my fist." So what? The champ has nothing to worry about from me. Satan is so strong that even the archangel Michael didn't try to fight him one-on-one. Instead, Michael said, "The Lord rebuke you" (Jude 9).

So when you fight the devil this week, instead of trying to prove how strong you are, tell God how weak you are. Instead of arguing you *can,* tell God you *can't.* Instead of saying, "I know I have the ability," tell God, "I don't have the ability." And then trust the Lord's strength and

His ability as you use His weapons to deal with the enemy in your life.

We are at war, but it's not like other wars. Christ has already won this war! All we have to do is enlist, put on our fatigues and our boots, and pick up our weapons, because it's time to march!

It's time to win some spiritual battles in every aspect of your life. This book was written to help show you how.

2

THE ORIGIN
OF THE BATTLE

Despite the occasional outbursts of terrorist bomb-ings in Israel, I can honestly say I never felt safer than when I was in the Holy Land. The Israelis live with the realization that they are in a constant state of con-flict. War could break out any day, even though everyone is talking about peace. Because the people of Israel live with the ever-present reality of conflict, everything they do takes that fact into consideration. So the Israeli gov-ernment goes to great lengths when it comes to protect-ing visitors.

I found out after our flight to Israel that there were two plainclothes Israeli security men on the plane, ready to deal with anyone who would try to disrupt our safe travel. When we got to Israel, two people asked us almost fifteen minutes' worth of questions about our luggage. Officials checked some of our bags.

One of them said, "I'm sorry to detain you, but over here we don't take chances. Your safety is our greatest consideration, and your enjoyment is our greatest desire."

On the streets of Israel, civilians are practically surrounded by Israeli soldiers and various security people. We were told that Israel doesn't have a high crime rate, and I can see why. The nation lives in a constant state of military readiness because its leaders understand that they are living on a battleground.

Even with this readiness, Israel still suffers some casualties. But imagine how the Israelis would suffer if they let down and started living as if they didn't have an enemy in the world.

Do you see where I'm going? The reason there are so many casualties among believers in spiritual warfare is that we have lost sight of the fact that we are in a perpetual state of warfare, which demands constant alertness.

There is another world, another dimension that sits outside our five senses, but that is equally real. It is the spiritual realm, and there is a conflict under way in this realm in which we are engaged.

But because so many Christians have been kept ignorant of this conflict for so long, they think people are their only problem. The Word of God teaches that what's really going on in our lives, families, churches, and the world at large is a battle that sits outside time and space, but that determines what happens in time and space. It is a spiritual battle.

In this opening section I want to fix the reality of spiritual warfare in your mind. We saw the nature of the battle, and now I want to talk about the origin of this global conflict. No one passage in the Bible puts this all together, so we need to look at several major passages that tell us how this warfare came about.

We don't have all the data on the origin of this warfare, but we have enough to give us the picture of what happened and why. If we can grasp and react properly to all that the Bible teaches us about this subject, we will be alert and prepared, and we will experience a greater sense of security and peace.

To understand the origin of spiritual warfare we have to go far back before time, into eternity past, when God created a body of beings called angels. He created them like Himself, in that they are spirit beings and God is spirit (John 4:24).

We know that angels are magnificent beings from their appearances in Scripture. When a person saw an angel, he or she was usually overcome and fell to the ground. Angels are beings of great light, just as God's manifestations of Himself in the Bible are often accompanied by a bright light (see Acts 9). All the angels are awesome creatures, but one angel in particular was glorious.

When God created this new order of beings to worship and adore and magnify Him, He decided to create one as a special masterpiece—Lucifer, the "brilliant" or "shining one" or "star of the morning." We are introduced to Lucifer in Ezekiel 28, one of the two key passages I want to cover in this chapter.

We need to start here because the conflict we are talking about originated in the angelic realm before the creation described in Genesis 1. Spiritual warfare began with Lucifer's rebellion against God in heaven. We'll deal with the connection between Ezekiel 28 and Genesis 1 below.

THE CAUSE OF SATAN'S REBELLION

In Ezekiel 28:1–10, we are told of the king of Tyre, a human ruler who came under God's judgment because his heart was swelled with pride. He even tried to make himself like God.

Then in verse 12, we are introduced to the power behind this rebellious and prideful king. It was Lucifer himself, this great being who came to be called Satan, the devil, Beelzebub, the accuser of the brethren, and so many other names and titles. Lucifer was the spiritual power influencing the king of Tyre, because, as we will see, a spiritual power always influences earthly actions because all around us rages a spiritual battle.

Lucifer's Perfections

So Ezekiel 28:12 begins a description of Lucifer before his rebellion against God. By understanding Lucifer before his rebellion, we'll have a better understanding of why he rebelled. Seeing what Lucifer was like will give us some insight into why he did what he did. Let's look at this description:

> You had the seal of perfection, full of wisdom and perfect in beauty. You were in Eden, the garden of God; every precious stone was your covering: the ruby, the topaz, and the diamond; the beryl, the onyx, and the jasper; the lapis lazuli, the turquoise, and the emerald; and the gold, the workmanship of your settings and sockets, was in you. On the day that you were created they were prepared. (Ezekiel 28:12–13)

This creature shone like the brilliance of the noonday sun. He didn't have to buy diamonds to wear. He *was* a diamond. He was covered with every kind of precious stone. Lucifer was God's master creation. He was glorious and perfect in every detail. And he could sing! The Hebrew word *sockets* in verse 13 could be translated "pipes." Lucifer didn't just play the organ, he *was* the organ. When he opened his mouth to sing, he sounded like a million-dollar organ. And why not? After all, he was created to lead all the other angels in the praise of God. So Lucifer was blameless, flawless, a masterpiece.

Lucifer's Exalted Place

Notice also that Lucifer occupied the most exalted place of all God's created beings. He was "in Eden, the garden of God." Verse 14 says, "You were on the holy mountain of God; you walked in the midst of the stones of fire."

Lucifer was near God's throne; he walked in God's holy presence. His access to God was awesome, greater than that of any of the other angels.

Lucifer's Lofty Position

Notice Lucifer's "job title": "the anointed cherub who covers" (v. 14). The cherubs, or cherubim, are the honor guard of the angels, the angels who have the responsibility to proclaim and protect the glory of God. They are the highest rank in God's hierarchy of angels.

Lucifer was at the top of the list. He was the highest-ranking cherub. He was the leader. He occupied the highest possible position that God could give to one of His creatures.

Lucifer's Terrible Pride

He had all of this, but then came that terrible day when, like the queen in the children's fairy tale, Lucifer stood for too long in front of a mirror.

Watch it when you stand in front of a mirror for too long, because the mirror has a way of reflecting your own glory back to you!

As Lucifer stood observing himself, he said, "Lucifer,

you're *bad*. Look at that jasper. Look at these diamonds. You don't have to be number two up here. Look at all your glory. You don't have to lead the other angels in worshiping God. You deserve some of that worship yourself."

We will consider the specific content of Lucifer's rebellion when we turn to Isaiah 14. Ezekiel 28:15–17 tells us that Lucifer lost his perfections, his place, and his position because "unrighteousness was found in [him]" (v. 15). "Your heart was lifted up because of your beauty" (v. 17).

Lucifer's great perversion was that he took the gifts of God and made them an end in themselves. He was lifted up with the greatest of all sins, the sin of pride. He rebelled against God because he forgot something.

It's mentioned several times in Ezekiel 28: "On the day that you were created" (v. 13); "From the day you were created" (v. 15). Lucifer forgot he was a creature. He forgot that his diamonds didn't show up by themselves. He forgot that his position as the anointed cherub didn't come because he woke up one day feeling "cherubic."

Lucifer forgot that the only reason he was so beautiful was that God created him that way. Lucifer stared into the mirror too long. Are you ever tempted to do that? Ever tempted to say, "Look at the business I have built," "Look at the clothes I am wearing"? The devil is still playing the pride game, and he's still conning humans into playing it with him.

Lucifer became awestruck with himself. He was like the woodpecker who was pecking away on a big tree. All of a sudden, lightning shot down from the sky and split the tree in half. The woodpecker flew away saying, "Look at what I did."

The angel who became Satan began to worship himself and wanted the rest of creation to worship him.

That's what makes pride such a terrible sin. Pride is self-worship. It is not just feeling good about ourselves. Pride makes us feel independent of God, so that we don't think we need Him. We think we are who we are because of what we have done.

So Lucifer looked in the mirror and said, "You're it. You don't have to take second place any longer." He forgot his creatureliness.

Lucifer's Diabolical Plan

When this shining angel chose to act on his pride, he began a plan of rebellion, a *coup d'etat,* against the throne of God.

Lucifer went to the angels and offered them the option of following him. He did this "by the abundance of [his] trade" (Ezekiel 28:16). What was his trade? His marketing effort among the angelic hosts.

Lucifer marketed himself, and one-third of the angels in heaven bought his plan (see Revelation 12:4). One-third of the angels went with Satan and said, "Yes, you're right, we don't need God anymore."

Lucifer led a revolt of angels, but he failed because he found out that glory belongs to God alone. God says in Isaiah 42:8, "I am the Lord, that is My name; I will not give My glory to another."

The punishment Lucifer received is recorded briefly here in Ezekiel 28. He was thrown out of heaven and cast "to the ground" (vv. 16–17).

We'll deal with the curse Lucifer received in the next section, so I just want to note here that Lucifer and his hosts were thrown down to the earth. They were evicted from heaven because God will not have any challengers to His authority.

We will meet this one who became Satan in the

Garden of Eden, where he was apparently on hand when Adam and Eve were created. Satan's pride was the cause of his rebellion, and his judgment was its culmination. He was no longer Lucifer, the shining one.

THE CONTENT OF SATAN'S REBELLION

To understand the content of Satan's rebellion, the details of his plan, we need to look at Isaiah 14. We might describe the nature of the devil's rebellion as negative volition. That is, Satan made some very bad decisions in his will.

We stop here and remember that God created the angels with volition, or the ability to choose. God did not mandate their loyalty and their obedience as if they were robots, just as He did not make us robots.

Satan had a will, and according to Isaiah 14, he exercised it five times when he said, "I will."

Isaiah 14 begins with God's pronouncement of judgment against a human king, in this case the king of Babylon (vv. 4–11). Then in verse 12 we read this statement: "How you have fallen from heaven, O star of the morning, son of the dawn! You have been cut down to the earth, you who have weakened the nations!"

This can be no one but the angel formerly known as Lucifer.

Why did God cut Satan down to the earth? God answers that in Isaiah 14:13–14. Satan reared up in rebellion and tried to tell God how things were going to be. Let's examine Satan's five volitional statements one at a time.

"I Will Ascend to Heaven"

"But you said in your heart, 'I will ascend to heaven'" (v. 13a). Satan didn't mean he wanted to take a tour of heaven. He already had access to the highest spot in heaven, the throne of God. He was already walking among the "stones of fire" (Ezekiel 28:14). He was already on the mountain of God.

Satan was not talking about a visit to heaven, but a takeover. In other words, he wanted to ascend to heaven with a view to occupying God's throne.

"I Will Raise My Throne"

Satan's hostile intentions are obvious from his second boast: "I will raise my throne above the stars of God" (Isaiah 14:13b). Job 38:7 says the stars refer to angels. Satan wanted to rule over all the angels. You may say, "Wait a minute. Wasn't Satan already in charge of the angels?" Yes, he was the number one cherub, the highest-ranking angel in heaven.

But Satan wasn't in charge the way God was in charge. Lucifer was saying, "Being the top angel isn't what I want. Every time I go down to the other angels, I have to tell them what God wants me to tell them. Every time I lead the angels in worship, I have to lead them to Him. Every time I hook up with the angels, the subject of our meeting is how great God is and why He deserves all the majesty and glory and worship.

"I'm tired of being the middle man between God and the angels. What I want to do is sit on the throne, give the orders, and accept some worship and glory."

Satan wanted the angels discussing *him* in their committee meetings. He wanted them figuring out how to serve him and make him look better. And he didn't want to answer to God anymore.

"I Will Sit on the Mount"

Satan's third boast was, "I will sit on the mount of assembly in the recesses of the north" (v. 13c). The Bible says that this mountain is the center of God's kingdom rule, where He controls the affairs of the universe (Psalm 48:2; Isaiah 2:2).

Satan didn't want to pray, "Thy kingdom come, Thy will be done," but, "My kingdom come, my will be done." He wanted to be managing the kingdom.

"I Will Ascend Above the Clouds"

Then Satan said, "I will ascend above the heights of the clouds" (Isaiah 14:14a). He was not talking about ascending above the clouds you see as you fly in an airplane. Many people have ascended above the clouds in airplanes. There's more to this boast than that.

The Bible associates clouds with the glory of God (Exodus 16:10; 40:34). His glory often appeared as a cloud. So the clouds are those things through which the glory of God is manifested.

Satan wanted glory. He wanted praise. He tempted Jesus by showing Him the kingdoms of the world and saying, "All these things will I give You, if You fall down and worship me" (Matthew 4:9). Satan wanted to be worshiped.

That's why Satan cannot hang out when we are worshiping God. He can't stand it because we are giving to God that which he so desperately wants for himself. Not only that, but when we worship God it reminds Satan of what he used to do.

Worshiping God is Satan's old job description. He used to bring God glory. But then Satan tried to share what can't be shared. He wanted to divide something that is indivisible, the glory of God.

God lives for His glory, for the demonstration of His greatness. Glory means to "show off, to advertise, to put on display." God is consumed with His glory because there is no one else like Him in the universe.

The reason you and I can't get stuck on ourselves is that there is always somebody better than us, prettier than us, smarter than us, better at business than us. But God is by Himself. There is no one like Him, nor will there ever be anyone like Him. So He will share His glory with none of His creatures.

"I Will Be Like the Most High"

Here is Satan's fifth and last rebellious claim: "I will make myself like the Most High" (Isaiah 14:14b).

This is really the statement of a fool. Here is Satan, creature that he is, looking up at the all-knowing, all-powerful, all-present God and saying, "I'm going to be like Him."

For Satan to be like God would mean there would be two Gods. But that isn't going to happen. God says, "Before Me there was no God formed, and there will be none after Me" (Isaiah 43:10).

"Thus says the Lord, the King of Israel and his Redeemer, the Lord of hosts: 'I am the first and I am the last, and there is no God besides Me'" (Isaiah 44:6). "I am the Lord, and there is no other; besides Me there is no God" (Isaiah 45:5). Not a lot of room for God-making here. God cannot replicate Himself.

When Satan said he was going to become like God, he was saying he envied the independence God has. God is totally independent. He is answerable to no one outside of Himself. And God is all-knowing. Satan tempted Eve by saying that if she ate the fruit, she would have knowledge like God's (Genesis 3:5).

This idea of being like God was Satan's sin, and it was hideous. One reason it was so hideous is that he wasn't tempted to do this by anyone else. There was nobody around to tempt him. He came up with this plan all on his own.

You and I can say somebody tempted us. That doesn't exonerate us, but at least we didn't come up with the sins we commit all on our own. But Satan had no outside pressure. He wasn't fighting a spiritual battle against a clever enemy. He rebelled on his own.

You may wonder why God allowed Satan to rebel against Him and live to tell about it. Why didn't God crush him like a roach?

We'll get into this in detail below, so let me just say here that one reason God permitted Satan's rebellion was to show the angels and us that when we don't live life His way, it doesn't work. Satan was determined to do it his way, and God let him do it his way. But the devil and his angelic and human followers will spend all eternity being reminded that rebellion against God cannot work.

THE CURSE OF SATAN'S REBELLION

God permitted Satan to carry out his rebellion, but He took control of the results. Satan raised himself up against God, but God slammed him to the ground. Satan learned that although he could control his decision, he couldn't control its consequences. We need to learn that too. You may do your thing, but after you do your thing God takes over. He controls the consequences.

Let me put it another way. As Satan learned, even when you sin, you sin according to God's rules, not yours. Satan would come to understand that he was not just the devil, he was the devil under God's absolute control.

The Devil's Immediate Sentence

Both Ezekiel 28 and Isaiah 14 address the judgment God carried out against His anointed cherub when Satan corrupted his character and sinned against God. Let's go back to Ezekiel 28. When "unrighteousness was found" in Satan (v. 15), God expelled him from "the mountain of God" and took away his place amid "the stones of fire" (v. 16). "I cast you to the ground," God told him (v. 17).

We know that the mountain of God has to do with His throne, the place from which He rules. So Satan lost his privileged place near God's throne. He still has access to God's presence, as Job 1 reveals. But now he can only come to God as a "visitor." Satan has no place in heaven anymore.

The devil lost his position as the "covering cherub" (Ezekiel 28:16). The stones of fire are the angels. Satan was removed from his exalted role as head of the angels.

He was also cast down to the ground, which Isaiah 14:12 tells us is the earth. Satan fell from heaven to earth, and he did not suffer his punishment happily. Revelation 12:12 warns those who dwell on the earth that Satan has come down with great anger, because he knows his time is short.

The Devil's Eternal Sentence

Isaiah 14:15 refers to Satan's ultimate sentence. "You will be thrust down to Sheol, to the recesses of the pit." Satan's eternal destiny is eternal fire.

Jesus stated this explicitly in Matthew 25:41. Speaking of His judgment on the Gentile nations at the end of the Tribulation, Jesus said He will pronounce this sentence to those on His left hand: "Depart from Me,

accursed ones, into the eternal fire which has been prepared for the devil and his angels."

The devil's final judgment will be executed at the
end of the millennial kingdom. "And the devil who deceived them was thrown into the lake of fire and
brimstone, where the beast and the false prophet are
also; and they will be tormented day and night forever
and ever" (Revelation 20:10).

When Satan is thrown into the boiling cauldron
called the lake of fire, the place of eternal torment, all of
those people who adopted Satan as their god will get to
live with their god forever. Hell was never made for human beings. It was created for Satan and the one-third
of God's angels who rebelled with him. But many people will go there because Satan is the god they wanted.

Satan was decisively and eternally judged for his sin.
The final portion of his sentence has not yet been carried
out, so right now he has access to the earth and he retains
some of his influence. This is crucial to our understanding
of spiritual warfare, because he is now our sworn enemy.

THE CONNECTION BETWEEN
SATAN'S REBELLION AND SPIRITUAL WARFARE

What we have been talking about in this chapter is
foundational to the reality known as spiritual warfare.

This is such an important point that I want to take a
few pages to show you how Satan's rebellion and his
curse are related to the cosmic conflict in which we are
engaged. How does all of this we have just covered tie in
with our warfare?

A Demonstration of God's Glory

The first thing we need to understand is that when
God permitted Satan's sin, and then judged him and his

rebellious angels, He did more than just pronounce their curse. He decided in His eternal wisdom to demonstrate something very important to these rebellious heavenly creatures.

See, Satan attacked God's very throne and trifled with His glory. So God said to Satan, "I am going to show you something. I am going to demonstrate to you and to the angelic world My power and glory. I am going to unfold before your eyes a plan that will demonstrate I am not to be trifled with."

So Satan was expelled from heaven and demoted to the earthly realm. That's the situation when we come to Genesis 1 and the beginning of creation. This is where things get interesting, because this is where spiritual warfare really began.

Notice the familiar statement in Genesis 1:2 that "the earth was formless and void, and darkness was over the surface of the deep." To put it another way, earth was a garbage dump, a wasteland. Everything was sort of floating together in a formless mass. It was a swamp. Later God had to separate the water from the dry land.

How did the earth become that way? It likely happened when Satan was thrown out of heaven and down to the earth. Whatever Satan takes over becomes a garbage dump, including our lives.

Some Bible teachers and theologians believe that Satan's rebellion and judgment occurred between Genesis 1:1 and 1:2, so that God's perfect creation became fouled when Satan fell. I believe Satan's fall happened before Genesis 1:1, somewhere in eternity past. But here is when he was thrown down to the earth.

Either way, the earth became a place of judgment because it became the holding cell for Satan and his angels until such time as their sentence is to be carried out.

The point is that wherever Satan resides, wherever he's in control, he creates chaos and garbage. That's why when Adam and Eve yielded to Satan, they were kicked out of Eden and the earth became a weed-filled wilderness.

Satan and his demons, the fallen angels, were limited to earth and its atmosphere as their primary realm of operation. They are still spirit beings, so they have access to the spiritual world. But their primary sphere of operation is earth.

So God decided to fix the wasteland called earth to demonstrate something very important to Satan and his demons and to the angels in heaven. Therefore, "The Spirit of God was moving over the surface of the waters" (Genesis 1:2).

God began to bring order out of the chaos. He created light to counter the darkness. He separated the waters from the dry land and began to dress the earth and fill it and the sea with all kinds of creatures.

Now let me show you what happened when God began to create. In Job 38:4–7, God asks Job where he was when God created the earth. God says when the angels saw His creative power, they "sang together" (v. 7).

Here were the angels of heaven, perhaps thousands of years after the fall of Satan had taken place. They saw light come to the dark earth, and they rejoiced. God was going to do something. What was He going to do?

God was going to make a creature of lesser stature than the angels to demonstrate to all the universe that even though this creature did not have angelic ability, angelic power, or angelic experience, if this lesser creature would trust and obey God, he would go farther than an angel in heaven who refused to trust God.

Here then is the connection between Satan's rebellion and spiritual warfare. That lesser creature was mankind

—you and me. God was saying to Satan, "I can take a creature of less beauty and ability than you, but who trusts Me, and I will do more with this weaker creature than you can do with all of your power."

In Psalm 8, David looked into the sky and was overwhelmed with the thought of God. He wrote:

> When I consider Thy heavens, the work of Thy fingers, the moon and the stars, which Thou hast ordained; what is man, that Thou dost take thought of him? And the son of man, that Thou dost care for him? Yet Thou hast made him a little lower than God, and dost crown him with glory and majesty! Thou dost make him to rule over the works of Thy hands; Thou hast put all things under his feet. (vv. 3–6)

Verse 5 can also be translated, "Thou hast made him a little lower than the angels," and that's the translation and interpretation I believe is called for in the context.

This is just like God. He came down to Satan's domain and said, "This earth is a wasteland. Let Me put My creative handiwork in it." God began to create, and all of a sudden the earth was filled with light and life.

Then, with Satan listening, God said, "Let Us make man in Our image" (Genesis 1:26)—just as He had made Lucifer and the angels in His image in that they were spirit beings. And God announced to Satan, "I am going to put man in charge of your house. He will have dominion over the earth, and rule over the birds of the air and the fish of the sea."

That explains why the serpent came to Eve and tempted her to doubt God. Satan wanted his planet back. Adam and Eve gave it back to him by their sin. And guess what God is in the process of doing today through His people? He is taking this planet back from Satan.

This is His plan, to display His power and glory to the angels of heaven and to Satan and the demons of hell.

A Demonstration of God's Justice

Let me give you a few more reasons that God permitted Satan to rebel and then judged him. God wanted to show His hatred of sin and His justice. He wants us to see through all of this that He is a holy and perfect God who judges sin.

God also wanted to reveal His wisdom. Paul said that God does what He does so that His "manifold wisdom" might be made known to the rulers and authorities in heaven (Ephesians 3:10). God wanted the angels to see the infinite wisdom of His plan of redemption.

A Demonstration of God's Grace

Here's another key to God's plan. Satan and the angels who followed him spurned God's goodness and grace. So God wanted to show them the glory of His grace when it is received by repentant sinners. God permitted sin in order that His grace might be shown to be greater (see Romans 5:20).

But this display of God's grace did something more. It allowed God to express His love while satisfying His demand for justice at the same time.

God can't just skip sin. Yet God loves us. How can He satisfy His justice that must deal with sin and also satisfy His love?

God did so by putting our sins on Jesus and punishing Him, thereby satisfying His holiness that demands that sin be paid for. Christ's death freed God to show His loving and forgiving grace to sinners who come to Him, confess their sins, and receive Jesus as Savior. This is the manifold wisdom of God.

A Demonstration of Hope

God also permitted sin to demonstrate that there is no meaning or hope in life apart from Him. He permitted Satan and us to have the ability to choose so that He could secure our obedience and service out of love, not out of fear.

God doesn't want people to love and serve Him because they are afraid He is going to lower the boom on them if they don't.

What God did in creation was to parallel man's situation with that of Satan. Satan was created a perfect being with a free will and the ability to choose. Adam was created a perfect being with a free will and the ability to choose.

Lucifer's homestead was called Eden (Ezekiel 28:13). Adam's homestead was called Eden. Lucifer was to oversee all of God's angelic creation; Adam was to oversee all of God's human creation. Lucifer had direct access to God in heaven; Adam had direct access to God when they walked together in the garden.

Mankind would parallel Satan and his angels in another way. The Bible says there are two classes of angels: elect angels and fallen angels. There will be two classifications of mankind: saved and unsaved, elect and fallen.

This is spiritual warfare. God created mankind to rule the earth. Satan came to Adam and Eve to take it back. That's why God had to become a man in the person of Jesus Christ, because a man had to take the earth back from Satan.

What we are experiencing on earth in terms of spiritual warfare has to do with something that is much bigger than we are.

THE CORRECTION OF SATAN'S REBELLION

This may seem like an unusual heading, because Satan's rebellion cannot be undone.

The Bible is clear that when he and the other angels sinned, their eternal doom was fixed. The death of Christ was for fallen human beings, not for angels (see Hebrews 2:16). The activity of Satan in the book of Revelation also shows that he will be the sworn enemy of God until his final doom is carried out.

But the effects of Satan's rebellion can be corrected in our lives if we will learn several important lessons that I want to leave you with in this chapter. These are also critical principles that will help you be successful in your spiritual warfare.

Guard God's Glory

If you want to correct the effects of Satan's rebellion in your life, you must learn that God will go to enormous lengths to guard and preserve His glory. God will spare nothing to preserve His glory.

If you try to interfere with God's glory, if you try to take from God that which belongs to Him alone, you are in trouble. A lot of people in the Bible had to learn that lesson the hard way.

Just ask King Nebuchadnezzar of Babylon (Daniel 4:28–37). If old Nebby were here, he would tell you, "Don't ever do what I did, standing on my balcony talking about 'Look at this great Babylon that I have built.'

"Don't ever do that because my nails started to grow, and hair started growing out all over me. I crawled like an animal for seven years, but I learned my lesson. When I got my sanity back, I let it be known that there's only one God in the universe. So let me tell you, God will bring you down to the dirt on your face, if He has to, to teach you this lesson."

This is why the serpent who tempted Eve was sentenced to crawl on his belly (Genesis 3:14). The serpent was used by Satan to steal the glory of God in the lives of Adam and Eve. And when you steal the glory of God, God will put you on your face. You'll be crawling in the dust until you give Him back His glory.

Ask King Herod Agrippa I (Acts 12:20–23). Herod took the podium to speak, and the people said, "The voice of a god and not of a man!" (v. 22).

Herod liked that. He said, "Yes, I am a god." But he was immediately eaten by worms and died because he did not give God the glory. There is no room in the universe for two Gods.

Humble Yourself Before God

The Bible tells us to humble ourselves before God (James 4:10; 1 Peter 5:6).

Let me clarify here. Humbling yourself does not mean that you go around saying, "Poor me, I'm nothing. I'm never going to be anything." That's not true humility. True humility is measuring yourself against the right standard and knowing where you stand in relation to that standard.

A little boy came to his father one day and said, "Dad, I measured myself, and I'm eight feet, four inches tall."

His father said, "Son, you know you're not eight feet tall."

"Yes, I am," the boy replied. "I measured myself, and I'm more than eight rulers tall." The father went to see what the boy was measuring himself with and discovered it was a six-inch ruler. You can always get taller if you're using the wrong gauge.

A lot of us think more of ourselves than we ought to think because we're measuring ourselves against the wrong people. We're comparing ourselves with each other instead of with God. We need to measure ourselves against the right standard. Sin is falling short of the standard, which the Bible says is the "glory of God" (Romans 3:23).

Pride was Satan's sin, and it will bring us down quickly. Pride is like a man's beard. It grows all the time, and you have to trim it every day.

The story is told of two brothers. One grew up to become a big-time professional man, and the other became a farmer.

The first brother was "Mr. Big Stuff." Nobody could tell him anything. One day he visited his brother on the farm and said, "Brother, when are you going to make something of yourself? When are you going to get a name?"

The farmer looked at him and said, "Do you see those stalks of wheat over there in my field? There is something interesting about that wheat. The stalks that are standing straight up have nothing in their heads. The ones that have something in their heads are bowing down to the ground."

Satan tried to become "Mr. Big Stuff" in the universe. He tried to stand up against God, but God laid him low. The people who know who they are and who God is lay themselves low before Him.

3

THE EXPANSION OF THE BATTLE

If you are being called to fight in a war, with all of the risks and sacrifice that warfare entails, you want to know what it is you're fighting for. You want to know if the cause is worth the cost.

You and I *have* been called to war. We're already at war, in fact. And what I want you to see in this chapter, and throughout the book, is that the cause for which we have been sent into battle is the greatest cause in the universe. We are part of a great, cosmic conflict to demonstrate and vindicate the infinite holiness and goodness of God and to bring Him glory.

As we saw in the previous chapter, Satan launched a direct attack on the throne and the person of God. So God judged Satan and evicted him from his heavenly position.

But rather than just annihilate Satan, God decided to make him a spectacle before the entire universe. God wanted the angels and all of creation to see His wisdom and power in action.

God set His plan in motion when He created Adam and Eve and told them to rule over the earth. Satan had already been cast down to the earth, so the earth was now enemy territory as far as God was concerned. But God invaded Satan's territory by placing mankind on earth. Up to this point, the battle had been confined to the heavenly realm. Up to this point, the participants were all spirit beings.

But when Adam and Eve showed up, the battle expanded to the earth. And the list of combatants expanded to include the human race. This all happened in Genesis 3, in which we find Satan's plan to take his territory back.

THE BATTLE LINES

But before we consider Genesis 3, which is so crucial to our understanding of spiritual warfare, we need to back up just a bit and set the stage for Satan's attack against our first parents.

You'll remember that one facet of Lucifer's creation was his volition, or freedom of choice. God created all the angels with the ability to choose because He wants His creatures to serve Him out of love, not out of necessity. Lucifer made his choice and became the devil.

God also created man and woman with the power of choice, for the same reason. Adam and Eve had the ability to choose whether they would love and obey God or disobey Him. To make their choice real and not just potential, God planted some trees in Eden.

According to Genesis 2:9, God filled Eden with every kind of tree imaginable for Adam's enjoyment and for food. In the middle of the garden God planted two particular trees, the Tree of Life and the Tree of Knowledge of Good and Evil.

Genesis 2:16–17 records God's instructions regarding the forbidden tree. If Adam ate from it, he would "surely die." The Hebrew text is very strong. No question about it.

What God was doing was re-creating the conditions of the original spiritual battle in heaven. That is, He placed His perfect creatures, Adam and Eve, in a perfect environment, with everything they could ever want. We know they were perfect because Genesis 2:25 says they were completely unashamed at their nakedness. They had no reason to be ashamed.

The point is that God now had a creature through whom He would demonstrate His power and His saving grace. But in order for God's grace to be made manifest, mankind had to have the power of choice. And in order for God to demonstrate His infinitely superior power, mankind had to be included in this angelic conflict called spiritual warfare.

This brings us to Genesis 3. Here was God's innocent couple, newly married, ready to serve Him and take planet Earth back from Satan. Satan had to make his move.

Why? If Adam and Eve made the right choice, they would live forever, the battle would be over, the victory would be won, and time—and Satan—would be no more.

Satan did not want that to happen, so he came after Eve. But why did he wait until Eve was created to launch his attack? Because he wasn't just after Adam. Satan wanted to destroy the entire race by destroying the progenitors of the race. He understood something we have forgotten, which is that whoever owns the family owns the future.

So he wasted no time in expanding the war. As soon

as God's instructions concerning the tree were given and Adam and Eve were married, Satan moved in to try to spoil God's plan and take back what he thought was his planet. Let's see his mode of attack, because it's the same basic strategy he uses against us today.

THE MODE OF ATTACK

Satan came at Eve with a subtle attack that cast doubt on the authority of God's word. He was so successful with this in the Garden of Eden that he has been using the same strategy ever since. You may have read Genesis 3:1–7 many times, but let's try to see it again through the lens of spiritual warfare.

"Now the serpent was more crafty than any beast of the field which the Lord God had made" (v. 1a). Satan knows how to dress for war! Forget the silly picture of a guy with horns and a long tail, wearing a red jumpsuit and carrying a pitchfork. Satan used a serpent, which apparently was an attractive creature at this point, to approach Eve.

Notice that the first conversation between a human being and the devil was about God. Satan didn't ask Eve, "How is the weather?" He didn't want to know about her gardening, or how she liked being married to Adam. He said, "Let's talk about God."

Why? Because this is a spiritual battle. And mankind was about to be thrust right into the middle of it. God gave a command concerning the tree in Genesis 2:17. Satan challenged God's word in Genesis 3, and Eve was smack in the middle of the battle. You and I are still there, by the way.

Questioning God's Word

Satan's first approach to Eve was to turn God's clear

statement into a question. "Indeed, has God said, 'You shall not eat from any tree of the garden'?" (v. 1b).

Satan was saying, "Eve, has God placed any limitations on you? Has He said no to you about anything in the garden?" In other words, "Is God being cruel and unfair to you? Are you suffering unnecessarily because God is being hard on you?"

Do you see the cleverness of the devil's strategy? God had said that Adam and Eve could eat freely from all the trees of the garden, except one. But Satan did not bring up the vastness of God's goodness. The devil only wanted to discuss the one restriction God had placed on mankind.

Satan always does this. He focuses on the one time God says no rather than on the many times God says yes. People think of the Ten Commandments as mostly negative. But the fact is that every time God says "You shall not," He is saying "You shall" to a whole list of legitimate things.

For instance, when God says "You shall not covet," He is saying, "You are free to enjoy to the full the things you acquire legitimately."

But Satan camps on the prohibition and causes us to ignore all the good gifts God gives us. Most parents have experienced this phenomenon at one time or another with their children. It usually happens at Christmas.

Your children give you a wish list of ten toys, and you buy nine of them. On Christmas morning, they open the nine gifts you bought them because you love them. But instead of saying, "Thank you for these nine great toys," the only thing they can say is, "Where is number ten?"

Questioning God's word is a trick of the devil to cause you to overlook and underappreciate God's goodness. That is why Paul says when you come to God in prayer about a need in your life, you are to come *with thanksgiving* to make your request known to God (Philippians 4:6).

Even when something is worrying you, or you are despondent, you are to come to God saying, "Thank You, Father, for who You are, for all that You have done for me, for Your grace that has saved me, for the answers to prayer I have seen in my life." That's coming "with thanksgiving."

But what do we do more often? We come to God with the attitude, "Why haven't You done this for me yet?" God's response is, "When you come to Me, start with all the good things I have done for you. Start with all the trees I have provided for you to eat from."

God wants us to come to Him with praise and thanksgiving because He has put a lot of trees out there for us to enjoy. But Satan will always try to get us hung up on the one tree we can't have.

I tell the young people in our church that instead of complaining to their parents for not getting them the most expensive tennis shoes available or the latest designer jeans, they should be saying, "Thank you, Mama and Daddy, that I eat every day. Thank you that I have a roof over my head every night. Thank you that I have clothes on my back and shoes on my feet."

We had better be teaching the next generation to be thankful, because they are in a spiritual battle too. And once a person starts focusing on what he doesn't have rather than on what God has done, he has just crossed over into enemy territory.

Changing God's Word

So Satan asked Eve, "Has God put any limitations on

you?" And Eve responded, "From the fruit of the trees of the garden we may eat; but from the fruit of the tree which is in the middle of the garden, God has said, 'You shall not eat from it or touch it, lest you die'" (Genesis 3:2–3).

We know Eve is in trouble already, because she is talking with the devil over what God said. In the process of doing so, she changes God's words at least three times.

First, Eve failed to mention that God said she and Adam could "freely" eat from all the other trees in the garden (Genesis 2:16). That omission minimized the provision of God.

That word *freely* is very important, because God was saying, "All of creation is available to you at no cost. You may eat freely, abundantly, to your heart's content. I have provided all this for you." God wasn't just good to Adam and Eve, He was *very* good. It didn't cost them anything.

Second, Eve added the prohibition against touching the fruit. God never said anything about not touching it.

Why is this important? Because Eve was turning God into a legalist. She was making God out to be a cruel killjoy who wouldn't even let her get near enough to the forbidden tree to feel its bark, let alone eat its fruit.

So many people think the Christian life is simply "You can't do this and you can't do that." That makes God look stale and miserly, not Someone you would want to follow gladly into spiritual battle. Eve's third change to what God said is a slight variation on the judgment He announced. God did not say, "Don't eat lest you die," as Eve repeated it to the devil. That makes the judgment sound like merely a possibility: maybe you will die, maybe you won't. Eve thus weakened the penalty.

But God's word of judgment in Genesis 2:17 was

much stronger than that. "You shall surely die." This is emphatic. Adam and Eve were *certain* to die if they disobeyed. God's judgment was guaranteed. Satan had driven a wedge of doubt into Eve's heart and mind. He had her beginning to wonder why God was withholding that one tree from her. She was about to forget the goodness and provision of God and start focusing on His one restriction.

Contradicting God's Word

Now Satan was ready to deliver his major strike. He flatly contradicted what God said. "The serpent said to the woman, 'You surely shall not die!'" (Genesis 3:4).

Here Satan challenged God's truthfulness. "What God said won't really happen. He wasn't telling you the truth."

Satan didn't stop after delivering his frontal attack. He went on to tell Eve his version of what the real problem was. "God knows that in the day you eat from it your eyes will be opened, and you will be like God, knowing good and evil" (v. 5).

In other words, the devil was saying, "Let me tell you what God is really doing here. God knows something He doesn't want you to know. You can be like Him."

What did Satan want more than anything else? To be like God. He was trying to get Eve to repeat his sin. This was a powerful temptation. "God is holding out on you, Eve. He's being selfish. He wants to be God all by Himself.

"But let me tell you the secret, girl. The answer is in this tree. If you take a bite of its fruit, you will know what God knows. You will be as powerful as He is. God doesn't want that to happen. But how would you like to be equal with God?"

Satan knew exactly what he was doing. The Tree of Knowledge of Good and Evil, standing in the middle of the garden, was a daily reminder to Adam and Eve that they were creatures, not the Creator. They had to obey and answer to a higher authority.

That's the same thing that bothered Satan. He had an exalted position. God had created him more beautiful than any other creature. But he was still a creature, not God.

So now the devil was trying to make Eve chafe under her restriction the way he chafed under his. By offering Eve the forbidden fruit, Satan invited mankind to join him in his rebellion. The spiritual warfare Satan launched in heaven was about to be expanded to earth.

THE PLUNGE INTO SIN

As Eve listened to the serpent's line, she looked at the Tree of Knowledge of Good and Evil. "When the woman saw that the tree was good for food, and that it was a delight to the eyes, and that the tree was desirable to make one wise, she took from its fruit and ate; and she gave also to her husband with her, and he ate" (Genesis 3:6).

This was not the first time Eve had seen this tree. But she had never seen it through Satan's eyes before. That was the difference. That's what Satan always does with sin. He wants to get us to see sin through his eyes. He wants to deceive us. As we will see later, this is a primary weapon in his arsenal.

The Entrance of Sin

The longer Eve looked at that tree, the more she just had to taste its fruit. She wanted to be what Satan wanted to be. She wanted to be like God. So she took the fruit and ate it. And then she said, "Adam, come here.

I'm not going down by myself. This is a family thing." And he ate too.

The Results of Sin

The minute Adam and Eve ate the forbidden fruit, they died just as God had promised. They became spiritually dead and alienated from God, just as Satan was alienated from God. And they fell under the curse of sin.

Our first parents knew right away that something was wrong. "The eyes of both of them were opened, and they knew that they were naked; and they sewed fig leaves together and made themselves loin coverings" (v. 7).

Sin produced immediate results. The Bible says that when Adam and Eve disobeyed, their fellowship with each other was broken. They were now conscious and ashamed of their nakedness. They hid their bodies from each other.

More important, their fellowship with God was broken, because the next time God came looking for them, Adam and Eve "hid themselves from the presence of the Lord God among the trees of the garden" (v. 8). They were now living in fear and shame. Their innocence was lost.

They had good reason to hide, because Adam's conversation with God in Genesis 3:9–12 brought out the truth: "I ate." The first pair disobeyed God because they let their feelings and desires take precedence over God's revelation.

Eve felt like she just had to have a piece of that fruit. Adam followed his feelings too. There's nothing wrong with your feelings, but your feelings should never cause you to lose sight of God's word. Our feelings must be in line with His revelation.

So Adam and Eve coveted something that was not theirs: the knowledge and glory of God. Satan is still tempting people to covet things that don't belong to them. We need to pay close attention here, because Genesis 3 teaches us a lot about the spiritual warfare we face every day.

The Curse of Sin

In one blink of time, the human race was handed over to the Evil One. Satan and mankind were now lined up against God in spiritual battle. So God began to take the situation in hand. He went down the line, pronouncing a curse against each participant in this first battle on earth.

The serpent was the first to be cursed. "On your belly shall you go, and dust shall you eat" (Genesis 3:14). God told this creature, "Do you want to be with the devil? Fine. I am going to put you down on your face in the dust where Satan is. You are going to become like him—worm food." Verse 15 is part of the serpent's curse, but I want to save it for later because it's a very special verse.

Eve's curse was a painful one. "I will greatly multiply your pain in childbirth, in pain you shall bring forth children; yet your desire shall be for your husband, and he shall rule over you" (v. 16).

This last phrase of verse 16 is very controversial, but the curse fits the sin. Eve took over, grabbing the reins of leadership from her husband. She acted independently of Adam.

So God's judgment of Eve was twofold. She would experience pain in childbirth. Every labor pain would become a reminder of her rebellion. Every birth pang would remind Eve of what she forgot (which was the same thing Satan forgot): that she was the creature, not the Creator. She was not God.

A lot of commentators take the word *desire* to mean that a woman would have a natural sexual desire for her husband even though the result, childbirth, was painful. But I don't believe God was talking about that desire. Eve had desired to dominate Adam, so her curse was to be dominated or ruled over by Adam.

To put it in blunt terms, man would dominate woman. Man would subjugate woman, be insensitive to woman. Does that excuse men who abuse women? Of course not! That's sin, and abusers are responsible before God for it. But every time you see an insensitive and domineering husband, it's a reminder of what happens when we mess with the Creator's plan. Spiritual warfare not only has a vertical dimension, between God and Satan. It has a horizontal dimension, between people.

Adam was the last to hear his curse. "Cursed is the ground because of you; in toil you shall eat of it all the days of your life. . . . By the sweat of your face you shall eat bread, till you return to the ground" (Genesis 3:17, 19).

Adam and Eve acted independently of God by eating the fruit. So God said to Adam, "Since you want to eat independently of Me, I am going to make it hard for you to eat now. You will have to work hard and sweat to earn your food."

When Adam and Eve let God feed them, He fed them abundantly and freely. But there were no more free meals now. Adam would have to go out and wrestle his food out of a cursed ground. He was going to have to work for a living. Every time a man comes home tired from a hard day's labor, he needs to remember Adam. Although work itself was instituted before the

Fall, hard work is a perpetual reminder that when you rebel against God, there's no more Paradise, no more eating freely from God's abundant garden full of trees.

This scene of judgment teaches us an important lesson for spiritual warfare: Rebelling against God isn't fun. All of a sudden, the thrill is gone. All of a sudden, that tree wasn't nearly as alluring to Eve as it had looked before. Now that chaos and destruction had set in, sin looked as ugly as it really is.

Here's another valuable warfare lesson. When Adam and Eve were obedient to God, God picked up the tab for their needs. But when they acted independently of God and imitated Satan's rebellion, they had to pay their own tab. And the price was very, very heavy.

So God turned the earth over to mankind. But then Satan overturned that by tempting mankind to sin and bringing the human race and the earth back under his dominion. God could have wiped out the whole mess in judgment, but He had a better plan.

THE CURE FOR SIN

Now we're ready for the best part of the story.

God told the serpent, through whom Satan was working, "I will put enmity between you and the woman, and between your seed and her seed; he shall bruise you on the head, and you shall bruise him on the heel" (Genesis 3:15). A man from the seed of woman—Jesus Christ—would one day crush and destroy Satan.

In other words, God said, "Satan, this battle is not over. It may appear that you won this round. But I am not going to change My plan. I am still going to work through a human seed."

So the situation now is that the world contains two distinct seeds, two offspring, the children of the devil who follow him, and the children of God who obey Him.

These two lines are so diametrically opposed that they cannot help but be at enmity with each other, just as their original "parents," God and Satan, are at enmity with each other. This means that our warfare on earth is a reflection of warfare in heaven.

The Evil Seed

God guaranteed that His seed would win the final victory, but Satan—being the tireless adversary that he is—said, in effect, "We'll see about that, God. This war is not over. It will be my seed against Your seed from now on. I'm going to get started on my seed right away."

And he did. Genesis 6:1–4 describes a unique event. Satan sent "the sons of God," a group of his fallen angels, to cohabit with human women and produce a race of men called "Nephilim." Then the text says, "the wickedness of man was great on the earth" (v. 5).

The sons of God were the angels of Jude 6, those who did not keep to their own domain. They got together with women and had children who were evil and demonic. Satan was attempting to produce his own seed, his offspring. God judged these wicked angels by confining them in the abyss, but Satan has been trying to develop his seed ever since.

The Godly Seed

Adam had been judged, but God had another word for him (Genesis 3:20–21). Adam heard God's prophecy of a coming Savior (v. 15), and then the text says he named his wife Eve, "because she was the mother of all the living" (v. 20).

The last *the* in this verse is in italics, meaning it

wasn't in the original language. Adam called his wife Eve because she was "the mother of all living." That's a powerful verse.

Adam was saying, "God, I believe that You are going to produce through my wife a seed that will crush the devil's head. And the way You know I believe You is by the name I'm giving to my wife. She will be called Eve, the mother of all people, including the living One who will someday win the battle with the devil and crush him."

Then in verse 21, "The Lord God made garments of skin for Adam and his wife, and clothed them." God provided a sacrifice to cover their nakedness—and to cover their sin.

The Divine Covering

Follow the sequence here. God judged Adam because he sinned. Adam would have to work the ground by his sweat until he died and returned to the dust himself.

But God also said there was going to be a Seed of the woman who would engage Satan in spiritual warfare and, unlike Adam, emerge victorious.

Adam heard this and said, "God, I believe You. I'm going to name my wife in light of my belief that she will produce the Seed who will fulfill Your promise."

So God said, "Because you have exercised faith, I am going to replace the leaves you sewed together by your own effort with My covering. Your covering will never work. Your covering will not solve the problem of sin. But I have a covering that will fix the problem."

Then God killed an animal, shedding its blood as a substitute for Adam and Eve. And God took the animal's skin and wrapped it around the two in the garden.

Now they had divinely provided covering rather than humanly provided covering. God covered them in His righteousness, rather than letting them stay covered in their own righteousness.

People have been trying to come up with their own covering for sin since the Garden. But the only thing that can cover you before a holy God is His covering. That's why all the way through the Old Testament, the people offered animal sacrifices. They were covering their sin before a holy God until the Seed of the woman, Jesus Christ (see Galatians 3:16; 4:4), would come and provide a permanent sacrifice through His own blood.

This contest is the real heart of spiritual warfare—and the good news is that it's no contest! Because Jesus Christ is God, He could not help but emerge victorious. And to show us how we can win over Satan just as Jesus won over Satan, God allowed His Son to be tempted by the devil (Matthew 4:1–11).

Jesus beat the devil in the desert by using the Word of God. Remember that in Genesis 3, Satan attacked the word of God and won over Adam and Eve. But in the desert, Jesus—called the "last Adam" (1 Corinthians 15:45)—used the Word to win over Satan.

Jesus did everything right where the first Adam did everything wrong. Adam ate outside of God's will. Jesus refused to do so. Adam disobeyed God's word. Jesus obeyed it perfectly. So what the first Adam messed up, the last Adam fixed up.

Nobody but Jesus could have been the Seed of the woman. All men were fallen in sin. So up in heaven, God the Father said, "Who will go and defeat Satan?"

God the Son said, "I will go."

God the Father said, "I need Somebody who is willing to be born of a woman. I need Somebody who can meet Satan face-to-face in the wilderness and defeat him. I need Somebody who will go to another tree and hang on it to bring mankind back into the garden. Then I need Somebody to rise from the dead to demonstrate that I won the victory over hell and Satan."

And Jesus the Son said, "I will go."

At just the right time, Jesus was born of a virgin and came into this world to be our Savior, our Deliverer, and our victory over Satan, sin, and hell.

So the *real* spiritual battle is already over and won. But Satan continues to fight, and he wants to take as many people down with him as he can. We must stand against him and defeat him the same way Jesus defeated him, through the power and Word of God. This is our battle.

The war is real, but isn't it great knowing you are on the winning side? If you know Christ, the curse of sin is lifted. You don't go from dust to dust. You go from dust to glory.

4

THE SCOPE
OF THE BATTLE

It's easy to be a soldier in a parade. The weapons aren't loaded, there is no enemy to be found, and all your leader has to do is make sure you keep in step.

But when you're in a war, your weapons are always loaded, the enemy is in sight, and your commander is telling you what to do in order to stay alive and win the battle.

Far too many believers in Jesus Christ think they are in a parade instead of a war. They dress up nice, smile and wave, and want to know how to keep in step rather than how to go to war. That's why we have so many casualties on the spiritual battlefield. You can't fight a war while marching in nice, straight lines. The British redcoats found that out when they came to the American colonies.

Someone might say, "How do you know we're in a war?" That's easy. Besides the casualties, we also have a lot of prisoners of war, believers who have been taken captive by the enemy in some area of their lives. You and I are in a battle, for sure—smack in the middle of it.

God created mankind to rule the earth and demonstrate His power to Satan and the angelic world. But now "the whole world lies in the power of the evil one" (1 John 5:19).

Satan has an agenda, which is to keep the world of unsaved people under his control and render Christians ineffective in spiritual warfare, bringing us down to daily defeat. Let's consider the scope of the battle.

SATAN'S FOUR FRONTS OF ATTACK

Satan is on the attack in four arenas of our lives. Since the Garden of Eden, he has widened the battle to include all of life, and he is attacking on all four fronts simultaneously. I want to review these four arenas from chapter 1 briefly, then talk about Satan's method of attack and our weapons of defense and counterattack.

The Individual Front

The devil's first battlefront is our individual lives. The apostle Peter said, "Be of sober spirit, be on the alert. Your adversary, the devil, prowls about like a roaring lion, seeking someone to devour" (1 Peter 5:8).

To put it bluntly, Satan is after you. No matter who you are or what your status, he wants to overthrow and defeat you. I referred above to Christian prisoners of war. The devil has some Christians in POW camps because of alcohol, drugs, pornography, fear, discouragement, depression, and a whole host of other problems.

There are a lot of names for these things. But in the spiritual realm, the fact is that believers who are being held captive by the devil in things like these are prisoners of war. The devil is after individual Christians, seeking to capture and destroy them spiritually.

The Family Front

The second front where Satan attacks the people of God is in their family life. We saw this in the Garden when Satan tempted Eve. Eve gave the fruit to Adam, and the family came under the authority of hell. We saw it in Genesis 6, when a group of fallen angels cohabited with women and produced offspring as part of Satan's plan to create a demonic family and race.

It should be obvious why the family is so important to Satan. According to God's curse on the serpent in Genesis 3, from then on the battle would be waged between the seed of the woman and the seed of the serpent. The offspring of these two lines, the godly line and the ungodly line, is key to the fight.

Satan wants to destroy your family not only because he wants to destroy you, but because he wants the next generation too. If Satan can get to the next generation by messing up our homes, then he has us, our kids, and the homes *they* will establish someday, because our children will be ill equipped to raise their children properly. It becomes a generational problem.

This is why Satan loves to see divorce among Christian couples. If he can get husbands and wives fighting each other over their disagreements and personality conflicts and preferences, then they will miss the bigger battle altogether. It's not just about personalities; it's about war in the spiritual realm.

The tragedy is that we as Christians are still fighting flesh and blood, rather than the principalities and powers and world forces that are devastating us (Ephesians 6:12).

We must fight for the family because whoever controls the family controls the future. We have to fight against men walking away from their families because they're tired or things are getting hard. We have to fight against women being so in love with the workplace that they neglect their "seed," the next generation, at home. Satan wants your family and mine.

The Church Front

The enemy has also opened a third front, which is the church. Here he promotes disunity, division, and discrimination through things such as personality squabbles and power struggles, and through more serious problems such as doctrinal error, racism, chauvinism, and culturalism.

The devil wants to split up the family of God, because Satan understands something that many Christians don't. He understands that God does not work in a context of disunity. There must be harmony in the body of Christ if we are going to see the power of God in action.

So if our enemy can split God's people along racial, class, gender, or cultural lines, if he can get people making decisions based on personal bias rather than on divine truth, he has won a major battle.

But when you're in a war, you don't care about the color, class, or culture of the person fighting next to you, as long as he is shooting in the same direction you are. We're in a common battle against a common enemy, so we'd better learn to get along.

One reason our communities are in disarray is that the churches in these communities have not come together to bring the power of God to bear on the problems. And one reason the churches have not come together is that we are not very good about making the distinction between membership and fellowship. This is a very important distinction.

For instance, our church in Dallas has a doctrinal statement that a person must affirm to become a member. We may have things in that statement that distinguish us from other churches or groups of Christians, but these things should not extinguish our fellowship with Christians from other groups.

In other words, if you belong to Jesus Christ we can have fellowship, even though we may not dot all of our *i*'s and cross all of our *t*'s alike. If Jesus Christ and His truth is the standard, then we can have fellowship in Christ even while our church membership is distinct. It is incumbent upon us to maintain fellowship without compromising membership.

Paul said we must be "diligent to preserve the unity of the Spirit in the bond of peace" (Ephesians 4:3). Satan wants to attack and split the church, because if he can do that he negates divine power.

The Society Front

Here's a fourth place where Satan has opened a battlefront. We get a glimpse of Satan's activity in the society at large in Daniel 10:13–14, where an angel reveals to the prophet Daniel that Satan is the energizing force behind the rulers of the nations.

Now don't misunderstand. I'm not saying that all human rulers are demonically inspired. It's easy to see Satan's power behind a Hitler or a Stalin and behind the various dictators and warlords who are destroying lives and nations today. Thankfully, not every nation is ruled by people like this. But it is important to recognize a spiritual warfare principle here. Since it's true that the whole world lies in Satan's power, then we have to recognize he exerts influence over the world's leaders and structures.

Once we understand this principle, we realize that the answer to our culture's woes lies much deeper than just electing the right person to office. That's certainly important, but there is a bigger battle going on here.

Until we begin to trace our individual, family, church, and societal problems back to their spiritual source, Satan will continue to take spiritual POWs in bunches.

You may feel that Satan has taken you prisoner in one or more of these areas. Your problem may go all the way back to childhood in the form of an abusive parent. You may be repeating destructive patterns in your family that were present in your birth home.

Whatever the case, you may have been a prisoner of war so long that you think and act like a POW. Identifying Satan's areas of attack is one important step toward your liberation. Another is to find out *how* he attacks us.

SATAN'S METHOD OF ATTACK

Satan not only knows *where* to get at us, but he also knows *how* to get at us. That's why we need to understand the method he uses to defeat us and make us spiritual POWs.

In 2 Corinthians 10:3–5, the apostle Paul reveals the devil's primary battle strategy. This is incredibly important information:

Though we walk in the flesh, we do not war according to the flesh, for the weapons of our warfare are not of the flesh, but divinely powerful for the destruction of fortresses. We are destroying speculations and every lofty thing raised up against the knowledge of God, and we are taking every thought captive to the obedience of Christ.

The first thing Paul wants us to know is that we can't use secular or fleshly weapons to fight spiritual battles. The reason so many Christians are losing the battle is that they are trying to beat the devil using the world's weapons. They are looking to the secular world to help them with their spiritual need.

If your problem, your struggle, your need is induced and orchestrated by your spiritual enemy, your flesh can't win the fight. Unless you choose a spiritual response, all the time, effort, and resources you spend trying to fix the problem will ultimately be a waste of time, a Band-Aid on the situation.

Paul says our methods are not of the flesh because our enemy is not of the flesh. Some of us have been wrestling with things day in and day out for years. Those are battles, no matter what other name we may give to them. And if God speaks to it, it is a spiritual battle.

And if your battle is a spiritual battle, it needs a spiritual cure. You don't fight cancer with skin lotion. You don't fight a brain tumor by taking two aspirin and lying down. Those kinds of problems demand another kind of help. So do spiritual problems.

An Attack on the Mind

The text we cited above tells us that Satan targets his attacks on our minds. We know that because Paul talks about "speculations," "the knowledge of God," and "taking every thought captive" (2 Corinthians 10:5).

Where do speculations come from? The mind. Where is knowledge rooted? In the mind. Where do thoughts come from? The mind. It is all in the mind. So the Christian who wants to trade his or her spiritual POW status for freedom must learn to think differently.

When Satan attacks a Christian's mind, he starts building what Paul calls "fortresses" ("strongholds," NIV and KJV). The devil builds a place from which he can operate, and he means for that fortress to be permanent. He plans to take up residency there.

Satan makes himself at home, in other words, and he gets a grip on the mind until people begin thinking there is no way to overcome this problem, no way to save this marriage, no way to unify this church, no way to make a difference in our world.

Whenever you hear a Christian saying, "No way, it can't be done. I've tried everything, and it just doesn't work," you're looking at somebody who has allowed Satan to build a fortress in the mind. However that fortress got there, it was constructed by the Evil One.

A fortress or stronghold is a mind-set that holds you hostage. It makes you believe that you are hopelessly locked in a situation, that you are powerless to change. That's when you hear people saying, "I can't, I can't, I can't."

The only reason you say, "I can't," when God says, "You can" is that Satan has made himself at home in your head. In computer terms, he has you operating by the old information that was on the hard drive of your mind before you became a Christian.

See, the Bible says before we were saved, we were operating by a godless way of thinking, a thought system that was vain and empty. Satan controlled the keyboard that entered data into our minds and put it on the screen of our lives to be lived out.

But when we came to Jesus Christ, He gave us a new drive in our minds with new data to control the way we live. Every believer has this new data, but many of us are still living by the old data that will not be erased completely until we get to heaven. Even though we are on our way to heaven, we are still being programmed by the enemy in some areas.

That's why Paul had to write this passage in 2 Corinthians. He wanted to help believers who had become trapped into thinking the enemy's way—which all of us have done at one time or another.

The Formation of Partitions

How is Satan able to pull off this kind of influence in a Christian's mind? He does it by raising up "lofty thing[s]" (2 Corinthians 10:5). A lofty thing is a partition, a wall.

We have a couple of classrooms in our church building that have partitions we can pull to divide a large classroom into two rooms. The reason for drawing a partition is to keep the two activities or classes on each side from mixing with each other.

Why does Satan want to raise up a partition in our minds? Because he wants us to be what James 1:8 calls "double-minded" people. We'll get to this term later, but the idea is to divide our minds. When this happens, we keep that which is of God on one side, and that which is not of God on the other. We literally have two minds—two sides of the room, if you will.

Satan's partitions are "raised up against the knowledge of God" (2 Corinthians 10:5). Satan wants to block divine information crossing over to the other side of your brain. He wants to block the knowledge of God in your life, to keep it from infiltrating the other side of the room.

That way, you can go to church with your problem

or your sin and hear the Word of God. But when Satan raises the partition, the biblical data you heard on Sunday are not transferred to Monday. So you come to church with your problem and leave with your problem, and all you had in between was a nice song and a sermon. Satan erected his partition and blocked the knowledge of God.

Satan wants to block the knowledge of God in your life for the same reason he wanted to block the knowledge of God in Eve's life. He knows that if you ever take God seriously, you're going to live life as it was meant to be lived.

The devil doesn't want you to do that. Instead, he wants to keep your mind divided. He wants to make you a spiritual schizophrenic.

What does a schizophrenic saint look like? This is someone who can smile and praise God in church, and then turn into a completely different person out in the parking lot. A schizophrenic stands up for Jesus in church, yet is a "secret saint" at work. Nobody knows this person belongs to Christ. He is for God one minute and for self the next.

Satan wants you to have two minds. A person with two minds is never really sure who the enemy is. He is a confused, and ineffective, spiritual warrior.

An Illustration of a Partition

Before we get to the solution to Satan's attack, I want to show you a classic illustration of this kind of double-minded, partition thinking. It's in Matthew 16:13–24.

Jesus asked His disciples, "Who do people say that the Son of Man is?" (v. 13). They gave various answers, and then He asked, "But who do you say that I am?" (v. 15).

Simon Peter had the answer. "Thou art the Christ, the Son of the living God" (v. 16).

Peter was thinking with his right mind here. He knew who Jesus was, and he wasn't ashamed to say it. And Jesus not only commended Peter for his answer, but He also guaranteed that the church would be founded on Peter's confession, and He gave Peter the keys of the kingdom (vv. 17–19).

So everything was fine. Then in the next breath, Peter became a tool of the devil when Jesus started telling His disciples that He was going to die and be raised again (v. 21). "Peter took Him aside and began to rebuke Him, saying, 'God forbid it, Lord! This shall never happen to You'" (v. 22).

Peter was telling Jesus, "Lord, You don't know what You're talking about. Nobody is going to take Your life. I've got my sword, and I'll cut off some ears!"

Jesus' response to this schizophrenic saint was stunning. "He turned and said to Peter, 'Get behind Me, Satan!'" (v. 23). In other words, "I am not going to call you by your real name because right now you are thinking like the devil. You are acting as his mouthpiece."

Peter thought he was speaking for God when he said, "God forbid it, Lord!" He thought he was representing God. But Satan had raised a partition in Peter's mind, and at that moment Peter had taken sides with the devil.

The devil didn't understand why Jesus came to earth, but he was trying to frustrate God's plan. Peter was agreeing with the devil's plan. He was thinking and speaking out of two sides of his mind. He was a double-minded man.

Even your good thoughts, if they don't agree with God's thoughts, are wrong thoughts. Peter believed he had a good thought. But it was a godless thought, because if Jesus hadn't gone to the cross you and I couldn't be saved.

That's why Jesus went on to say in Matthew 16:24, "If anyone wishes to come after Me, let him deny himself, and take up his cross, and follow Me." Denying yourself includes bringing down the partitions in your mind. It means saying no to your thoughts when they conflict with God's thoughts.

We cannot let Satan build strongholds in our minds and divide our thinking. God's thoughts must always be superimposed over our thoughts.

Satan's attack plan is to get to our minds and erect barriers that keep us from obeying God and enjoying victory. But Paul tells us that we can counterattack and destroy Satan's attempts to build a base of operations in our lives.

THE GOAL OF OUR COUNTERATTACK

Satan wants to build his fortress in your mind, but he needs a piece of ground to build it on. He needs a corner of your mind where he can erect his stronghold.

But you don't have to yield any ground at all to the enemy. God has given you and me the power to counter Satan's attack, to overrun and destroy his fortresses.

Tearing Down Fortresses

Back in 2 Corinthians 10:4, Paul says our spiritual weapons can destroy Satan's fortresses.

Weapons such as prayer, reading the Word, obedience, meditation on Scripture, fasting, and service can blow up the devil's strongholds. And that's what we must do. These fortresses don't need to be remodeled. God doesn't tell us to capture them, change the locks, and use them for Him. Satan's fortresses must be torn down.

Destroying Partitions

We also need to pull down those lofty partitions (v. 5). These include "speculations," those rebel thoughts that take us far away from the knowledge of God. We must say, "This thought is from the devil. I judge it in the name of Jesus Christ. Partition, come down."

See, you are not responsible for every thought that flashes into your mind. Satan can plant thoughts in our minds. But you are responsible for what you do with it once it is there. Our job is to recognize and dismiss evil thoughts.

Taking Our Thoughts Captive

That's the idea behind Paul's statement about "taking every thought captive to the obedience of Christ" (2 Corinthians 10:5). This is war language. When the enemy sends us one of his thoughts, we need to grab that thought and take it hostage.

We can do this by telling ourselves, "This thought is not like God's thoughts. It is against God and His revealed will. No matter how good this thought makes me feel, no matter how much I may want to do it, it's a thought out of hell, sent from the enemy. In Christ's authority I am going to make it my captive and dismiss it."

When we can do this successfully day in and day out, we are going to start winning some serious spiritual victories, because whoever controls the mind controls the battle. When you start taking all those roaming enemy thoughts captive, Satan no longer has any influence over you, and you are operating with the mind of Christ.

But you have to take each thought captive to Christ.

No army can afford to have enemy troops running around loose behind its lines, wreaking havoc and sabotaging its weapons and defenses.

You may be thinking, *Tony, this sounds too easy.* If you have been a spiritual POW for very long, you may think Satan's strongholds are too hard to conquer. You may think the battle is hopeless, the problems too great.

But I think this is one reason we have so many problems. We make the Christian life harder than God makes it. Yes, there are difficult problems. I don't want to minimize that. But many of the problems we're facing are not as difficult as we make them, because we approach them with a defeatist mind-set.

What is the difference between a person God delivers in twenty-four hours and a person who takes twenty-four years to get free? I submit that in most cases, the difference is in the mind. When the thinking changes, the actions change. And then the fortress comes down.

Let me give you an example of how this works. Joshua and the army of Israel came to the city of Jericho (Joshua 6). It was surrounded by a high wall. It looked impregnable. It was a fortress.

You know the story. God told Israel to march around the city for six days, and then march around it seven times on the seventh day. Then the priests were to blow the trumpets, the people were to shout, and the wall would fall down.

Imagine Joshua saying, "Excuse me, Lord, but this is a war. These people are the enemy. They are strong. Would You please give me my military instructions?"

Joshua didn't do that, of course. He obeyed God, and when the priests blew the trumpets and the people shouted, that wall that had stood for years came down instantly. The wall fell because the people tore it down

God's way. If they had used human methods, they would have wound up defeated.

THE METHOD OF OUR COUNTERATTACK

This is the question we always face: Are we going to use human or divine methods? It saves a lot of time and grief to use God's method. Let's see what is involved in His method for countering Satan's attack on our minds. I want to look at several passages in the book of James.

Come to God in Faith

The apostle James has solid advice for us when we are facing a difficulty in life. If you need wisdom for your problem, James says, ask God (1:5). But you need to ask a certain way:

> Let him ask in faith without any doubting, for the one who doubts is like the surf of the sea driven and tossed by the wind. For let not that man expect that he will receive anything from the Lord, being a double-minded man, unstable in all his ways. (vv. 6–8)

The double-minded person, who is trying to operate from a human and divine viewpoint at the same time, knows what everybody else thinks and what God says, and is trying to entertain both views. That kind of person won't receive the answer he needs from God. You're wasting your time if you are trying to mix and match God's way with man's way.

Go to the Root

If we are going to counter Satan's attack with an offensive of our own, we need to address the root cause of the problem, not just the symptoms.

The root cause is not what someone is doing. A person may say, "I have a drug problem." No, you have a drug symptom. "I have a moral problem." No, you have a moral symptom. "I have an alcohol problem." No, you have an alcohol symptom. The symptom is what you do. The root is the thinking that makes you do it.

James says, "Draw near to God and He will draw near to you. Cleanse your hands, you sinners; and purify your hearts, you double-minded" (James 4:8). There are two things to do here.

Cleansing the hands refers to confessing and getting rid of the wrong things we are doing. But notice that James goes beyond the hands to the heart. We must purify our hearts, because if we merely stop doing wrong things without dealing with the internal problem that caused the wrong behavior, we will soon go back to the wrong behavior.

This is why so many people's New Year's resolutions fail and why so many Christians' good intentions never get fulfilled. What they are doing is not the main problem. They need to fix the root that is producing the fruit.

See Sin God's Way

How do we deal with the real problem? How do we fix our thinking? How do we cleanse our hearts?

James answers that in James 4:9–10. He says, "Be miserable and mourn and weep; let your laughter be turned into mourning, and your joy to gloom. Humble yourselves in the presence of the Lord, and He will exalt you."

A lot of people misinterpret the promise at the end of verse 10. James is not saying that God will exalt you to some high position in society. He is saying that God will exalt you above your problem, above that which is keeping you down and making you a spiritual POW.

But before God can lift us up, He has to take us low. God wants us to weep and mourn over our sin. He wants us to start seeing our sin the way He sees it. When we do that, then we'll get the help that God gives.

But that help won't come as long as we are light-hearted about sin. Satan's goal is to get us to laugh and joke about sin, to take it lightly so we don't do anything about it.

James says we ought to be mourning over our sin, not laughing. We ought to be crying in the presence of a holy God. It's time to take the offensive against sin, confessing, "Lord, this is not just a problem; this is sin. This is not a bad habit; it's rebellion against your holiness. This is not just something that everybody does; it's something I ought not be doing."

When we begin to see sin the way God sees it, then we will experience what the psalmist meant when he said, "The Lord is near to the brokenhearted, and saves those who are crushed in spirit" (Psalm 34:18; see Psalm 51:17). The Lord says in Isaiah 66:2, "To this one I will look, to him who is humble and contrite of spirit, and who trembles at My word."

Going down low before God in contrition and humility may not seem like the way to launch a spiritual attack against Satan, but that's exactly what it does. When you say to God, "I'm as low as I can possibly get, and unless You raise me up, I'll never get up," then God can begin to do something.

When God sees you go down low in mourning over your sin, He can reach down and pick you up. That's grace, God doing for you what you could never do for yourself.

We get this kind of help when we deal with our double-mindedness and get serious about our sin. Then we will see God invading Satan's prison camp and setting some POWs free.

Practice Warfare Praying

If all of this sounds foreign and even a little scary to you, I'd like to introduce you to a new way of praying. I want to help you begin to use God's Word like a sledgehammer to break down some walls and destroy some fortresses. Let me tell you about what is often called warfare praying. If we are going to be soldiers, we may as well learn to pray like soldiers.

This is a new way of praying for many believers. It is praying God's Word back to Him and standing on it for victory in spiritual battle and release for Satan's captives. God has such a high view of His Word that if you ever learn to pray His Word back to Him, you'll have power in prayer you never knew existed.

This kind of praying goes well beyond the safe, polite, general prayers that many people pray. We pray, "Bless me today, Lord. Be with me today." We make vague requests and offer bland sentiments that don't move the hand of God or make even a crack in Satan's fortress.

We need to start talking straight about our needs and using God's Word to crack the foundations of hell. Look at the way Jesus dealt with Satan. When Jesus was being tempted in the wilderness, He hammered the devil with the Word. Jesus shattered the devil's temptations by confronting him with Scripture. Jesus said we too must live by every word that comes from the mouth of God.

I have a friend who was once trying to tear down a wall with a sledgehammer. He hit it once, but nothing happened. He hit it a second time, and still nothing happened. Then he hit that wall ten, twenty, and thirty blows, but it didn't crack.

Finally, on the thirty-ninth blow of the sledgehammer, a tiny crack appeared in the wall. So he hit the wall a few more times, and now he had a spiderweb of a crack. He knew he was on his way, so he kept on hitting the wall until it began to shatter. And after a while, he didn't need his sledgehammer anymore. All he needed was a hammer and chisel to do the rest.

Are you praying about a problem or a situation that's so tough you wonder if it will ever be resolved? You say, "I hit it with the hammer of prayer one time, and nothing happened." Hit it again. Keep pounding on that wall with the Word of God until you see that first hairline crack. Then start praying even harder, because you know that wall is ready to come down.

Don't think I'm saying you have to do it all by your effort. Warfare praying is so powerful because our Helper is so powerful.

Here's an example of what I mean. In 1996 the Texas Rangers, the major league baseball team in our town, were fighting for a division championship. On the last Friday night of the season, the Rangers were trying to win a game that would clinch their title.

But the game went into extra innings, late into the night. The Rangers wound up losing in fifteen innings, but their fans danced in the aisles anyway.

That's because the Rangers got some help. There was another game that night out in California, and the word came over the scoreboard. The team chasing the Rangers had lost as well, clinching the division title for the Rangers. They couldn't pull it off by themselves, but somebody elsewhere in the country took care of the enemy for them.

When Satan attacks, you don't have to fight him all by yourself. Just be faithful to do what God has asked you to do, and there is Somebody on the other side of the heavenlies to take care of the enemy for you. And even if you lose a game or two, you'll still be a winner because "greater is He who is in you than he who is in the world" (1 John 4:4). God can make you a winner over Satan and his attacks.

PART TWO

YOUR ASSISTANTS

5

THE EXISTENCE
OF ANGELS

One day several years ago, I put some food on the stove to warm up. While it was warming, I lay down on the couch. Unfortunately, I fell asleep—and I can still remember lying there and almost hearing a voice inside of me saying, "Get up. Get up."

I turned over and tried to ignore the feeling. But it got louder: "Get up! Get up!" So I jumped up, wondering what was going on. Then I remembered the food on the stove, and I ran into the kitchen. I got there just as flames began rising over the stove.

I got to that mess just in time to grab it off the stove, take it to the sink, and put it out. Women may shake their heads that I didn't smother the fire by putting the lid on the pan. Anyway, when the water hit that stuff, it was so red-hot that it exploded right in the sink. Then I realized how close it was to exploding on the stove and starting a serious fire.

My response that day was, "Lord, thank You for Your angelic wake-up call that brought me to life."

I did not make that reference to angels flippantly. I firmly believe that this incident was an example of angelic activity in my life as a child of God. My guardian angel was doing his job that day.

You probably have a similar story of being "touched by an angel" in your own life. Maybe it was that time you were nodding off behind the wheel and you suddenly awoke just in time to steer away from disaster. I believe times like that are instances of angelic activity.

As we begin our second section, which will deal with God's holy angels, it's time to restate a foundational thesis of this book. The physical, visible realm is greatly affected by the spiritual, invisible realm that the Bible calls the "heavenly places." What happens in the spiritual realm controls and influences what happens in the visible realm.

So the better we understand the invisible spiritual realm, the more prepared we will be to wage successful spiritual warfare against our adversary the devil.

I don't have to tell you that angels are in vogue. You can find "angel clubs" and stores that specialize in angelic collectibles. Angels have hit prime time on television and in films. Both *Time* and *Newsweek* magazines have featured angels on their covers. The world is fascinated by the idea of helpful supernatural forces operating in the world.

But a lot of what we see about angels in the popular culture is inaccurate and trite when we compare it to what the Bible teaches about angels. They are an invisible army of beings who manage history for God. They aren't just cute, friendly creatures who want to protect you and make you feel good about yourself. Angels have much more significance than the culture is giving them, and it's biblically impossible to talk about angels without discussing God.

We will investigate that significance in the next four chapters. It's time to get past the popular, secular view of angels and understand what is really happening in the angelic realm.

In the course of doing so, we will deal with some things that we don't fully understand. But that's OK, because there are a lot of things about life that we don't fully understand. So let's ask and then try to answer the question, Who are the angels?

ANGELS ARE CREATED BEINGS

The first thing to know about angels is that they are created beings.

We will see in the next section that several traits of the holy angels are also true of demons. That's because, of course, the demons are themselves fallen angels, created in purity and power until they followed Satan in his rebellion. So we will see some similarities between angels and demons.

Created for God's Purposes

According to Colossians 1:16, the angels were part of the original creation: "For by Him [Christ] all things were created, both in the heavens and on earth, visible and invisible, whether thrones or dominions or rulers or authorities—all things have been created by Him and for Him."

There is something very important in this verse. Notice that the object or focus of creation is Christ. Everything was created for Christ. The angels were not created as an end in themselves, but for God's divine purposes.

In fact, in Colossians 2:18 Paul says that one tenet of false teaching is the worship of angels. One problem with all the attention being placed on angels today is that people get too focused on angels, watching for the angels to show up, and forget to focus on Christ.

This verse in Colossians reminds us that people can misuse divine truth. As people see and hear more about angels, the temptation may be to worship the created angels rather than the Creator of the angels. So Paul says, "Don't do it" (see 2:16–19). But that is not to deny the reality of the angelic realm and the truth the Bible teaches us about angels.

Created to Serve and Worship

Angels were created to be "ministering spirits" (Hebrews 1:14), to serve God and His people, not to be worshiped. Every time in the Bible when an angel appeared and a human being fell at that angel's feet, the angel told the person to get up and not worship him (see Revelation 22:8–9).

Angels were also created to give God endless worship around His throne. Far from wanting worship, the angels find their delight in praising God (Psalm 148:2). We can learn a lot about worshiping God from angels, His full-time worshipers.

When were the angels created? The Bible gives us a clue in Job 38, where God asks Job:

Where were you when I laid the foundation of the earth! Tell Me, if you have understanding, who set its measurements, since you know? Or who stretched the line on it? On what were its bases sunk? Or who laid its cornerstone, when the morning stars sang together, and all the sons of God shouted for joy? (vv. 4–7)

The "morning stars" are the angels. Job is told that when the earth was made, the angels formed a choir and celebrated. Therefore, angels were created before the earth was created. We know this also because the angelic conflict began in heaven before it spilled over to the earth.

Were the angels singing just because God hung the earth out in space? No, they were singing because of what God was going to do on the earth He created and hung in space. They didn't understand the details of redemption, but they knew that God was going to defeat Satan and somehow vindicate His righteousness, which He ultimately accomplished by sending His Son to earth.

ANGELS ARE SPIRIT BEINGS

The second thing we need to know about angels is that they are spirit beings.

Hebrews 1:14, which we cited above, is just one of a number of Bible references that tell us angels are spirits. Satan and the demons are spirits too, and that's why our spiritual battle is not against "flesh and blood" (Ephesians 6:12). The angels are immaterial, invisible beings.

But even though this is true, angels can become visible to carry out specific, sovereignly directed supernatural activity on the earth. They did so on a number of occasions in Scripture.

One of the most familiar examples of this is Genesis 18, when Abraham welcomed three strangers to his tent. One of the visitors was the Lord Himself, and the other two were angels. The Lord announced to Sarah that she was going to have a baby, the promised seed Isaac (who, we might note, continued the righteous seed begun in the Garden of Eden).

Abraham invited the three strangers to stay for a meal—and in the process of showing hospitality to them, he found the provision of God for the miracle he and Sarah needed to produce a child at their greatly advanced ages.

The two angels who visited Abraham were also God's provision for Abraham's nephew Lot, for it was the angels who went on to Sodom in Genesis 19 to warn and rescue Lot from destruction.

Occasions like this are why the Bible says, "Do not neglect to show hospitality to strangers, for by this some have entertained angels without knowing it" (Hebrews 13:2). Sometimes, when God wants to accomplish a specific work in a believer's life, He will direct one of His invisible angels to become visible to that believer, but the believer may not recognize that he is seeing an angel, since angels appear looking like men.

The "strangers" the writer of Hebrews was talking about were fellow believers who traveled about from place to place in that day and often needed lodging. The writer is saying that we should not refuse our hospitality to other believers, because God may be sending us the answer to our prayers. If we slam the door on people who need our help or hospitality, we may be slamming the door on God's answer or His provision.

ANGELS ARE PERSONAL BEINGS

Here is another characteristic of God's holy angels. They are personal beings because they exhibit the three qualities of personhood: intellect, emotion, and will.

Angels must have intellect or intelligence, because

they are able to carry out God's commands and converse with human beings when the occasion demands it.

They also use their minds in other ways, because Peter says the angels are intensely curious to understand human redemption (1 Peter 1:12). They have to look on from the outside because there is no redemption for fallen angels.

Angels also have emotions. When they see a human being get saved, they break out in rejoicing (Luke 15:10). Why do angels get so excited over each person's salvation? Because it means one more victory for God in the angelic conflict.

In other words, the excitement of angels is related to spiritual warfare. The battle of eternity is for human souls because the eternal destiny of angels is already fixed. Demons can't be redeemed, and the angels who remained loyal to God are confirmed in holiness.

Satan is trying to keep the unsaved unsaved, and God is working to snatch the unsaved from their danger of the flames of hell. Every time God snatches somebody out of hell into heaven, the angels throw a party.

So when you tell someone about Christ and see that person come to faith in Christ, you send the angels into ecstasy. They are in this battle with us, and they know that salvation means another victory for the kingdom of God.

As personal beings, angels also have wills. At the time of Satan's rebellion, they were able to make a choice. It was through his will that Lucifer became the devil, and it was through their wills that one-third of the angels became demons.

Angels have all the attributes of personality. So when we talk about angels, we are not relating to forces or inanimate objects. Angels are personal.

ANGELS ARE INNUMERABLE

The question used to be asked, "How many angels can stand on the head of a pin?" I don't think that old conundrum has ever been answered, but one thing is sure: Trying to count the number of God's holy angels for any purpose would be a waste of time. They are without number.

In one of his visions, the prophet Daniel saw God take His seat on the throne of judgment. Attending God were "thousands upon thousands" and "myriads upon myriads" of His angels (Daniel 7:10).

A myriad is ten thousand, so we are talking about a minimum of tens of thousands of angels, but the vastness of this description suggests millions. And that number does not even begin to do justice to the scene Daniel saw.

Since angels do not procreate (Mark 12:25) and do not die, however many God created initially is the same number that exists today. Try to imagine how many angels God created, and then recall that one-third followed Satan (Revelation 12:4). When it comes to spiritual warfare, the action must be heavy with untold millions of angelic beings engaged in the battle!

There's one other important place where the angels show up in all the strength of their numbers, and that is in worship. Hebrews 12:22 tells us that when we come into God's presence in worship, we are joined by "myriads of angels." We will have more to say about the angels and worship later.

ANGELS ARE GLORIOUS BEINGS

Angels may be servants, but they are also glorious beings. Every appearance of angels in the Bible is a glorious thing to behold.

Beings of Light

One of the most glorious appearances of an angel is the angel who appeared to Daniel. The prophet writes:

> I lifted my eyes and looked, and behold, there was a certain man dressed in linen, whose waist was girded with a belt of pure gold of Uphaz. His body also was like beryl, his face had the appearance of lightning, his eyes were like flaming torches, his arms and feet like the gleam of polished bronze, and the sound of his words like the sound of a tumult. (Daniel 10:5–6)

This is a being of glory. Daniel's angelic vision was so overwhelming that even though the men with him didn't see the angel, they were overcome with a sense of dread and took off (10:7). And when Daniel saw and heard the angel, he fell on his face (vv. 8–9). The sight was more than he could handle.

Because angels are glorious beings, when they show up, light follows them. This happened with the apostle Peter in a jail cell in Jerusalem. "An angel of the Lord suddenly appeared [in Peter's cell], and a light shone in the cell" (Acts 12:7).

Remember that Daniel said the angel he saw had the appearance of lightning. Throughout Scripture, the appearance of an angel has some sort of light or other glory associated with it. That's one reason angels are called stars, because like the stars in heaven they are flames of fire.

Reminders of Divine Reality

This goes back to a fundamental principle, which is that for everything visible, something invisible corresponds to it. This is important for us as Christians because when we look at the things around us, we must learn to look for the unseen things that are behind the visible things.

If all you can see is the things around you, you are functioning as a natural person. That's not a compliment for us, because as Christians, we want to be supernatural men and women. That is, we want to perceive divine reality and see things from the divine viewpoint.

Let me tell you one of the devil's favorite tricks. He wants to keep you seeing things only from a physical standpoint. He does not want you to see the spiritual reality behind the physical reality, because that way you won't get down to the truth of whatever it is you are facing.

The devil wants you to focus on the surface stuff because that's what he did. If the angels are glorious, imagine how much more glorious and beautiful Satan must have been as Lucifer, the one in charge among the angels.

Lucifer was so beautiful and so magnificent that his beauty went to his head and he tried to challenge God. God's holy angels are glorious beings, but unlike Satan they do not use their beauty to try to dazzle anyone.

ANGELS ARE FUNCTIONAL BEINGS

A sixth trait of angels I want you to see is that they are functional beings. That is, they have a job to do—three basic jobs, in fact.

Worshiping God

The first job of angels is the one we mentioned above, that of worship. There are angels who praise God continually, without ever ceasing (see Revelation 4:8).

So when we come into the presence of God, we join the angels who are already there. This means that we never worship alone, because there is not one nanosecond of time in which God is not receiving the adoration of His angels.

That's a problem for some people who can't understand how God can be worthy of all that worship. But the answer is simple. There is no being in creation greater than God. He is the Creator of all, and the Lord of all. He is the only One worthy of the adoration that the countless hosts of angels give Him. They have no problem praising God. It's what they were created to do.

Executing His Will

The second thing angels do is execute the program of God. To put it another way, the angels are God's staff members, who carry out His will and His Word. The psalmist wrote, "Bless the Lord, you His angels, mighty in strength, who perform His word, obeying the voice of His word!" (Psalm 103:20).

As we will see in more detail when we examine the organization of angels, there are various levels and orders of angels who execute God's plan in His universe. The Bible tells us about the cherubim, the seraphim, and the four living creatures, those angelic beings we might call the elite or the top echelon. Under these angels are the angels we might call the "workers," the ones who carry out the Lord's will.

Ministering to the Saints

This is the third job of angels, and the one that many people find the most interesting.

Hebrews 1:14 says that angels are sent "to render service for the sake of those who will inherit salvation."

If you are a believer, you have one or more angels assigned to you, what we commonly call guardian angels.

Guardian angels are only sent to minister to saved people (Hebrews 1:14). This is one problem with all of the popular stuff being shown and written about angels today. The people who claim to be "touched by an angel" are not believers in many cases, and really have nothing to do with God's kingdom program.

But the Bible is clear that angels are not just spirits out there floating around, waiting to rescue anyone who happens to need a hand. We might say that the ministry of angels is not available to the general public.

God uses angels for His specific kingdom purposes, and if it's not related to the kingdom, He is not necessarily interested in someone being "touched by an angel." Where angels are involved, they are ministering to the saints in cooperation with the will of God.

The Bible specifically says that children have guardian angels, and that these angels "continually" behold the face of God (Matthew 18:10). Therefore, Jesus warned, don't despise these little ones, because they have some very powerful defenders.

The story of Peter's release from prison by an angel gives us another example of guardian angels. After the angel led Peter out of the prison and Peter realized he was free, he went to the house of Mary, where the church was gathered, praying for him.

In verses 13–17 of Acts 12 we read the unusual story of Peter's reception at Mary's house. He knocked on the door, and a servant girl named Rhoda answered. She heard Peter's voice, and she ran to tell the others that he was at the door.

The others did not believe Rhoda, and when she kept insisting that it was Peter, they said, "It is his angel"

(v. 15). But Peter kept knocking, and when they opened the door, they saw him and were amazed.

The point is that there was a belief in the early church that believers had angels assigned to them. Peter obviously did, because his angel showed up and got him out of jail!

ANGELS ARE POWERFUL BEINGS

The seventh and final trait of angels I want to discuss is their tremendous power.

In 2 Thessalonians 1:7 Paul says that when Jesus Christ returns, He will return "with His mighty angels in flaming fire." The angel who rolled the stone from the mouth of Jesus' tomb (Luke 24:2, 4) did so without any trouble. Objects in nature are no problem for angels, because they have power.

Power over Nature

In fact, the Bible says that angels have power in nature. I want to look at a number of passages here and then draw some conclusions.

In the book of Revelation, angels are very active in the arena of nature. "After this I saw four angels standing at the four corners of the earth, holding back the four winds of the earth, so that no wind should blow on the earth or on the sea or on any tree" (Revelation 7:1). That's a tremendous picture of power over nature.

Now I want to look at the prophet Ezekiel's vision in Ezekiel 1:4–5:

> And as I looked, behold, a storm wind was coming from the north, a great cloud with fire flashing forth continually and a bright light around it, and in its midst something like glowing metal in the midst of the fire. And

within it there were figures resembling four living beings. And this was their appearance: they had human form.

Ezekiel saw four amazing creatures that he later identified as cherubim (Ezekiel 10:15). These can be identified with the four living creatures of Revelation 4:6. Ezekiel saw them moving across the sky with great manifestations in nature—that is, the wind, a great cloud, flashing fire or lightning, and a bright light.

We are saying that the angels are very powerful beings, even wielding power over nature under God's direction. I would like to suggest something to you relative to angels and nature, based on this description in Ezekiel 1.

Manifestations in Nature

I believe that the elements of nature such as thunder and lightning are sometimes manifestations of God's angels. Let me illustrate what I mean.

When I was growing up in Baltimore, every weekend I would go to visit my grandmother, who lived on a nearby street. I would be sitting watching television, and sometimes it would start to thunder outside. Lightning would flash, and the rain would come.

My grandmother would say, "Tony, turn off the television!"

I'd say, "Why, Grandma?"

She would answer, "Because God is talking to us."

I would say, "Grandma, God is not talking. I'm in the middle of this show." But she got angry if I didn't turn off the TV, because her argument was that when God was talking, you should pay attention.

My grandmother may not have had the application of Scripture exactly right, but the principle behind her conviction is solidly biblical.

The prophet, in Ezekiel 1, said, in effect, "I saw the wind. And when my eyes were opened and I was able to look inside the wind, I saw angels moving there."

Let me establish this concept further with this extended quote from Psalm 18, a glorious statement of the power of angels:

> Then the earth shook and quaked; and the foundations of the mountains were trembling and were shaken, because [God] was angry. Smoke went up out of His nostrils, and fire from His mouth devoured; coals were kindled by it. He bowed the heavens also, and came down with thick darkness under His feet. And He rode upon a cherub and flew; and He sped upon the wings of the wind. (vv. 7–10)

These verses are a virtual repetition of 2 Samuel 22:8–11, in which David described God's great deliverance from David's enemies. God is pictured as coming down to earth to move in behalf of His people, and His activity is accompanied by a series of natural phenomena.

Notice that verse 10 of Psalm 18 says symbolically that God did this by riding "upon a cherub," one of the highest echelon of angels. The cherub's movements are connected with "the wings of the wind."

Verses 11–15 of Psalm 18 continue this description of God's movement in history being manifested through all manner of natural phenomena. You can read those verses and note all the references to meteorological activity and other occurrences.

When God moves in history, He often does it through angels. That's why angels play such a prominent role in the book of Revelation. The entire book is a record of God carrying out His end-time plan through the ministrations of angels.

ANGELS ARE GOD'S CREATURES

Here's a question that may have occurred to you, because it has occurred to a lot of other people. If angels are so great and so powerful, why not go looking for them? Why not seek an angelic visitation or an angelic blessing if they are God's servants just waiting to serve the saved?

I want to answer this from Hebrews 1, where the writer says concerning Jesus:

[Jesus] is the radiance of [God the Father's] glory and the exact representation of His nature, and upholds all things by the word of His power. When He had made purification of sins, He sat down at the right hand of the Majesty on high; having become as much better than the angels, as He has inherited a more excellent name than they. . . . And when He again brings the first-born into the world, He says, "And let all the angels of God worship Him." And of the angels He says, "Who makes His angels winds, and His ministers a flame of fire." (vv. 3–4, 6–7)

The writer of Hebrews acknowledges that angels are awesome, but they are merely the servants and the worshipers of Jesus Christ, who is God.

We know the names of Gabriel and Michael, two angels who are mentioned in the Bible. They are glorious beings, but Hebrews says don't get too excited about angels' names. Get excited about Jesus' name, because His name is more excellent than that of any angel.

Don't go looking for angels; go looking for Jesus. Don't go looking for your guardian angel. He has already found you. Go looking for Jesus.

Angels are God's ministering servants, but when it comes to Jesus, God the Father says, "Thy throne, O

God, is forever and ever" (Hebrews 1:8). When God addresses the angels He says, "Give Me a little wind here. Give Me a little earthquake there. Give Me a little lightning over here." But when God addresses Jesus, He says, "O God."

Only Jesus is the Son of God. Only Jesus is God Himself, the second person of the Trinity. Angels are Jesus' created, obedient servants, His worshipers who will exalt Him forever. Jesus is the name to know.

6

THE MINISTRY
OF ANGELS

Sometimes, when we need to get a package across town in a hurry either from our church office or from the Urban Alternative headquarters in Dallas, we call a local messenger service.

The service sends a messenger, a courier, who picks up our package and delivers it for us. The messenger's only job is to deliver our message to the right person, without changing it in any way.

GOD'S MESSENGERS

That's exactly what angels do. The word *angel* itself means "messenger." God's holy angels are His divine messengers, His "courier service." We have talked a little bit about what angels do, and in this chapter we are going to examine their ministry in detail. But knowing that angels are God's messengers gives you the fundamental, overarching picture of what they do.

I want to look at five areas of this messenger service,

the ministry of angels. And then I want to close this chapter by examining a critically important text relative to the ministry of angels in your life today.

Angels Are Messengers of God's Word

First of all, angels are messengers of God's Word. They played a part in the delivery of the Law to Moses.

In his defense before the Jewish council, the church leader Stephen said that the nation of Israel received the Law "as ordained by angels" (Acts 7:53; see also Galatians 3:19). According to Hebrews 2:2, the law was "spoken through angels."

When Moses sat down to write the Pentateuch, the first five books of the Bible, also called the Law, he was guarded from error by the superintending ministry of the Holy Spirit. That's true for every writer of Scripture (2 Peter 1:19–21).

But let me stop right here and clarify the relationship between the ministry of the Holy Spirit and the ministry of angels. This is critical for our understanding, especially in this chapter where we will see so much of the angels' ministry of guidance and protection.

The question is, If the Bible says the angels are doing all of this, how does their work relate to the role of the Holy Spirit? The two relate in this way.

The Holy Spirit is *God*. He is not just another spirit being or an angel; He is fully God, the sovereign third person of the Trinity. That means the angels are His messengers too. They act under His command. The Holy Spirit directs the angels in their ministry with and to God's people. So let's not confuse the Spirit's ministry with that of the angels.

The interplay between the Holy Spirit and the angels is evident in the recording of Scripture. The Spirit was the Guide when Moses wrote, but the angels were involved in the delivery of God's law. In some way, under the Spirit's direction the angels oversaw the transmission, protection, and integrity of the written Word.

Angels were also active in delivering the message concerning the coming of the living Word, Jesus Christ. Recall the Christmas story, and you'll remember that from beginning to end, angelic messengers were key to the unfolding drama of God's work.

Angels appeared to Zacharias, Mary, and the shepherds (Luke 1:11, 26; 2:9), and at least three times to Joseph (Matthew 1:20; 2:13, 19, 22).

Angels Are Messengers of God's Protection

Angels are not only messengers of God's Word. They are messengers of God's protection.

There is a wonderful illustration of this in 2 Kings 6:8–23, the story of Elisha and the way God supernaturally protected His prophets using His angels. You are probably familiar with this Bible story. Elisha had been advising the king of Israel concerning the movements of the king of Aram, or Syria.

The king of Syria became furious over this, so when he discovered that it was Elisha doing this, he plotted to capture Elisha. He found out Elisha was living in Dothan, so the king sent his army to surround Dothan and take Elisha (vv. 11–14).

I love what happened next. Elisha's servant got up the next morning and went outside to see an army circling the city. He went to Elisha and said, "'Alas, my master! What shall we do?' So he answered, 'Do not fear, for those who are with us are more than those who are with them'" (2 Kings 6:15–16).

Then Elisha prayed that God would open the young

man's eyes so he would see what Elisha saw. God answered Elisha's prayer, and his servant saw that "the mountain was full of horses and chariots of fire all around Elisha" (v. 17). Those were God's protecting angels, and they delivered Elisha from the Syrians in a supernatural way.

Let me show you something here. Elisha's servant wanted to get really practical. "What are we going to do?" Watch out for Christians who always want to be practical. You need to hang around Christians who want to be *supernatural,* not just practical.

Why? Christians who live supernaturally are able to look beyond what is visible to the eye. They understand that they're in a spiritual battle, so they aren't limited by what they see around them. They can see God's solution. And they can help you see it too.

So your attitude ought to be, "Lord, if there's something I'm not seeing, show me, so that I won't react just to what I see—the enemies. But I'll react to what You are doing. Please open my eyes."

We saw in Acts 12 that an angel delivered Peter from prison. But this was actually the second time this had happened to Peter. Earlier, the high priest and his pals put all the apostles in prison (Acts 5:17–18).

But according to verses 19–20, "An angel of the Lord during the night opened the gates of the prison, and taking them out he said, 'Go your way, stand and speak to the people in the temple the whole message of this Life.'"

Here's another way God delivers His protection to us through the angels. In the middle of the story about the rich man and Lazarus (Luke 16:19–31), Jesus said this about the death of Lazarus: "It came about that the poor man died and he was carried away by the angels to Abraham's bosom" (v. 22). The angels transported Lazarus to heaven.

Why would Lazarus need an angelic escort into the heavenly realm? In order to get from earth to heaven, he had to pass through enemy territory.

We have noted that Satan is the prince of the power of the air (Ephesians 2:2). Battles are going on in heavenly places between the forces of Satan and the forces of God in order to control the events of history. And if hell had its way, it would never let you out of that grave to get to heaven.

But you don't have to worry about hell winning even after you die, because you get an escort to glory. Lazarus was protected and escorted through enemy territory into heaven and the presence of God. That's protection! So angels are the messengers of God's protection. They protect us every day, and they escort us to heaven. We will never know until we get to heaven how many times God's angels bailed us out here on earth.

Angels Are Messengers of God's Provision

Here is another ministry of angels that ought to encourage all of us. The angels are messengers of God's provision.

In Psalm 78, the writer is rehearsing God's provision for Israel in the wilderness wanderings. The psalmist refers to the manna that God "rained down" on the people (v. 24). Then we read this statement: "Man did eat the bread of angels" (v. 25).

Manna was basically cornflakes from above, little white flakes that rained down from heaven to supernaturally supply the people's need. What God did was tell the angels to deliver food to the Israelites. They were the messengers of His provision.

A lot of times when God answers our prayers, we think the answer just showed up. No, it was delivered by God's couriers, His angels. They deliver His provision.

Angels also ministered to Jesus after His temptation in the wilderness. I've seen that area. It's a dry, dusty, blazing hot place. I can imagine how emaciated Jesus must have been from forty days and nights of fasting in that desert, and how exhausted He must have been from dealing with the devil.

When it was all over, "The devil left Him; and behold, angels came and began to minister to Him" (Matthew 4:11). They brought Jesus food and water, God's provision for His weakness.

But please notice that the angels didn't show up until the battle was over. Here's a great lesson for spiritual warfare. It wasn't until Jesus had defeated the devil that God sent angels to provide His food.

A lot of us who don't want to deal with the devil are still waiting for the food. That is, we want God to answer prayer and supply our needs when we haven't resisted the devil, applying against him biblical principles that give us spiritual victory.

Could it be that one reason God hasn't answered your prayer yet is that you haven't yet faced the spiritual issue behind the need? The angels came only after Jesus had achieved victory.

The prophet Elijah also experienced God's provision through angels—but in his case the help came after spiritual defeat. First Kings 18 tells the story of Elijah's incredible victory over Jezebel's prophets of Baal on Mount Carmel.

But unlike Jesus, Elijah had a big letdown after Mount Carmel and ran for his life when Jezebel threatened him. Elijah even gave up and asked God to take his life (1 Kings 19:1–4).

Elijah had lost his spiritual equilibrium. He was afraid and defeated, but God was not finished with His prophet. So He sent the angel of the Lord to cook a little meal for Elijah and wake him to eat it. Elijah ate and drank and gained new strength (vv. 5–8).

So whatever your situation today, don't stop praying. God may be getting an angel ready to come with your provision. Even when it looks like nothing is happening, don't give up. God and His angels are at work.

Angels Are Messengers of God's Judgment

The popular idea of angels today is that they are little floating beings full of sweetness and light. Angels deliver God's protection and provision, but they are also messengers of His wrath and judgment.

We see an awe-inspiring picture of this in Revelation 15:1, where the apostle John records: "I saw another sign in heaven, great and marvelous, seven angels who had seven plagues, which are the last, because in them the wrath of God is finished."

Revelation 15 gives us a tremendous picture of God equipping His angels for fearsome judgment. They are given "seven golden bowls full of the wrath of God" (v. 7), and then in 16:1 they are commanded to go and pour out the bowls on the earth.

God has ordained that the angels deliver judgment against His enemies (see Matthew 13:41–42; 2 Thessalonians 1:7–8). In Psalm 78, the writer says God sent "a band of destroying angels" against Egypt when Pharaoh would not let the Israelites go (v. 49). You'll remember that the tenth plague against Egypt was the death of all the firstborn children.

What the psalmist is saying is that the plagues of Egypt were caused by angels. They are actively engaged in spiritual warfare today, and the Bible says that angels will execute God's final judgment against His enemies. This will be spiritual warfare raised to a higher level.

The Bible gives us some sobering examples of the angels delivering judgment against people who oppose God. One of the most amazing accounts is the death of Herod Agrippa that I mentioned earlier (Acts 12:20–23).

The people of Tyre and Sidon, the area north of Israel, wanted to make up with Herod. So he came one day in all of his royal finery and begin speaking to them. As he spoke, the people started shouting, "The voice of a god and not of a man!" (v. 22).

Herod said, "I like this."

But God didn't like it, because Herod refused to give Him the glory. So God dispatched an angel to strike Herod down, and he died an awful death.

Let me give you another principle of spiritual warfare. I don't care how healthy, wealthy, or good-looking you are. Mess with God's glory, and it doesn't matter that the doctor gave you a good report last week. Mess with God's glory, and you deal with His angels. They are agents of His judgment.

A lot of people have trouble with this concept. But we have to realize that while God is good and kind and loving, He is also just and holy. And His justice demands judgment against that which violates His holiness.

So God's angels will deliver someone to hell as surely as they will deliver someone to heaven. We need to take seriously the warning of Hebrews 12:29: "Our God is a consuming fire." It is "a terrifying thing" to fall into His hands (Hebrews 10:31).

Angels Are Messengers of God's Guidance

Here is the fifth and final "messenger service" of angels that I want you to see. God uses angels again and again to guide His people.

The birth of Jesus was filled with instances of angelic guidance. Angels disrupted Joseph's sleep several times to show him what to do.

God may allow His angels to disrupt your sleep or trouble the waters of your life to get your attention. He may want you to rethink the direction you're heading in, or pray more about a situation.

We see two great examples of angelic guidance in the book of Acts: the ministry of Philip in Acts 8, and Peter's vision of the sheet full of unclean animals in Acts 10. In Philip's case, notice that he did not get specific instructions from the Holy Spirit until he had obeyed the angelic leading. The angel told Philip where to go, and then the Spirit took over.

An angel also appeared to Cornelius (Acts 10:3–8), and he obeyed. At the same time, the Spirit was dealing with Peter (vv. 9–16). So God may use an angel to get you started. The angels fulfill the guidance ministry that is delegated to them, and the Holy Spirit takes over the rest.

God has a course for your life. Satan's job is to distract you and throw you off course. But if you stay committed to the Lord, you don't have to worry about reaching your intended destination. The angels know which road you need to take. You just have to stay open to the Spirit of God.

GOD'S MINISTERS

For the remainder of this chapter, I want to unfold a brief but very important passage of Scripture, John 1:45–51.

This story is important for our purposes because in it Jesus reveals a truth about the work of angels that we need to understand and appropriate for our lives today. He does so by linking His ministry with one of the most well-known incidents in the Old Testament, what we know as Jacob's ladder.

The Ladder to Heaven

John 1 records Jesus' call of His disciples. One of the men He called was Philip (v. 43), who went immediately to his friend Nathanael and told him, "We have found Him of whom Moses in the Law and also the Prophets wrote, Jesus of Nazareth, the son of Joseph" (v. 45).

Nathanael was skeptical, so Philip invited him to come and meet Jesus (v. 46). Jesus saw Nathanael coming and said, "Behold, an Israelite indeed, in whom is no guile!" (v. 47).

Nathanael was taken back by this, and asked Jesus how He knew him. Jesus revealed to Nathanael that He had seen him earlier when he was sitting under a fig tree, before Nathanael ever thought about coming to see Jesus (v. 48). Nathanael knew he was dealing with Someone special, so he confessed, "Rabbi, You are the Son of God; You are the King of Israel" (v. 49). Then come the verses I want to focus on:

> Jesus answered and said to him, "Because I said to you that I saw you under the fig tree, do you believe? You shall see greater things than these." And He said to him, "Truly, truly, I say to you, you shall see the heavens opened, and the angels of God ascending and descending on the Son of Man." (vv. 50–51)

Jesus told Nathanael that because of his affirmation and his faith, he would see heavenly, angelic activity occurring in his life. I want to consider the implications of what Jesus said.

Why did Jesus call Nathanael an Israelite without guile? I believe it wasn't only because He knew that Nathanael had a sincere heart. Jesus said this because He knew what Nathanael was thinking about as he sat under that fig tree.

Jesus' words grabbed Nathanael for the same reason. That is, they revealed to Nathanael that Jesus knew his thoughts, and that shook him up a little bit.

So what was Nathanael thinking about? He may have been thinking about an Old Testament Israelite in whom there was plenty of guile—Jacob the deceiver.

Specifically, Nathanael may have been pondering the incident in Genesis 28, when Jacob saw a ladder reaching into heaven and angels going up and down on it. Jesus referred to this event when He told Nathanael that he would see greater things in his life.

Jesus was saying something important about Himself and the ministry of angels, and it wasn't just for Nathanael. It's for all of God's people. The word *you* in John 1:51 is in the plural.

In other words, if you and I are plugged in to the right source, we will also see heaven operating on our behalf by virtue of the activity of God's angelic host. When you're engaged in spiritual warfare, there's nothing better than knowing that you are connected to heaven and heaven is connected to you. So let's find out what was happening here by turning back to Genesis 28.

Jacob's dream of the ladder reaching into heaven occurred in a place he would later name Bethel. The reason Jacob was there was that he had deceived his father, Isaac, and stolen the blessing of his older brother, Esau. Esau got mad and threatened to kill Jacob, so his mother, Rebekah, told him to leave town until Esau cooled down.

So here was the deceiver Jacob—Mr. Guile himself —on the run, stopping to spend the night under the stars. He put his head on a stone pillow and went to sleep.

Then the Bible says, "He had a dream, and behold, a ladder was set on the earth with its top reaching to heaven; and behold, the angels of God were ascending and descending on it. And behold, the Lord stood above it" (Genesis 28:12–13a).

In verses 13–15, God reaffirmed to Jacob His covenant promises to Abraham. God told Jacob He would give him a land and many descendants and make him a universal blessing. Then God left Jacob with a wonderful promise of His abiding presence until all of His purposes had been fulfilled.

Jacob did not deserve all of this, but God chose to bless him as an act of sovereign grace. God gave Jacob a glimpse into heaven as reassurance of His presence because Jacob was going to accomplish God's purposes.

Jesus promised Nathanael, and us, the same heavenly presence when we commit ourselves to living for Him and accomplishing His purposes.

Notice the Bible says that the ladder was set on earth, but its top reached to heaven. If we are going to be spiritually successful on earth, we must hear from heaven. Remember one of the foundational principles of spiritual warfare: Everything that happens on earth is precipitated by something that has already happened in heaven. So if you are going to have on earth what you need for victory, it must come from a connection you have in heaven.

The problem with many of us is either that we don't realize God has set up a ladder for us, we don't know where our ladder is, or we don't have the ability to see to the top of our ladder.

Jacob saw his ladder, and when he woke up from his dream he said, "Surely the Lord is in this place, and I did not know it" (Genesis 28:16). Jacob realized that he had been in God's presence.

This wasn't just a dream. God was making a supernatural disclosure of Himself. Jacob got God's ladder, and he received some awesome things with it. Let me tell you four things that come with God's ladder.

Four Blessings of the Ladder

First of all, God's promises come with His ladder. There at Bethel, God confirmed to Jacob the promise He had made previously to Jacob's ancestors Abraham and Isaac (Genesis 28:13–14).

The Scripture says that God has many "precious and magnificent promises" (2 Peter 1:4). One of the tragedies today is that many of us don't know the promises that God has made, based on His name and His character, and that He is committed to fulfill if we live according to His will and claim them.

Why are God's promises so important in this spiritual battle we're fighting? Because many of us are suffering defeat after defeat by virtue of not knowing and using the promises of victory God has for us.

One thing Satan has done successfully is keep us ignorant of God's promises. And because of that ignorance, we're discouraged when we ought not be discouraged. We're complaining when we ought not be complaining. We're fussing when we ought to be giving thanks—all because we don't know what God has promised.

If you know what God has promised you in His Word, when you're in a difficult situation you can get on your knees and say, "Lord, I'm in a mess, but I want to thank You for Your precious and magnificent promises. I want to thank You for what You told me You will do. I want to thank You that You have the power to do it. I want to thank You that You are bigger than my problem, and in the name of Jesus Christ I claim Your promise."

This is why knowledge of the Word of God is critical in spiritual warfare. God has His angels going up and down the ladder, but they are sent according to His Word.

A second thing that came with the ladder was God's presence. Jacob said God was there, and yet he didn't even know it (Genesis 28:16). God's ladder is there. The angels are there to minister to us. But sometimes it's easy to miss their activity.

Jacob's response reminds me of the story of a man whose house was being engulfed in a flood. He was standing on the roof, praying, "Lord, I trust You to deliver me from this flood."

A man came by in a boat and said, "Come on. Get into the boat." But the man on the roof was afraid to risk the boat. So he said, "No, God will deliver me."

Then a helicopter flew over the man and dropped him a line. But he was afraid to be pulled up into the helicopter, so he refused the line. "God will deliver me."

But the man drowned. He woke up in heaven and said, "Lord, why didn't You deliver me?"

God said, "I sent you a boat and a helicopter."

A lot of times we don't recognize the presence of God. Jacob did not, because he was not spiritually sensitive until after this event.

A third blessing that comes with the ladder of God is the protection of God. "I will keep you," He told Jacob (see Genesis 28:15). Let me tell you something. When you are properly linked to heaven and the angels are ministering to you up and down the ladder, you can relax.

Why? Nothing can happen to you outside of God's will. When you are in God's will, He will keep you for whatever purpose He has for you. Nobody can take what belongs to you when earth is properly linked to heaven. God will keep you.

Many of us don't ask God to do what He is willing and waiting to do because we don't really believe that He's able to do it. We don't see the ladder that connects us to heaven. So instead we quit the battle, we run from it, or we say, "I can't."

God says you can, because "greater is He who is in you than he who is in the world" (1 John 4:4). The devil deceives us and says, "Greater is he who is in the world than He who is in you." If we don't see the ladder, we act out Satan's will rather than God's will. With God's protection, we can be confident in any situation.

The fourth thing you get with the ladder is God's provision. We saw that above in the story of Elijah (1 Kings 19).

Elijah was scared and he ran, but God took care of him through an angel. The prophet even wanted to die. But even when you're at your worst, God can take care of you. And He can take care of you from beginning to end. So when you have a difficulty, don't run *from* God; run *to* God.

One day my little granddaughter got scared by a dog that was barking in our yard. She came running to me, crying and screaming, "Poppy! Poppy! The dog's going to get me!"

She jumped up into my arms, then she looked at me and looked at the dog. She did the same thing again, then stuck her tongue out at the dog.

Where did she suddenly get all of that confidence? The dog didn't change, but now she wasn't on her own. She was in someone else's arms. She was looking at me and not just at the dog.

You can't look only at your circumstances. You can't ignore them. You don't need to pretend that a problem isn't there. But the issue is what you do with your circumstances. If you run to God and climb into His arms, you will see things from a totally different perspective.

YOUR LADDER

What will it take for God to let you see His ladder—His supernatural, angelically supported presence on earth? There are two conditions.

Faith in God's Word

Nathanael first believed in Jesus based on what Jesus said. The importance of the Word is also seen in Jesus' own temptation (Matthew 4:1–11), where Jesus countered the devil with Scripture.

If you are going to see heaven open up, and witness the supernatural presence of God on your behalf through His angelic host, you will have to take His Word seriously.

Jesus said, "Nathanael, because you believed, you will see." Jesus Himself was ministered to by angels because He said to Satan, "This is what the Word says."

Many believers are not seeing heaven opened because they are saying, "This is what I think." "This is what my mama said." "This is what my daddy said." No, you won't see your ladder unless you are operating from the perspective of God's Word.

When you are faced with something that contradicts the Word, you must remind yourself that that contradiction is a lie. Lies are among Satan's most potent weapons. It's a lie when Satan says you are bound by habits or addictions or guilt. You have been set free in Jesus Christ. If you have a problem or an addiction, the problem is real. But its authority over you is a lie. According to the authority and power of God's Word, you can overcome any problem. Believing the Word releases the angels. Satan runs from the Word. It burns him to handle it. That's why he wants to distract us from the Word.

Faith in God's Son

Nathanael also confessed his faith in God's Son. "You are the Son of God; You are the King of Israel" (John 1:49). Nathanael acknowledged Jesus as God and as Israel's Messiah, and Jesus told him he would see heaven opened. Nathanael would see his ladder.

Nathanael's open faith stands in contrast to another group of Jesus' followers, introduced in John 2:23–25. They were disciples of uncertain loyalty, for although the Bible says they believed in Jesus, it also says that Jesus "was not entrusting Himself to them, for He knew all men" (v. 24).

In other words, Jesus was not going to draw back the clouds of heaven and let these people see what Nathanael would get to see because they were not ready to commit themselves fully to Him.

They wanted to follow Jesus from afar. They wanted to be "Secret Service" saints. As a result, Jesus would not entrust Himself to them. He would not release the angels to move out from heaven and come down to earth on their behalf. In the words of Matthew 10:33, "Whoever shall deny Me before men, I will also deny him before My Father who is in heaven."

So when you get down on your knees and pray,

"Lord, I need Your power in my life; I need Your deliverance," God is going to check out your testimony before the world. What is your public confession? Are you a member of the spiritual CIA? Are you a covert operative for the kingdom?

If there is no public confession of Christ before the world, then there will be no private blessing from Christ in the world. You cannot be a secret disciple and see heaven open.

That's what a lot of people want. They want public blessings, but they want to be private Christians. They want a public display of heaven to solve their problem, but they don't want to be a public testimony for Jesus Christ. But there must be a confession to see heaven open and the angels moving.

In Genesis 28, Jacob saw a ladder. But according to John 1:51, the ladder is Jesus Christ. Angels only move up and down the ladder called Christ. If He is not your ladder, if your faith is not in Him, you won't see the angels and you won't see divine help.

THE INVISIBLE WORLD

Let me give you a great verse to consider as we wrap up this chapter. Paul says in 2 Corinthians 4:18 that we need to keep looking "not at the things which are seen, but at the things which are not seen; for the things which are seen are temporal, but the things which are not seen are eternal."

The previous two verses, verses 16–17, help to set the context. The mature Christian is one whose life is guided by the unseen realities of the spiritual world, not by the five senses. It's not that these things are wrong; they just aren't enough.

The focus of your life must be derived from the invisible world. You say, "But how do I see that world?"

Paul tells us in Colossians 3:1–2. "If then you have been raised up with Christ, keep seeking the things above, where Christ is, seated at the right hand of God. Set your mind on the things above, not on the things that are on earth."

God wants you to live on earth with a heavenly perspective. He wants you to see life through heavenly sunglasses. He wants the spiritual world to be the "tint" by which you look at the things of earth, so that your mind is functioning from a divine as opposed to a human perspective.

Abraham did this. He was able to leave his home in Ur and go out to a place he had never seen, living in tents in a strange land, because he saw something that wasn't visible to the eye. "He was looking for the city which has foundations, whose architect and builder is God" (Hebrews 11:10).

Abraham functioned in time from an eternal viewpoint. He saw the ladder to heaven, and it affected where he lived and how he lived. His nephew Lot was exactly the opposite.

All that Lot could see was earth, so when it came time to choose, he chose to move toward Sodom (Genesis 13:10–11). Lot made a decision based on the physical world, and he lost everything. Abraham made a decision based on the spiritual world, and he gained everything.

The writer of Hebrews goes on to say that all of the godly patriarchs and matriarchs "died in faith, without receiving the promises, but having seen them and having welcomed them from a distance" (11:13). Moses was willing to endure "the reproach of Christ" because he saw "Him who is unseen" (11:26–27).

My hope is that when you understand the ministry of angels, you will begin to see heaven opened and see a ladder. You'll see a new connection between the visible and the invisible worlds. My prayer is that you will see heaven and earth come together, and you'll be able to testify that God intervened.

When that happens, make sure you do what Jacob did. Let's go back to Genesis 28 one more time.

When Jacob woke from the dream in which he saw the ladder and heard God's promises, he said to himself, "How awesome is this place! This is none other than the house of God, and this is the gate of heaven" (Genesis 28:17).

Then Jacob took his stone pillow and made an altar out of it (v. 18). In other words, Jacob worshiped God. He poured oil on the stone as a way of sanctifying and dedicating the place, and he made a vow to God.

The message to us is clear. When God opens heaven, don't wait until you're in church next Sunday to worship. Stop where you are and praise Him. Turn the place into a place of worship. Rededicate your life to the Lord the way Jacob did (see vv. 20–22).

I want you to see two things in particular about Jacob's vow. "If God will be with me ... then the Lord will be my God." This is a very important vow because up to this point, Jacob had been his own god.

I don't mean he was an atheist. He was a follower of Yahweh. But when it came to his life's decisions, Jacob had been saying, "I'll take control of my own life. I'll do things my way. I'll help God out."

But after he saw the ladder, Jacob said, "God, You are God in my life. Anybody who can connect heaven and earth like this has to be in charge."

Finally, look at verse 22: "And this stone, which I

have set up as a pillar, will be God's house; and of all that Thou dost give me I will surely give a tenth to Thee."

Even though this was long before the Mosaic Law had been given and the tithe commanded, Jacob was ready to give a tenth of everything he had to the Lord because he saw heaven and earth come together.

When you see heaven and earth come together, when God sends His angels to minister in your life, you will have no problem giving back to Him anything that He commands.

7

THE OPERATION OF ANGELS

Not long ago I went to the grocery store with my wife, Lois, and I came across a very interesting magazine. It was displayed right out front, where I couldn't miss it. The title leaped out at me: *Angel Times.*

I have to admit I was shocked to see it. The magazine had a picture of a beautiful female angel on the cover, although the Bible doesn't say anything about female angels. Every article in the magazine reflected our culture's new, faddish infatuation with angels. Everybody seems to be high on angels and wants to be "touched by an angel."

Besides a magazine and all the television programs about angels, angel jewelry is popular. Recently I met a woman who excitedly showed me her angel pin, a cute little cherub on a pin.

And of course, we have always had the chubby little Valentine angels who sort of float around and shoot people with their love arrows.

If someone wants to wear an angel pin, I have no problem with that. But when I see all of this stuff relating to angels, I can't help but reflect on the true biblical nature of angels: awesome, fierce, blazing creatures who inspired fear and trembling whenever they showed up.

In the Bible, one of the first things angels always had to say when they appeared was, "Fear not." They are terrifying creatures who surround the throne of God and who exist to do His bidding.

In this chapter I want to talk about the operation of angels. And the point I want to make is simply that angels always operate along God-established and God-ordained lines of authority.

Angels do so because of a fundamental principle about the nature of God. According to 1 Corinthians 14:33, "God is not a God of confusion." He's a God of order. So anything that originates from Him must be done "properly and in an orderly manner" (v. 40). Therefore, God's angels must operate in an orderly fashion.

One of Satan's major goals is to bring about confusion, disruption, disharmony, and disorder. He does this because he knows that God will not act in an environment of conflict, chaos, and confusion.

So, for example, the reason Satan wants you and your mate to be fussing and battling each other is that he knows God will not answer a husband's prayers when his attitude toward his wife is not in God's order (1 Peter 3:7).

God steps back from confusion because it is against His nature. Rebellion and lack of order are in antithesis to His very being. His angels operate under His authority because God does everything in an orderly way.

So let's find out how God's angels operate, and then

in chapter 8 we'll see how to bring the angels' ministry to bear on our behalf as we wage spiritual warfare. Let me note that as we conclude this section in these two chapters, we will be returning to some familiar passages. But these texts are so rich that I want you to see different facets of them than we saw in previous chapters.

ANGELS ARE ORGANIZED BY AUTHORITY

The first thing we need to understand about the way angels operate is this: they are organized by authority.

Paul writes in Colossians 1:16, "For by Him [Christ] all things were created, both in the heavens and on earth, visible and invisible, whether thrones or dominions or rulers or authorities—all things have been created by Him and for Him."

I've read this verse for years, but it wasn't until I came to this study that I saw a couple of things that are important for our understanding of the way God's creation works.

First, the fact that Paul talks about Christ creating both earthly and heavenly rulers and authorities underscores a main point we have been making all the way through this book. That is, there is parallel activity going on in creation between the visible and the invisible world.

These two realms operate in conjunction with each other, so that what happens in the invisible realm is mirrored in the visible realm. In other words, where there's a visible earthly king, spiritual rulers are also operating.

Not only that, but each realm is organized along definite lines of authority.

We know that Paul's reference to thrones and dominions refers to both the angelic and the demonic order because Satan mimics everything God does. God's angels are organized along a clear chain of command. The enemy has his own ranks of demons too (Ephesians 6:12). As the anointed cherub, Satan himself used to be at the top of the angelic chain of command. He was the ruler under God of the angelic realm.

Then the Bible mentions another archangel, Michael (Jude 9).

There are also the cherubim, who are what we might call the angelic guard. It was two cherubim who were put at the gate of the Garden of Eden to keep Adam and Eve from going back into the garden. Cherubim have a major role to play in protecting the glory of God.

The seraphim are concerned with the holiness and worship of God. We met these awe-inspiring creatures in Isaiah 6. When they worshiped, the whole temple shook. They worship God twenty-four hours a day. Another order or tier of angelic beings is the living creatures of Revelation 4. They are unusual creatures engaged in serious worship.

This is the angelic order, with each rank of angels functioning under the higher rank. We get a good picture of this angelic order of authority in Revelation 12:7, which describes a war in heaven in which Michael and his angels went to battle against Satan and his angels.

Here are two angelic armies, under the authority of their respective leaders who were squaring off against each other.

Angels Understand the Importance of Authority

Angels are not only organized by authority, but they understand the importance of being under authority. Michael the archangel appreciated the importance of authority.

Michael Versus Satan

In the verse mentioned on the previous page, Jude 9, we see Michael calling on God's authority to deal with Satan. "Michael the archangel, when he disputed with the devil and argued about the body of Moses, did not dare pronounce against him a railing judgment, but said, 'The Lord rebuke you!'"

As an archangel, Michael was Satan's counterpart. That's important because most people think God is Satan's counterpart or opposite. No, God has no counterpart. He is the all-powerful creator. Satan is a created being. If you want to find a counterpart to Satan, look in the angelic world, not at God. God is in a class all by Himself.

Notice that even though Michael is a powerful archangel, he was very careful in the way he dealt with the devil. Michael knew that Satan had a higher authority than he did, even though both were archangels.

Michael never forgot who he was, and he never forgot the position Satan held. So even though they were in face-to-face conflict over Moses' body, Michael never tried to leave or usurp his position of authority. He understood that the only way he was going to win his battle against the devil was by invoking the authority of the Lord.

You Versus Satan

If Michael, the awesome archangel of God, had to be careful in dealing with Satan, how much more careful should you and I be?

If you are going to defeat the devil in your life, you are going to need access to God's authority, because you are going to encounter situations where it will take more than the power of positive thinking to deliver you. You're going to need divine intervention, which means you have to be operating under divine authority just like the angels.

Let me give you a biblical illustration of what I'm talking about. In Matthew 8:5 Jesus came into Capernaum, a little town off the Sea of Galilee. There He met a Roman centurion who said, "Lord, my servant is lying paralyzed at home, suffering great pain." Jesus said, "I will come and heal him" (vv. 6–7). But notice the centurion's response:

> Lord, I am not worthy for You to come under my roof, but just say the word, and my servant will be healed. For I, too, am a man under authority, with soldiers under me; and I say to this one, "Go!" and he goes, and to another, "Come!" and he comes, and to my slave, "Do this!" and he does it. (vv. 8–9)

Matthew 8:10 says that Jesus was astounded by the level of this man's faith. This Gentile soldier understood something that many of God's own people in Israel did not understand, which was the principle of authority. Because the centurion understood the military chain of authority, he knew that he could appeal to a higher authority, Jesus, to do for him what he asked.

If you need help with a circumstance that is too big for you to handle, you need to invoke the principle of authority. When you draw on the divine authority you have in Christ, even though you are the one with the problem, it is God's authority that will bring about the solution.

Jesus says this kind of living takes a kind of faith that not many people have. Many times, we go about doing our thing and then ask the Lord to bless it, rather than appealing to His authority to intervene and do *His* thing in the situation. This Roman soldier said to Jesus, "If You will just speak the word, my problem will be solved because You have the authority."

What the centurion did is a reflection of the way the angels operate. They operate by authority, appealing to the greater to assist the lesser in a problem that is too much for the lesser to handle.

Children do this when they have trouble with a teacher and appeal to a parent, invoking parental authority.

If you're not operating in authority as a way of life, don't suddenly call on God for help when you get in trouble. That's what a lot of people want—convenient authority. They don't want God's authority over them until they need it.

This is like a child who wants his parents to come through for him when he has been living an independent life and ignoring their authority. That is a misuse and abuse of authority.

The angels understand authority, and that's why Michael invoked God's authority when he faced the devil.

ANGELS ARE LOYAL TO THEIR AUTHORITY

Here's another reality about angels and authority that we need to see. Angels are very loyal to their authority.

This is true both for God's holy angels and for the demons. After the rebellion of Satan, there are no more defections on either side of the angelic world. The angels who followed Satan have already been consigned to eternal condemnation, and the angels who remained true to God were confirmed in righteousness.

We can see an illustration of this loyalty in Matthew 12. Jesus had cast a demon out of a man, and the people were saying, "This man cannot be the Son of David, can he?" (v. 23). They were wondering if Jesus might be Israel's Messiah.

When the Pharisees heard this, they wanted to crush any talk like that because they hated Jesus. So they accused Jesus of casting out demons by the power of Satan.

Jesus replied, "Any kingdom divided against itself is laid waste; and any city or house divided against itself shall not stand. And if Satan casts out Satan, he is divided against himself; how then shall his kingdom stand?" (vv. 25–26). We should never expect Satan to go against himself.

Jesus went on to apply this to Himself in Matthew 12:28–29 when He said that He cast out demons by the Spirit of God. Then He used this illustration: "How can anyone enter the strong man's house and carry off his property, unless he first binds the strong man? And then he will plunder his house."

Jesus was saying that He was able to plunder Satan's house because He is stronger than Satan. And the reason He can overcome whatever Satan is trying to do in your life is that what He is doing is greater than what Satan is trying to do.

So when it comes to the angelic realm, there is complete loyalty. Satan will never betray himself. God will never betray His kingdom. It's only *people* who want to vacillate between the two kingdoms.

Angels don't vacillate. Angels don't sit on the spiritual fence. You don't see angels with one foot in the world and one foot in heaven. Angels are full-time with God or full-time with Satan.

This principle of loyalty is important for our lives

and our spiritual warfare. How much of the power of God you see in your life depends on whether you are a full-time or a part-time saint. If you're a part-time saint, then don't expect to see a full-time presence of God, because friendship with the world is hostility toward God (James 4:4).

The only way you're going to see God's authority operating in your life is if your total allegiance is to His kingdom. God has called us to be full-time disciples, and it is in that realm that He transfers His authority to us (Matthew 28:18–20).

ANGELS EXERCISE AUTHORITY THROUGH PEOPLE

Here's a fourth principle by which angels operate. One of the primary ways they carry out their ministry in history is through people.

Again, this principle applies to both good and evil angels. Paul warns, "The Spirit explicitly says that in later times some will fall away from the faith, paying attention to deceitful spirits and doctrines of demons" (1 Timothy 4:1).

Demonic Control

This verse clearly says that some of the teaching that will come in the last days is demonic in origin. But how does this teaching come? Through liars (1 Timothy 4:2), men who try to get God's people to abstain from that which He has provided.

In other words, the demons are promoting Satan's agenda through people they control. These may even be people who don't know they are being controlled by demons. But they are teaching demonic doctrines and leading people astray from the truth.

This is why it is so important that you not only stay

in tune spiritually yourself, but stay around people who are spiritually in tune. One of the gifts of the Holy Spirit is the gift of discernment. We need discernment to tell if a problem or situation is being promoted by demons. If it is, then the solution needs to be spiritual, not just human.

This is why the Bible tells us to "test the spirits" (1 John 4:1). The first and most important test is found in verses 2–3. Every spirit that confesses Christ is from God, and every spirit that does not confess Christ is not from God. This test alone will help you sort out a lot of false teaching. We need to discern what is influencing people to do what they do and say what they say.

This is also important because even though we as believers cannot be demon-possessed, we can be demon-influenced. We can allow Satan's way of thinking and acting to control us.

Demonic Delays

I want to go back to Daniel 10 once again, this time to look at the matter of angels exercising their authority through human beings. Daniel had been praying and fasting for understanding from God for three weeks when an angel appeared to him (v. 5).

By the way, this angel was not a cute, chubby little Valentine cherub. Read Daniel 10:6–9 and you'll see that Daniel fell on his face and the men with him ran away when he saw the angel. This was an awesome creature.

The angel had to reassure Daniel and stand the prophet up so he could deliver his message. Then look at what the angel told Daniel:

> From the first day that you set your heart on understanding this and on humbling yourself before your God,

your words were heard, and I have come in response to your words. But the prince of the kingdom of Persia was withstanding me for twenty-one days. (vv. 12–13a)

Here is a battle in heaven between an angel and a demon called "the prince of Persia." The demon had this title because he was exercising his power through people in the earthly kingdom of Persia, influencing this kingdom to oppose God's plan through Daniel and Israel.

Notice that the battle had begun the moment Daniel started praying three weeks earlier. The demon was able to delay the good angel in delivering God's answer to Daniel.

Before we go any further, let me draw some crucial implications from this passage.

Daniel 10 shows us that whether we receive an answer to our prayers often has everything to do with a battle we cannot see, because Satan wants to stop God's answer from getting through.

You say, "Then why doesn't God just wipe out all the demons and His human enemies and clear the way? Get rid of them all, and then we wouldn't have to worry about it."

God could do that, of course. But He has chosen to win the spiritual battle using different weapons. He wants to demonstrate that when His people are living in obedience to Him, they are greater than Satan and his hordes of demons who are operating in rebellion against God.

So if you are praying and the answer hasn't come yet, you need to be praying, "Lord, if You are using Your angel to send the answer to my prayer, I pray that You will provide him with whatever support he needs along the way to defeat whatever tries to delay or stop him."

Daniel didn't quit praying when his answer didn't come. If you don't know that this unseen activity is going on, you may think that God either doesn't care or that He is mad at you. If you don't realize that the angelic world is seeking to exercise authority through people on earth, you will react unbiblically rather than persevering in prayer.

Angelic Help

As awesome as he was, the angel who appeared to Daniel had been unable to break through the demonic resistance. He couldn't get God's answer through to Daniel.

But then he invoked the principle of authority and sent for Michael to help him: "Then behold, Michael, one of the chief princes, came to help me, for I had been left there with the kings of Persia" (Daniel 10:13b). Michael overruled the resistance of the demon of the kingdom of Persia and got the answer through.

What God did for Daniel, He can do for you. So don't get discouraged or frustrated if your answer doesn't come or if it doesn't seem like God is working. Your answer is tied to events outside you, beyond you, and above you. And God may be using His angelic channels, so hold on until your answer comes.

My point is that behind nations and events, there is angelic activity. Later in the book of Daniel, Michael is called the angel "who stands guard over the sons of your people" (Daniel 12:1). The reason the Arabs can't wipe out Israel is that Israel's wars are not just about human conflict. There is an archangel involved who says, "You will not be able to destroy this people."

ANGELS ARE ACTIVATED BY AUTHORITY

This is our fifth point about the operation of angels. They are activated by authority.

I'll have a lot more to say about this in the next chapter, so I don't want to steal that thunder here. But I want to make a point about the activation, and possibly the deactivation, of angels from an important New Testament passage concerning the issue of authority.

The passage is 1 Corinthians 11, where Paul sets down this foundational principle of authority: "I want you to understand that Christ is the head of every man, and the man is the head of a woman, and God is the head of Christ" (v. 3).

Then Paul goes into a discussion of praying and prophesying with and without head coverings. Whether this passage refers to a woman's long hair or to a covering over the hair is debated, but Paul's thesis is that the woman should have her head covered when engaging in these activities, as a sign of her submission to God-ordained authority.

Then Paul makes this summary statement in verse 10: "Therefore the woman ought to have a symbol of authority on her head, because of the angels." Let's talk about what this means.

First Corinthians 11 has to do with the church's worship and how that worship is supposed to work. What I believe Paul is saying here is that in order for the angels to do what they're supposed to do, the people for whom they are doing it must do what they are supposed to do.

Paul has argued that it is a disgrace and a sign of rebellion against authority for a woman to pray or speak in church with her head uncovered. If a woman did that and signaled her rebellion with the angels watching, she would rebuff the angels.

The woman is not the only person under authority here. Men are to operate under the authority of Christ. And Paul says that even Christ is subject to God the Father. Men and women are equal in essence, but they are distinct in function. And when you rebel against that chain of command, you lose access to the angelic involvement and activity in your life.

I suspect that many women are not seeing the power of God operating in their lives, are not seeing their prayers answered, are not seeing God intervene in their circumstances, because they have decided to address things by means of rebellion rather than by means of biblically based obedience.

The same thing can be said of men. When we rebel against the authority of Christ over our lives, we place ourselves outside God's protective angelic hedge, and the enemy has a field day with us. The angels are activated when God's people are operating according to His principles of authority.

ANGELS ARE UNDER GOD'S AUTHORITY

My last point is simply a reminder that the holy angels are under God's sovereign authority.

That's good news for you and me, because one reason we are going to win this conflict called spiritual warfare is that the angels are under God's authority.

The Temptation to Worship Angels

In fact, the danger in a study like this is that as you begin to get plugged into these spiritual realities and begin to recognize angelic activity in your life, you will be tempted to worship angels.

People in the Bible who saw angels often faced the temptation to worship them, because they are such overwhelming creatures. But let me just note a couple of texts in the book of Revelation that should lay this temptation to rest.

When the apostle John saw the angel in Revelation 19, he said, "I fell at his feet to worship him. And he said to me, 'Do not do that; I am a fellow servant of yours . . . ; worship God'" (Revelation 19:10).

Again in Revelation 22:8, John fell at the feet of an angel to worship him. And again, the angel said, "Do not do that" (v. 9). No angel of God ever accepts worship. The angels know whose authority they are under and who is worthy of worship.

Only one angel ever tried to steal God's worship, and his name was Lucifer. No angel has tried it since. The angels always direct all worship to God.

A Demonstration of God's Authority

Let me close this chapter by reminding you of a classic case that demonstrates the authority of God over the angels. It's the story of Job.

You recall what happened. God called the angels together for a conference in heaven, and He allowed Satan to attend the meeting (Job 1:6). You have to be pretty confident in your power to allow the enemy into your planning sessions.

But not only did God allow Satan to enter His presence, God took the initiative to point out His servant Job to Satan. "Have you considered My servant Job? For there is no one like him on the earth, a blameless and upright man" (Job 1:8).

This was not a case of Satan looking for Job. According to verse 7, Satan was just roaming around on earth, looking for someone to devour like the roaring lion he is (1 Peter 5:8).

So God pointed out Job, and Satan replied, "Does Job fear God for nothing? Hast Thou not made a hedge about him and his house and all that he has, on every side? Thou hast blessed the work of his hands, and his possessions have increased in the land. But put forth Thy hand now and touch all that he has; he will surely curse Thee to Thy face" (Job 1:9–11).

Satan issued a challenge to God as part of the angelic conflict. Satan wanted to embarrass God by proving to Him that Job was not the man God thought he was.

So God gave Satan permission to take everything Job had except his life or his health (Job 1:12). Here was Job, minding his business, going to work every day. Suddenly everything he had was gone, including his children. But Satan could not cross the line God had drawn, because God was firmly in control and Satan was under His authority.

Even later, when Satan again challenged God and was allowed to afflict Job with a terrible disease, God demonstrated His absolute control over the angelic realm by again drawing a line Satan could not cross (Job 2:6).

There is a whole chapter's worth of principles for our spiritual warfare in the life of Job. His faithfulness to God is incredible, despite the fact that he didn't know what was happening or why—and God never really told him. Job didn't understand all the ramifications of his circumstances, but he understood that he was part of something bigger, and he demonstrated his submission to God's authority.

So the angels operate by authority. They function along lines of authority that are clearly marked out by

God, and the extent to which we will see the operation of angels in our lives is the extent to which we bring ourselves under God's authority as a way of life, like Job did. When we do that, then we can call on that authority for help in our time of need.

8

THE ENLISTMENT OF ANGELS

As we finish this section of the book, I want to talk about enlisting the help of angels, or how we can position ourselves so that God can release His angels to minister on our behalf.

We know from Hebrews 1:14 that angels are ministering spirits assigned to those who will inherit salvation. That is, angels have been given responsibility to serve those who know Jesus Christ.

Let me clarify something before we begin. I do not mean to suggest that you and I can force the angelic world to do anything we want. The angels obey their boss, who is Jesus Christ. We have no authority in the angelic realm on our own. Our authority comes from our relationship with God through Jesus Christ.

Although we have authority by virtue of our position, not our obedience, we cannot expect guidance or answers to prayer unless we are obedient to God. But when we are in right relationship with God, He is predisposed to release angelic activity on our behalf as we carry out His purposes. It's a matter of our putting ourselves in position for God to minister to us through the ministry of angels.

The means by which we enlist the angels to minister on our behalf is no great mystery or secret. The holy angels of God are active in their assistance of us when we worship Him.

ANGELS ARE CREATED FOR WORSHIP

The Bible says that when we come to worship God, we join the company of "myriads of angels" (Hebrews 12:22). The theology here is very straightforward. Angels were created for the worship of God. In fact, they are always looking into the face of God (Matthew 18:10). And when we join them in doing what they do best, God activates them on our behalf.

So what I want to do in this chapter is help you understand the implications of this statement as we look at the various categories of worship and learn what it takes to see the activity of the angels in our lives. I want to begin with a great passage we have visited before, Isaiah 6. In this text the angels and worship come together in a powerful way.

We know from Isaiah 6:1 that the prophet had his great vision "in the year of King Uzziah's death."

That historical note may not mean much to you, but it meant a lot to Isaiah because under King Uzziah, Israel had finally flourished. It had come into its own. Under King Uzziah, Israel had become a power to be reckoned with. And yet, Uzziah had died.

It could be that as you read this, your Uzziah has died—something in your life that you were counting on to keep things steady has disappeared. It could be your job or your health or some other circumstance. But whatever it was, it's gone. The hope you were placing in that thing or that set of circumstances is no longer available to you.

Isaiah's vision came at just the right time, because he and his nation were hurting. But he did the right thing in that he bowed before the Lord. It was in recognizing His proper relationship before God that Isaiah joined the angels, and the angels moved on God's behalf in his life:

> In the year of King Uzziah's death, I saw the Lord sitting on a throne, lofty and exalted, with the train of His robe filling the temple. Seraphim stood above Him, each having six wings; with two he covered his face, and with two he covered his feet, and with two he flew. And one called out to another and said, "Holy, Holy, Holy, is the Lord of hosts, the whole earth is full of His glory." (Isaiah 6:1–3)

When Isaiah went into the temple in Jerusalem, he was suddenly transported to the temple in heaven, the realm that the New Testament calls heavenly places. And what did he see? He saw angels—the seraphim—doing in heaven what Isaiah came to the temple to do on earth, which was worship.

Whenever you and I worship God, we join the angels, because for them, worship is nonstop activity. The Bible says the seraphim had six wings. With two wings they covered their faces, because they could not look directly on the awesome glory of God. With two other wings they covered their feet, symbolizing humility in God's presence. And with two wings they flew, ready to do God's bidding.

Please notice that four of the seraphim's wings are for worship, and two are for working. If you spend more time in worship than in working, then you'll know what you're doing when you go to work because you have been in God's presence.

ANGELS ARE ENLISTED BY OUR PRAISE

These opening verses give us the setting of the vision, and also reveal the first area of worship in which the angels are involved.

One of the fundamental elements of worship is praise. In the midst of his worship, Isaiah heard the seraphim calling out their praise to God. They spoke antiphonally, calling out to one another, perhaps from each side of the temple. One group spoke, and the other answered in response.

Transformed by Praise

I want you to see something here. Isaiah saw the Lord seated on a throne, "lofty and exalted." We call this attribute of God His transcendence, the fact that He is infinitely far above and distinct from everything in the universe.

But the angels also sang, "The whole earth is full of His glory" (Isaiah 6:3). This is the immanence of God, His nearness to His creation. Both are true of Him. He is "out there," and yet He is also right here.

Follow me on this. Isaiah went to the temple to worship because King Uzziah died. Isaiah's earthly circumstances were a mess. But when he went into the temple, he learned something he couldn't learn in the newspaper. The newspaper headlines said, "The King Is Dead." But the temple "newspaper" headlines said, "The King Is Alive."

Do you see the difference? Which newspaper are you going to read? Which headline are you going to believe? If you look at your circumstances through earthly eyes only, they may look bad. But when you come into the temple of God and learn what God is about, it changes the way you view your circumstances. Isaiah saw God.

When you come into the house of God to worship, things can change. Maybe on Saturday your King Uzziah died. Your world took a tumble. But then you saw God on Sunday, and there was new hope. There was a new sense that all was not lost. That's what God does when you worship.

Cleansed by Repentance

When Isaiah saw and heard the angels worshiping, something happened: "The foundations of the thresholds trembled at the voice of him who called out, while the temple was filling with smoke" (Isaiah 6:4). This wasn't a tame little worship service!

Isaiah—who was the most spiritual man in Israel—saw all of this and cried out, "Woe is me, for I am ruined!" (v. 5). He was saying, "I thought I was good until I came in here. I sing my songs, but I don't sing so that the building shakes. I believe in God, but I've never seen Him like this."

Isaiah got to see God as He really is, and as a result the prophet saw himself as he really was. He saw how unlike God he was. When you get a new view of God in His holiness, you get a new view of yourself. And it's not pretty.

The word *woe* means "undone," literally "coming apart at the seams." Isaiah saw his sin and the sin of his people, and he confessed, "I am a man of unclean lips, and I live among a people of unclean lips; for my eyes have seen the King, the Lord of hosts" (v. 5).

Commissioned by Praise

It was at this point that the angels got active. After Isaiah let God and not the death of King Uzziah define his circumstances, the angels started to move. Verses 6–8 of Isaiah 6 describe the prophet's cleansing by a seraph that flew to him with a burning coal from the altar.

Why did God send an angel to purify Isaiah? God had a mission for him. "Then I heard the voice of the Lord, saying, 'Whom shall I send, and who will go for Us?' Then I said, 'Here am I. Send me!'" (v. 8).

Now Isaiah received his mission. He discovered what he was supposed to do with his life. Because he went into the temple to worship the Lord, he wound up joining the angels in bowing before God. And when God saw that, He sent the angels to prepare Isaiah for his mission.

You say, "But I'm confused." Praise God in your confusion. Why? Because you are praising the One who can unconfuse your confusion.

Another Example of Praise

There's another great example of the power of praise in 2 Chronicles 20. Jehoshaphat, the king of Judah, was in trouble. He was being invaded by three armies (v. 1).

So Jehoshaphat went to prayer. "O Lord, the God of our fathers, art Thou not God in the heavens? And art Thou not ruler over all the kingdoms of the nations? Power and might are in Thy hand so that no one can stand against Thee" (v. 6).

That's not how most of us would start our prayer if three armies were invading us. We would start our prayer with, "God, how could You let this happen to me?"

But Jehoshaphat started praising God for who He is.

Then the king praised God for what He had done. "Didst Thou not, O our God, drive out the inhabitants of this land before Thy people Israel?" (v. 7).

Then notice what Jehoshaphat said in 2 Chronicles 20:9. "Should evil come upon us, the sword, or judgment, or pestilence, or famine, we will stand before this house and before Thee . . . and cry to Thee in our distress."

Do you hear what he was saying? Jehoshaphat was saying, "Lord, whatever happens, we are going to worship You." And because he worshiped, he could say, "O our God, wilt Thou not judge them? For we are powerless before this great multitude who are coming against us; nor do we know what to do, but our eyes are on Thee" (v. 12).

Jehoshaphat and Judah not only worshiped, but they put worship ahead of military strength. According to verse 21, the king commanded the praise singers to lead the army into battle. He knew that in order to win this fight, he needed God's help. If victory was to be gained, it would be gained by God's presence and power.

No wonder we read in verse 22 that when the singers began singing and praising God, He ambushed and routed their enemies.

We buy all kinds of stuff to solve our problems. We pay people to listen to us talk so we can solve our problems. We hire businesses to come up with solutions. But often God is saying, "If you would just praise, I would take care of that for you."

Worship is what gets God's attention and enlists the help of His angels. And in this passage, worship is what prompted God to come to the aid of His people and rout their enemies.

So here's a great principle for spiritual warfare. Learn to praise God, and He will take care of the enemy.

ANGELS ARE ENLISTED THROUGH PRAYER

Here's a second element of worship that will enlist the angels on our behalf. When God's people pray, they move heaven.

Prayer and the Angels

Prayer and the presence of angels are tied very closely together in Scripture. Many times when God sent an angel down to earth, it was in response to someone talking to the Lord. We saw this happen several times in the book of Daniel.

The experience of Peter in Acts 12 is another good example. Peter was in prison, and the church was praying. God sent an angel, and Peter was miraculously released. The only bad thing was that the church was shocked when God answered their prayer. If you want to move the hand of God, pray like you expect something to happen.

God is sovereign and will make the ultimate decisions about our lives. But never let it be said in heaven that a lot of blessings were never delivered to you on earth either because you didn't pray or because you prayed but didn't expect anything to happen.

If you have a legitimate request or need, take it to God in prayer and expect an answer. Abraham interceded for Lot (Genesis 18), and two angels came to deliver Lot and his family from Sodom.

Prayer in the Lions' Den

We can't talk about prayer and the angels without going to Daniel 6, the great story of Daniel in the lions' den. Many of us need to review this account because we're being devoured by people and circumstances in our lives. A lot of people are in the lions' den today. Let's see what to do.

Daniel's problem started when his enemies persuaded the king to forbid prayer to any god but him for thirty days. They knew that Daniel would ignore the king's edict and pray to God. They were right (Daniel 6:10).

Daniel was a praying man, but please notice that prayer did not keep him from getting thrown into the lions' den. People think, *Because I pray, nothing bad should happen.*

Not necessarily. Because you pray, you're not *alone* if something bad should happen. That's a big difference.

Daniel wound up in the lions' den, but God honored His praying servant and sent an angel to shut the lions' mouths. Daniel was able to announce his own deliverance to the king the next morning (v. 22).

The lions lost their appetite through angelic intervention. Daniel could have tried all he wanted to close the lions' mouths himself. A lot of us are doing everything we can to close the mouths of the things that are devouring us. But it doesn't work.

Maybe God's angels can do a better job with the lions in our lives than we can. But to get God's angels working on our lions, we have to get God's attention. And one way to get God's attention is through prayer.

Prayer in the Garden

Jesus understood the importance of prayer because He functioned as a man while He was on earth. In Luke 22:41, we find Jesus in prayer in the Garden of Gethsemane just before His crucifixion.

"He withdrew from [the disciples] about a stone's throw, and He knelt down and began to pray, saying, 'Father, if Thou art willing, remove this cup from Me; yet not My will, but Thine be done.' Now an angel from heaven appeared to Him, strengthening Him" (Luke 22:41–43).

Jesus was praying that He might be spared the cup of suffering that awaited Him at the cross. But then He submitted His will to the Father's will, and God the Father sent an angel to strengthen Jesus so He could accomplish the Father's will.

There's nothing wrong with praying that God will do certain things in your life. Jesus prayed fervently and specifically that God would remove the cross from His life.

But then after He made His request, Jesus made it clear that what He wanted most was what God the Father wanted.

Tell God what you want when you pray. That means you can't just pray, "Bless me today, Lord." That is a wasted prayer, because you haven't asked for anything. Vague prayers get vague answers. If you are still alive at the end of the day, you can assume that God blessed you that day.

Don't be afraid to be specific in prayer. Tell God the desires of your heart. And when He gives you some of those desires, praise Him.

Prayer and Angelic Strength

There is another kind of praise for answered prayer. This is not praise because we received what we asked for, but praise because even though God denied or delayed our request, He gave us the strength to accept what He sent us.

When you pray, God will either give you what you asked for, or He will give you strength to deal with what He wants. Jesus was strengthened by an angel after He submitted to the Father's will and needed strength to go to the cross.

So when you pray, "Thy will be done," God's strength will be yours. Prayer is a powerful way to enlist God's help, which may come through His angels.

ANGELS ARE ENLISTED BY SUBMISSION

A third aspect of worship that can bring you angelic assistance is submission, which simply means coming underneath appropriate, God-appointed authority.

Jesus in the Garden of Gethsemane was also the perfect example of proper submission expressed in worship as He submitted to His Father's will.

Angels and Authority

We have already made the point that angels always operate under authority themselves. You will never get angelic help from God if, for instance, you're a wife who is fighting the legitimate authority of your husband, or a husband who refuses to bow to Christ's authority over you. Angels know when we are operating in proper submission.

In Acts 19 we read about an unusual incident when a group of Jewish exorcists tried to imitate Paul's power over demons:

> Some of the Jewish exorcists, who went from place to place, attempted to name over those who had the evil spirits the name of the Lord Jesus, saying, "I adjure you by Jesus whom Paul preaches." And seven sons of one Sceva, a Jewish chief priest, were doing this. And the evil spirit answered and said to them, "I recognize Jesus, and I know about Paul, but who are you?" And the man, in whom was the evil spirit, leaped on them and subdued

all of them and overpowered them, so that they fled out of that house naked and wounded. (Acts 19:13–16)

The angelic realm knows whether a person is functioning under authority. The demon knew that these men had no authority to be doing what they were doing. They had no right to be using the name of Jesus the way Paul used it. So the demon knew that they were totally unprotected, and he messed them up.

No Submission, No Authority

If you're not under authority, your own authority is limited. God does not trust full use of His authority to people who have not first learned submission. Even Jesus "learned obedience from the things which He suffered" (Hebrews 5:8).

The apostle James makes this crucial connection when he writes, "Submit therefore to God. Resist the devil and he will flee from you" (James 4:7). Most people start quoting this verse by saying, "Resist the devil." But the first step is to submit to God. Come under His authority.

Why? Until you're submitted to God you won't have the power to resist the devil. But when you are in submission to God, the devil can't handle you because you are operating under God's authority.

Nathanael, our friend we met a few chapters ago, got to see the angels in action because he recognized Jesus for who He is and came under Jesus' authority by responding to His call to discipleship (John 1:46–51).

Isn't that what you want to see in your life, the angels of God moving up and down the ladder of Jesus, bringing answers from heaven to your needs on earth? It won't happen until you come under the authority of

Christ and exercise the responsibility you have under His authority.

But when you get all of that lined up properly, you will see the angels in action, addressing needs on earth from the resources of heaven.

ANGELS ARE ENLISTED BY WITNESS

Let me mention one more thing in closing, the issue of your witness. We talked about the relation between your witness and the work of angels in an earlier chapter, but I want to mention it again here.

In Luke 12:8–9 Jesus said, "Everyone who confesses Me before men, the Son of Man shall confess him also before the angels of God; but he who denies Me before men shall be denied before the angels of God."

Jesus said your witness, or lack thereof, is an issue that involves the angels. This is because the angels are messengers who wait for God's instructions to bring the answers to earth.

So if you are a Christian who can never seem to speak a word for Christ, He will deny you angelic assistance when you come with your needs and requests.

But if you are not ashamed to be publicly identified with Christ, if you don't mind other people knowing that you belong to Him, He will not be ashamed to say before the angels, "She is one of Mine. Take her the answer."

I want to close with four powerful verses from Psalm 103:

The Lord has established His throne in the heavens; and His sovereignty rules over all. Bless the Lord, you His angels, mighty in strength, who perform His word, obeying the voice of His word! Bless the Lord, all you His hosts,

you who serve Him, doing His will. Bless the Lord, all
you works of His, in all places of His dominion; bless the
Lord, O my soul! (vv. 19–22)

This is an awesome picture of worship. Angels worship the Lord. His people worship Him. Even His works
worship Him.

What about you? Worship is powerful because God
is looking for worshipers (John 4:23). When you worship, you exalt the Lord. And when He is exalted, when
He is lifted up, He sends the angels on your behalf.

PART THREE

YOUR
ADVERSARY

9

THE CHARACTER OF SATAN

We have looked at the pride and rebellion of Satan, how he went from being the anointed cherub of God to the archenemy of God. We have also dealt with the way in which Satan carried his battle against God from heaven to earth, bringing with him one-third of the angels when God banished him to this planet.

Now that we have looked at the battlefield and identified the combatants, we need to study our enemy and his forces in more detail before we move on to the resources God has given us for spiritual warfare.

So for the next few chapters, I want to talk about Satan's character, strategy, and helpers. Then we will get to the best part—his defeat at the hands of Jesus Christ.

THE CURSE OF SATAN

Satan's evil character was formed the moment he let his pride cause him to rise up in rebellion against the throne of God.

This creature went from a beautiful, perfect being named Lucifer, living in the light and glory of heaven, to Satan the prince of darkness, banished to the earth. And he fell with the speed of lightning.

That's what Jesus said in Luke 10:18 when He told the seventy disciples He had sent out, "I was watching Satan fall from heaven like lightning." This is one of many Bible passages that speak of Satan's judgment by God and the curse imposed on him. His curse was evident in his change of name and his change of destination.

A Change in Name

We know that before his fall, this angel's name was Lucifer (Isaiah 14:12 KJV). But in Luke 10:18 Jesus called him Satan.

People's names were very important in the Bible, because names reflected character. The names of God reflect God's character. The name given to Christ's followers at Antioch, "Christians" (Acts 11:26), reflected their conversion and allegiance to Him.

The names given to Lucifer after his fall reflect his character. "Satan" is one of those names. It means "adversary" or "opposer." His curse is revealed in the fact that he went from "Lucifer," meaning "shining one," to a name meaning adversary, the one who opposes everyone and everything associated with God.

When you rebel against God, it will always affect your character. When you oppose God, you are not the same person you used to be. That's why being right with God is so important. Rebellion changes your character.

Satan's character was corrupted so completely that God gave him a different name. Lucifer had lost his brilliance and his righteousness, so he got a name that reflected his fallen status.

Actually, the Bible has a number of names for our enemy. Satan is one name we are very familiar with. Another is the devil, which means "accuser" or "slanderer." The word *Satan* is used about fifty-five times in the New Testament, and *devil* is used about thirty-five times. The devil is the great accuser of God's people. That's why the saints rejoice when the devil is finally "thrown down" by God (Revelation 12:9).

The devil's nature is revealed in the great contest of Job 1–2. By accusing Job of serving God for gain, Satan was slandering both Job's character and God's character. Remember, everything our enemy does is ultimately directed at God. The devil hates God and wants to do anything he can to injure God's reputation so that He does not get the glory due Him.

The devil can't touch God, so he seeks to destroy God's glory by attacking His people. This is why the devil is regularly in God's presence, accusing and slandering the saints to hinder God's glory and keep us from being blessed.

The idea of an accuser suggests a legal setting, a court scene. We need to understand that God operates His universe like a court. He gave Israel His law, and throughout the Old Testament we find God bringing a charge against His people when they broke that law.

Lucifer himself was brought into the court of heaven, charged with rebellion, found guilty, and sentenced to the lake of fire, as we will discuss below. His fellow rebellious angels were also sentenced to eternal fire.

Now the devil is on death row, even though he is being allowed to operate for a period of time. He has taken the role of prosecutor, bringing charges against us before God, accusing us of all sorts of things, slandering us and God.

The great thing is that we have a "defense attorney,"

Jesus Christ, to defend us by pleading His blood (1 John 2:1). The sad thing is how often we fail and do wrong things that give substance to the devil's accusations.

So when the Bible calls our enemy "the devil," God wants us to understand that our adversary is also our accuser.

The Bible has many other descriptive names and designations for Satan. For example, he is called "the god of this world" (2 Corinthians 4:4) and "the prince of the power of the air" (Ephesians 2:2) because right now, he's in control of this planet. Satan has demonized this world.

Here's a very revealing passage about Satan. Jesus said, speaking of our enemy, "The thief comes only to steal, and kill, and destroy" (John 10:10).

Look at the evil titles Jesus gave to the devil. He is a thief who wants to steal your joy, your effectiveness for Christ, and anything else he can take from you. He is a killer, "a murderer from the beginning" (John 8:44).

Because of Satan, Adam and Eve died. Because of Satan, Cain killed Abel. And because of Satan, all the children of Adam will die someday. Satan would kill you and me if at all possible. He is a destroyer who wants to wreck everything and everyone God has made.

Let me give you one more name for the devil that's very revealing of his character. It's found in Revelation 12:1–9, a key passage that gives us a lot of information about our enemy's names, character, and activity.

I referred to this text briefly earlier, but this time I want to focus on verse 3, where the devil is called the "great red dragon" (this is where people get the idea that Satan wears a red jumpsuit). He is then repeatedly referred to as a dragon in the verses that follow. And notice that John also calls the devil "the serpent of old" (v. 9), a reference to his deception in the Garden of Eden.

A dragon is basically a serpent on steroids. A dragon is an awesome, destructive creature, like the ones they used to portray in those old science fiction movies. A dragon may be mythical and not an actual being, but the Bible draws on the imagery of a terrifying, destructive beast to characterize Satan.

Other terms are used in the Bible to describe Satan, but we have enough here to make our point. When Lucifer fell, he got a litany of new names that tell us who he is and that warn us to be on the alert for his attacks.

A Change in Destination

Lucifer got something else hung on him besides new names. He also got an eternal death sentence. Since we talked about Satan's eternal destiny earlier, let me just note it again and then talk about Satan's new destination.

Jesus said that the lake of fire "has been prepared for the devil and his angels" (Matthew 25:41). It is called "the lake of fire and brimstone" (Revelation 20:10), where the devil will be cast along with his followers for eternity.

There was never any possibility of redemption for Satan or his angelic followers. Speaking of Christ's incarnation and death for sin, the writer of Hebrews says, "He does not give help to angels" (Hebrews 2:16). The Cross did not include a provision for Satan's sin.

Why no provision for Satan? I believe that part of the reason is that he sinned against too much light. Lucifer was perfect in every detail. He had firsthand experience with God. He lived in God's very presence. He knew what he was doing. He wasn't seduced by any tempter. Satan entered into his rebellion with his spiritual eyes wide open. There was no remedy for him.

When Adam and Eve followed Satan in his rebellion and sinned against God, the human race received the same penalty that Satan received—spiritual death. But God did something for mankind that He did not do for Satan and his angels. God displayed His grace to us, providing us a way of salvation (Ephesians 2:8–9).

Satan's sin was so terrible that there was no grace for him. But God chose to extend His grace to mankind to demonstrate His power and goodness to the entire angelic world.

Satan thought he had won the battle for mankind when he succeeded in the Garden. But Satan did not count on God's grace, an attribute of His character that did not come into play until sin was present. Grace can only be measured against sin.

What God did by showering His grace on sinners was step into Satan's domain and plunder it. Satan had mankind in the fearful grip of physical and spiritual death (Hebrews 2:14–15), but God used death itself—the death of Christ—to defeat Satan at his own game.

The result is that Satan is not only condemned to eternal death himself, but he is also defeated in his purpose of taking the entire human race with him to destruction. Salvation is God's statement to Satan that he is a beaten foe.

THE CONTEST OF SATAN

We have already learned enough about Satan to know that even though he has been decisively and eternally defeated by Jesus Christ, he is not about to lie down and quit. He is still engaged in a great contest, a great war, against God for the souls of men and women. And he has some potent weapons at his disposal.

The Weapon of Power and Wealth

Did you know that the devil can give you a lot of stuff?

Well, he can, because this world has been "handed over" to him temporarily. And as the devil told Jesus in His temptation, "I give it to whomever I wish" (Luke 4:6). Satan can give people power, wealth, friends, and fun on a mammoth scale. Scripture says that "the whole world lies in the power of the evil one" (1 John 5:19). So Satan can do you some earthly good, but when he does it he has something bad in mind. It's sort of like those letters you get in the mail from credit card companies, congratulating you on your "outstanding credit history" and making you feel special because you have been hand-selected from among the masses to receive one of their cards with a high-dollar limit.

These letters actually make you think you've accomplished something and you deserve a reward. But credit card companies are not out to do you a favor. They have one overriding concern, which is the interest they hope to collect from you. The buying power they want to give you comes with a high price tag.

I'm not trying to equate credit card companies with the devil. But a similar principle is at work. Satan can give you "buying power," but he will be there to collect heavy interest when the bill comes due. And the interest he seeks to collect is your destruction.

The Weapon of Deception

Everything Satan does is wrapped up in lies, because deception is at the heart of everything he does.

Jesus said concerning the devil, "He . . . does not stand in the truth, because there is no truth in him. Whenever he speaks a lie, he speaks from his own nature; for he is a liar, and the father of lies" (John 8:44).

How many times have you ordered something from a catalog that looks like just what you wanted, but when the product arrives, it doesn't look nearly as good as it did in the catalog?

Satan knows how to put together a glossy, slick-looking catalog of temptations. He knows how to make things look good. But Jesus said that Satan is incapable of doing anything but lying. He is so thoroughly corrupt that lies are the bone and sinew of his nature.

Satan is the ultimate deceiver. He will either make a promise that he doesn't deliver on, or else he won't tell you the whole story. When the thing gets delivered, you find out it isn't what you thought it was, and you don't like what you're getting.

In fact, Jesus called the devil the "father of lies" because he gave birth to deception. He told the first lie to the angels who followed him in his rebellion. He continued lying in the Garden of Eden, and he has been at it ever since. He's out to deceive the whole world (Revelation 12:9). And the people he controls are his deceivers too (2 John 7).

If Satan is the father of lies, that means he has a family. Jesus prefaced His statement about the devil in John 8:44 by saying to the Jewish religious leaders, "You are of your father the devil, and you want to do the desires of your father."

Satan has a lot of kids, many of whom don't know that he is their father. But anyone who does not know Jesus Christ is a child of the devil. Some who claim to know Jesus Christ are still children of the devil.

We aren't the judge of people's hearts, but Jesus said that many people who call Him "Lord" will not enter heaven (Matthew 7:21). Why? Because they have been deceived by the devil into substituting their self-righteousness for God's righteousness.

The Weapon of Opposition

If Satan cannot get you to believe his lies or fall into one of his traps, he will turn around and oppose and resist anything you try to do for God. You can bank on Satan's opposition in your efforts to live for Christ, but that's a good sign because it means that Satan considers you worth opposing! He doesn't waste his time messing around with people who aren't doing anything.

People who never feel the devil's opposition probably are not doing much for God. See, the devil knows he cannot touch you and me in terms of condemning us to hell. So he is content to let us go our way as long as we don't try to invade his kingdom and make an impact for Christ.

But when we get serious about serving God, the adversary shows up. He's not about to stand by and let us plunder his kingdom. Remember, he's still determined to steal God's glory, so he is going to oppose anything that brings God glory.

It all comes back to the fact that we are in a war with a powerful enemy. But even soldiers in a war are given times of what is called R & R, "rest and recuperation" leave.

How do we get some R & R from Satan? By praising God. In fact, the stronger the opposition, the more you need to praise God in the midst of your opposition.

Satan can't handle praise. He's allergic to worship. He has to flee, because when we praise God, He shows up to enjoy our praises. And Satan cannot abide the presence of God. So if your adversary is opposing you hard right now, it's time to praise! When we praise, we resist Satan's opposition (James 4:7).

The Weapon of Accusation

Another potent weapon our enemy wields in his

contest against God is accusation, the aspect of Satan's character and work underscored by the name *devil*, the "accuser of our brethren" (Revelation 12:10).

To be effective, an accuser needs an opportunity to make an accusation. He needs something he can try to pin on the person being accused.

Paul urges us, "Do not give the devil an opportunity" to accuse us (Ephesians 4:27). Paul chose the right name for the enemy here, because the devil is the accuser or slanderer who seeks to tie us up with guilt.

When we give the devil an opportunity, an opening —in this case in Ephesians 4, by letting our anger get out of control—then at that point he has a legal right to accuse us before God.

The devil has been in God's court before. He knows what kind of Judge God is and how His court works. He knows that God is so righteous and so holy He has to deal with sin. So when we sin we give the devil the opportunity he needs to go into God's courtroom and lay a charge against us.

Satan cannot touch our salvation. But he is always ready to take advantage of our sin to ruin our lives.

This is so important because God's justice demands that He always deal with sin. He can't just skip it. When we as believers sin, we break our fellowship with God and give the devil an open door to operate in our lives. This is why the Bible urges us to deal decisively with sin (1 John 1:9).

If we don't, the devil turns that opportunity for accusation into a fortress. And when we allow him to build a fortress, we are in trouble because the devil now has undue influence over us. Don't let him bring you under his accusing control.

THE CONQUEST OF SATAN

The goal of any contest is conquest, victory. In Revelation 12:11 the Bible gives us three powerful weapons for defeating our adversary Satan, the devil who accuses us day and night.

The apostle John was looking ahead to that future day when Satan will be defeated once and for all, so the context of Revelation 12:11 is prophetic. But the weapons these tribulation saints used to defeat the devil are the same ones we can use today. This great verse says, "They overcame him because of the blood of the Lamb and because of the word of their testimony, and they did not love their life even to death."

We need three things to keep the devil from ruining us: the cross of Jesus Christ (which is absolutely foundational), our confession, and our commitment.

The Cross

The first thing you need to beat Satan is the cross, without which the other two weapons would not be possible. "The blood of the Lamb" is a reference to the death of Jesus Christ on the cross. The blood Jesus shed there not only purchased our eternal salvation, but it renders Satan powerless when we as believers are operating in the power of the Holy Spirit.

Please notice my caveat. Satan is not powerless in the sense that he cannot do anything. But Christ's blood renders Satan powerless in terms of his daily warfare against us when we are operating with the spiritual resources God has provided.

Let me show you what I mean. John 12:31–33 says that Satan was judged by the death—that is, the blood—of Christ. So if you are under the blood, you belong to

Christ. And as Paul says in Romans 8:31, "If God is for us, who is against us?" Paul goes on to ask in verse 33, "Who will bring a charge against God's elect?" Then in verse 34 he asks, "Who is the one who condemns?"

The one who tries to condemn us is the accuser, the devil. But look at God's answer to the devil's accusation: "Christ Jesus is He who died" (v. 34). So anyone, including Satan, who tries to condemn us has to undo and overcome what Jesus did when He died.

But that's not all Romans 8:34 tells us. Look at this verse again and you'll see that Jesus not only died, but He was "raised" from the dead. So our accuser has to overcome the resurrection of Christ as well.

It gets even better. Christ is "at the right hand of God." That's a reference to His ascension back to heaven, so we have a crucified, raised, and ascended Savior to answer any accusation against us.

And here's the topper. Not only is Jesus Christ at the right hand of God, the place of God's favor, but Jesus also "intercedes for us" (Romans 8:34c).

Christ is not sitting up in heaven wondering what's next on the agenda. According to 1 John 2:1–2, He is our divine defense attorney in heaven: "My little children, I am writing these things to you that you may not sin. And if anyone sins, we have an Advocate with the Father, Jesus Christ the righteous; and He Himself is the propitiation for our sins." The word *Advocate* means legal counsel, because this is a courtroom scene.

When Satan says to God, "Look at what Your child did. Look at what Your child thought. Look at what Your child said," then Jesus Christ rises to our defense as our attorney.

"Father, Satan has a point. Your child did that sin, but I want You to know that that sin has already been cov-

ered by My blood. I died to pay for this believer's sins,
and he has confessed that sin to Me. I have already covered that sin with My blood."

And God says, "Next case."

Remember that when we sin, we give Satan a legal
right to accuse us. But when we confess our sins (1 John
1:9), we are forgiven and cleansed through Christ's blood.

Then why does Satan keep coming with his charges?
Because he knows how often we skip over our sins and
don't keep our accounts up to date. And he knows that
sin in our hearts breaks our fellowship with God. Satan
is always looking for that little corner of our lives where
he can build a fortress.

Our Confession

A second weapon we can use in our conquest of Satan is our confession, "the word of [our] testimony"
(Revelation 12:11).

Our confession or testimony has to do with our
public identification with Christ. It has to do with how
we speak and live, whether we are adequately and accu-
rately reflecting who Jesus is, acknowledging Him
before the world, and pointing people to Him.

There is tremendous authority against Satan in our
confession of Christ, because of what Jesus said in
Matthew 10:32–33: "Everyone therefore who shall confess Me before men, I will also confess him before My
Father who is in heaven. But whoever shall deny Me before men, I will also deny him before My Father who is
in heaven." Jesus was not talking about salvation, but
about our willingness to confess before the world that
we belong to Him.

The authority over Satan comes because when we
confess Christ, He confesses us before His Father. That

is, He says, "Father, this believer is faithful to Me. She needs power over the Evil One, and I am signing off on her request so You will know I approve it."

So the question is, what have we done for Christ lately? If our lips are sealed about Christ at work, at home, or anywhere else, we don't need to bother asking Him for the power to conquer Satan. If Satan has silenced our confession, he has already won a victory.

If you and I are "secret agent" saints, if our witness is invisible, then the experience of our blessings is going to be invisible too. We are called to demonstrate God's glory, wisdom, and power. If we can't do that, we will still be talking about what God did for us two or five or ten years ago, instead of what He is doing for us today. But when we are ready to step out for Christ, He gives us great authority. In Luke 10, Jesus said to the returning seventy, "I have given you authority to tread upon serpents and scorpions, and over all the power of the enemy, and nothing shall injure you" (v. 19).

The words *serpents* and *scorpions* have to do with the devil, not the animal kingdom (Revelation 9:3; 12:9). In other words, these serpents or scorpions were those who carry out Satan's agenda. The seventy disciples who were willing to go out into the villages and witness for Christ had found that they had authority over Satan (Luke 10:17).

Our Commitment

The third weapon in our Revelation 12:11 "arsenal" is what I am calling our commitment. The saints in Revelation loved Christ more than they loved their lives. I'd say that is commitment.

Paul said, "I have been crucified with Christ" (Galatians 2:20). He also said, "For to me, to live is Christ, and to die is gain" (Philippians 1:21). Paul's only goal was that Christ be exalted in his life, even if it meant death (v. 20). That's the kind of commitment we're talking about here. Jesus said something interesting to those seventy disciples in Luke 10:20: "Do not rejoice in this, that the spirits are subject to you, but rejoice that your names are recorded in heaven."

Jesus was not downplaying the disciples' authority over Satan. He was reminding them not to lose sight of their primary focus, which was their relationship and commitment to Him.

In other words, our authority doesn't come from our power. It comes from our relationship with Christ. You don't go authority-hunting, you go Jesus-hunting. The closer you get to Jesus, the more authority you have.

That's the problem with many of the preachers you see on television. They're so busy telling people how to conquer Satan and putting on dramatic displays of their authority that Satan winds up getting way too much attention.

Let's never forget that power belongs to Christ, not us. We can only conquer Satan as we stay fully committed to the Lord. The thing to rejoice about is that we know Him.

An Object Lesson

I want to close this chapter with an amazing biblical account that puts some "skin" on this matter of conquering Satan. The story is found in Zechariah 3.

In a vision the prophet Zechariah saw Joshua, the high priest of his day, "standing before the angel of the Lord, and Satan standing at his right hand to accuse him" (v. 1). Joshua was a servant of God who evidently had done something wrong. So Satan came to be Joshua's accuser, to prosecute him before Jesus.

The text doesn't say Jesus was there, but "the angel of the Lord" in the Old Testament is a reference to Jesus in His eternal deity, before He came to earth.

So here is a classic courtroom scene, an instance of spiritual warfare in which Satan needs to be conquered. We have the throne of God, Jesus Christ as the intercessor, a man with sin, and Satan the accuser.

"And the Lord said to Satan, 'The Lord rebuke you, Satan! Indeed, the Lord who has chosen Jerusalem rebuke you! Is this [the man Joshua] not a brand plucked from the fire?'" (v. 2). Evidently this is one member of the Trinity addressing Satan on behalf of another member.

Joshua wasn't perfect. He was "clothed with filthy garments" as he stood before the angel (v. 3). He was dirty. He needed cleansing in his life. That's why he was standing there.

The angel of the Lord spoke to those who were near Joshua and told them, "Remove the filthy garments from him," and then said to Joshua, "See, I have taken your iniquity away from you and will clothe you with festal robes" (v. 4).

So Joshua appeared before the Lord in sin-stained robes. Satan came to accuse him. But God said to Joshua, "We are going to change your clothes because you have come into My presence with the help of My angel"— the pre-incarnate Jesus Christ.

Joshua got a new turban, and then the new garments (v. 5). Notice the last phrase of verse 5. This all happened "while the angel of the Lord was standing by."

The lawyer was in the courtroom, dealing with Satan's accusation. God won the case, so he told Joshua, "If you will walk in My ways, and if you will perform My service, then you will also govern My house and also have charge of My courts, and I will grant you free access among these who are standing here" (vv. 6–7).

God told Joshua that if he would live for Him and serve Him, God would grant him protection from defilement and give him access. Satan was conquered, and Joshua was forgiven and set free.

The Emancipation Proclamation freeing America's slaves was signed in 1863. But not all slaves got the message right away, so they still thought like slaves, walked like slaves, acted like slaves, and allowed themselves to be treated like slaves.

When you met Jesus, He set you free from Satan's kingdom (Colossians 1:13). But it's possible to be spiritually emancipated and yet still live in bondage to Satan's accusations and intimidation.

Satan will never change his character. He will never give up the contest until he is tossed into the lake of fire. Satan will be Satan for eternity, but he has been conquered by the blood of Jesus Christ.

If you want to make that conquest real in your everyday Christian life, recognize the strategies of your enemy. Be on the alert for his attacks. And stand against Satan in the power of the blood. He will have to flee when you come into the presence of Jesus Christ to praise Him and have Him change your garments by the confession and cleansing of sin.

10

THE STRATEGY OF SATAN

The story is told of a farmer who was constantly having his watermelons stolen by thieves.

The farmer came up with a brilliant idea to thwart the thieves. He poisoned one watermelon, then put a sign in his watermelon field that read: "Warning: One of these watermelons has been poisoned."

The next day the farmer went out to find that none of his melons had been stolen, because the thieves didn't know which one was poisoned. He was quite satisfied that his idea had worked and that he would not have a problem with theft anymore.

But two days after the farmer put up his sign, he came out to his field to find that his sign had been altered. Someone had scratched through his message and had written, "Two of these melons have been poisoned." Our farmer friend had to destroy his whole crop because now he didn't know which other melon was poisoned.

That's what it is like dealing with the devil. No matter what you come up with, he can come up with something better. No matter what sign you put up, he can change the wording. No matter what strategy you devise, you can't outwit this fellow.

Satan has a definite strategy, and it can be understood in one word: deception. Satan's strategy for your life and mine is to deceive us. He is the master deceiver. He is the camouflage king.

The reason Satan has turned to deception is that he cannot outpower God. Satan tried to overcome God in heaven, and that gamble failed. Satan's power will never be a match for God's.

Evidently, in his rebellion Satan forgot that God can do something he cannot do, which is create something out of nothing by simply speaking it into existence. God looked at nothing and said, for example, "Let there be light." And light appeared.

Satan cannot create anything. All he can do is manipulate and maneuver what has been created. Since he cannot match God's power, Satan has to maximize the power he has, and deception is his strong suit. He has turned deception into an art form.

THE POWER OF SATAN'S STRATEGY

Just because Satan is no match for God, that doesn't mean he is powerless. In fact, I want to begin the discussion of Satan's strategy by looking at the power of his deception.

In 2 Thessalonians 2, Paul is correcting these believers' misconceptions about the day of the Lord. He writes:

Let no one in any way deceive you, for it will not come unless the apostasy comes first, and the man of lawless-ness is revealed, the son of destruction, who opposes and exalts himself above every so-called god or object of worship, so that he takes his seat in the temple of God, displaying himself as being God. (vv. 3–4)

Paul then says that this "lawless one," the Antichrist, will not be revealed until God's restraint is removed. Then, "That lawless one will be revealed . . . the one whose coming is in accord with the activity of Satan, with all power and signs and false wonders, and with all the deception of wickedness for those who perish" (vv. 8–10).

The appearance of the Antichrist will be Satan's crowning achievement in his plan to deceive the world. The Antichrist will be empowered by Satan, who will give this person great power to pull off the master deception. The "lawless one" will be so powerful that he will sit in the temple as God, and unsaved people will think he is God. That's power.

Satan's Authority

But we don't have to wait until the end times to see the power of Satan at work. How else can you explain the fact that people will give up everything they have to move in with a cult and put themselves under someone else's power, even to the point of committing suicide in the name of God? The only explanation is Satan's strategy of deception.

Where does Satan get the power he wields over people? He gets it from what I call his constitutional superiority over any man or woman. By constitutional superiority I mean that Satan is an angel, a spirit being. He does not have the limitations of flesh and blood. Therefore, you and I can't compete with the devil in our own strength. We can't outsmart the master deceiver. He has authority by virtue of his person. Satan's authority is given by God and limited by God, but it is still a greater authority than you and I exercise.

Satan's Experience

Satan is also powerful by virtue of his vast experience. He has untold years of experience at being the devil. You are not the first human being he has come up against. He has been against smarter and stronger people than you and me, and he has won.

One thing Satan has learned during all these years is how to transform himself, as we will see later in 2 Corinthians 11:14. He can make himself look like one of the good guys. He is the master chameleon as well as the master deceiver. He can become any color he needs to be in order to pull off his lie. He seeks to camouflage himself and his plans.

Satan is so good and so experienced at deception that the Bible says one day he will deceive all the nations of the world (Revelation 20:8). This world is a puppet, and Satan holds the strings.

Satan's Organization

Another reason that Satan is so powerful in carrying out his strategy is that he commands a massive organization of evil (Ephesians 6:12). Satan's organization is well run and heavily disguised. It reminds me of the Mafia. Do you know the address of Mafia headquarters? Can you pick out the members of the Mafia as they walk the streets? The Mafia has camouflaged itself in the midst of legitimate business.

Many of these men wear suits and ties and carry briefcases just like other people. They operate legitimate-looking businesses behind which they hide their crimes. We know that they are out there and that they are powerful, but they're hard to identify. They control crime and prostitution and money-laundering business- es, but it's hard to find them.

Well, Satan heads a spiritual Mafia that controls peo- ple and even whole nations. People wonder how a nation can produce a Stalin or a Hitler. The explanation is the massive work and deception of Satan. That's how powerful he is.

THE PROGRAM OF SATAN'S STRATEGY

Let's consider the program of Satan's deception. What is he hoping to achieve by working his strategy of deception on the world and on God's people?

Satan's program is to produce such a wonderful counterfeit of God's works and ways that he leads us astray. Paul wrote to the Corinthians, "I am afraid, lest as the serpent deceived Eve by his craftiness, your minds should be led astray from the simplicity and purity of devotion to Christ" (2 Corinthians 11:3).

Notice that Paul's illustration of Satan's deception is Eve, which takes us back to Eden. We have already vis- ited Genesis 3 in detail, but Satan hasn't changed his program. He is out to get us going in the wrong direc- tion, just as he led Eve astray.

The devil wants to make you turn left when you ought to turn right. He wants to make you miserable when you ought to be happy, taste defeat when you ought to have victory, and ruin your life when you ought to have a successful life.

Satan is a counterfeiter—and the better the counter- feiter, the fewer the number of people who realize they're carrying counterfeit money. In fact, you can buy groceries and gas and furniture with counterfeit money. The problem comes when those bills hit the bank and are shown to be worthless.

A Counterfeit View of Ownership

You'll remember that Satan told Eve she could be like God. He knew that was a counterfeit promise because he had tried it himself. But he's still tempting us to take things into our own hands, to set up our own kingdoms, to try to live independently of God.

"You don't have to be anybody's slave, not even God's slave," is Satan's message. His theme song is "I Gotta Be Me." The devil wants you to believe that you don't have to answer to God anymore.

But that's a myth. This universe is God's house, and He's just letting us live in a borrowed room for a while.

At one time or another, most parents have to have an "ownership" discussion with their teenagers. A teenager gets mad, goes to his room, and cranks up the music because he doesn't want to hear what his parent is saying. So the parent confronts his rebellion and tells him to turn the music down. He responds, "I can do whatever I want in here. This is *my* room."

Wrong. This is when a parent brings out the homeowner papers and informs the child that since his parents are paying for the house it belongs to them, not him. He is simply occupying a room that they let him sleep in.

If he wants his own room, he needs to buy his own house and furniture. Then he can have any room he wants. But until then, it's the parents' room on loan to him, and the parents call the shots.

Teenagers need to understand the concept of ownership and authority because that's the way God's world works. There's a big difference between being the owner of the house and a guest in the house. One of the foundational verses in Scripture is Psalm 24:1: "The earth is the Lord's, and all it contains, the world, and those who dwell in it."

Satan may temporarily control a lot of this world's assets and use them against believers, but he even does that within the limits of God's permission. Ultimately, it all belongs to God. Your job is not really yours. It is God's job; He's just letting you hang around to work it. Your money is really God's money that He is letting you use. The same goes for your house, your car, and your clothes.

Everything you have belongs to God. And the moment you say, "It's mine" in the sense of ownership as opposed to stewardship, what you've done is insult God by saying, "I want to be like the Most High."

A Counterfeit View of Good and Evil

After telling her that she could be like God, Satan also told Eve that if she ate from the forbidden tree, she would know good and evil. In other words, "You can make your own decisions about what's right and wrong. You don't need God telling you what's right and making you feel guilty for doing what you want."

I once had a person tell me, "I'm never coming back to Oak Cliff Bible Fellowship." When I asked why, he said, "Because I want sermons that make me feel good. I don't need anybody telling me what to do." That is exactly what Satan told Eve.

Youth speaker Josh McDowell's national "Right from Wrong" campaign gives us an excellent example of what happens when a culture makes its own rules. McDowell discovered that many Christian young people in solid evangelical churches differ very little from their unsaved friends in their views of truth, morality, and ethics.

Where did these teenagers get ideas that pretty much match what the unsaved world believes? From a culture that has bought into Satan's counterfeit of what is good and what is evil. He's the one who suggested that human beings could discern between good and evil on their own and, therefore, could make their own choices about what's right and wrong.

A Counterfeit View of Life and Death

Satan also told Eve, "You won't die if you eat from this tree. God was lying to you."

In other words, "There are no consequences to your actions. You can do whatever you want without suffering any penalties. God won't do anything about it."

But the death God warned Adam and Eve about did come to pass. They lost their innocence, their relationship with Him, and their home in the Garden. And physical death followed as the inevitable consequence of their spiritual death.

Counterfeit Views of Truth

Let me tell you a secret. Satan cannot stand truth. He does not want you to believe something simply because God said it. Our enemy has all kinds of systems in place to lead us away from objective truth, that which is independent of what we may think or what we may have experienced. Let me mention some of Satan's counterfeits for truth.

One is called *relativism,* the idea that truth is ever-changing, always on the move. In this view, what is true today may not be true tomorrow. You hear this when young people say, "Well, back in your day that may have been true. But that was then, this is now."

Another of Satan's counterfeits is *subjectivism,* which says that truth is strictly personal. You know you have encountered subjectivism when you hear the old line, "Well, that may be true for you, but it's not true for me." For these people, truth is a matter of personal choice, like choosing a dress or tie.

Empiricism is still another of Satan's phony substitutes for truth. Empiricism says that truth resides only in what we can see and feel and measure. Truth depends on evidence and data you can gather and evaluate.

Satan snares some people in the trap of *existentialism,* the teaching that truth is found in what you can experience. The idea that there is a revealed body of truth that never changes is irrelevant to existentialists. The only thing that matters to them is what is happening at the moment.

For still others, truth is purely logical. It can be arrived at through syllogisms. This is *rationalism.* If you can get the right formula, then you'll find the truth. This is the realm in which most science is conducted. Science proposes hypotheses and formulates equations, and based on logical deduction it announces, "Mankind is the product of evolution." Rationalism seeks to explain life on this planet without reference to God.

Let me just mention three more of Satan's counterfeits for truth. One is *phenomenalism,* the belief that if something happens outside the normal course of events, it has to be true.

People in this camp are swayed by the devil's counterfeit miracles. We read earlier that the Antichrist will be able to work all kinds of signs and wonders by Satan's power (2 Thessalonians 2:9–10). But just because something looks miraculous doesn't mean it is from God.

Satan deceives many people by doing that which is outside their normal frame of reference. They say it's a miracle. But the test is whether the incident is in agreement with the objective truth of Scripture. Satan can imitate the miraculous.

Another counterfeit is *pantheism,* the belief that God is synonymous with His creation. To pantheists, God is in everything and everything is God. We have God in us too, so we can be gods.

Pantheism is a very ancient form of paganism, but it looks new and exciting today because it is dressed up in new clothes called the New Age movement. But it's the same old lie.

The final false view of truth I want to mention is *pragmatism,* the idea that truth is whatever works. You hear this all the time. Someone will say, "If it works for you, that's great." These are the practical folks.

Whatever label you give to Satan's deception, the basis is the same. Satan hates objective truth, and he'll try to lead people astray from it every time.

A Counterfeit View of Christianity

Satan even has his own fake form of Christianity. He has phony doctrine (1 Timothy 4:1) as well as being able to produce phony miracles. The devil even has a counterfeit communion table. That's why Paul said, "You cannot drink the cup of the Lord and the cup of demons" (1 Corinthians 10:21). Satan also offers a counterfeit spirituality (Galatians 3:2–3) based upon a counterfeit gospel (Galatians 1:11–12).

And to propagate his program, the devil has his own false teachers. Paul warned the church at Corinth of men who were "false apostles, deceitful workers, disguising themselves as apostles of Christ" (2 Corinthians 11:13). Since Satan can make himself look like one of the good guys (v. 14), he can do the same for his servants.

THE PROCESS OF SATAN'S STRATEGY

We've seen that Satan's strategy is powerful and purposeful. Our enemy has a well-laid-out program to deceive and destroy. We need to look at the process of his deception, how it actually works. It occurs in four distinct stages.

Stage One: Desire

The apostle James outlines the process by which Satan deceives people. It begins with the desire: "Let no one say when he is tempted, 'I am being tempted by God'; for God cannot be tempted by evil, and He Himself does not tempt anyone. But each one is tempted when he is carried away and enticed by his own lust" (James 1:13–14).

Stage one in Satan's plan is the arousal of a desire. Even legitimate desires become a problem when Satan tempts us to meet a legitimate desire in an illegitimate way. The process of temptation often means trying to get us to meet a good need in a bad way.

The desire for food is good, but gluttony is sin. The desire for sex is legitimate, but immorality is sin. The desire for sleep is good, but lying in bed all day is laziness and sin.

Satan knows you can't just skip the desire, because our desires are God-given. So the enemy wants to control how your desires are met. This is the issue in temptation. Satan wants your desires to master you, rather than your mastering your desires. He wants the desire to take control. It's called addiction.

Stage Two: Deception

In stage two of the process, the illegitimate development of desire leads to deception, the moment when the person takes Satan's bait and finds out he has been deceived.

The idea here is of a fisherman. A smart fisherman doesn't just throw a bare hook in the water and wait. That hook has to be covered with some kind of bait for a fish to bite on it and get caught.

Satan is not just throwing bare hooks out in front of us. He doesn't say to a man, "Come on down to the local bar and let me get you addicted to alcohol so you can lose your job and your family, lose your self-respect and self-control, and wind up in a rehab center."

Satan is far too smart to let his hooks show. He covers them with enticing bait. He invites a person down to the friendly neighborhood tavern for one drink, then two, three, and four, until that person's desire for alcohol overcomes all his other desires and commitments. He has been thoroughly deceived.

Satan deceives us by planting an evil thought or idea in our minds. He can't make us do anything, but he can build deceitful castles of desire in our minds.

King David found that out. Look at what happened when he saw Bathsheba bathing. He could have turned away, but Satan got him to keep looking and then thinking and then acting.

On another occasion in David's life, the Bible says that "Satan stood up against Israel and moved David to number Israel" (1 Chronicles 21:1). David got the idea, "I don't need God. I have a big enough army to take care of it myself." But seventy thousand people died because of David's sin.

Peter asked Ananias, "Why has Satan filled your heart to lie to the Holy Spirit?" about the money Ananias and Sapphira had received from the sale of their land (Acts 5:3).

This couple's desire to sell their land and give the money to the church in Jerusalem was legitimate. And the money they earned from the sale was legitimate income. If they had just given a certain amount and been up front about it, there would have been no problem. But Satan tempted them to twist their story and say they had given it all, and they died.

Satan knows how to intertwine our desires with his twisted plans to lure us into his deception. But we still have to bite on the hook.

Stage Three: Disobedience

So desire leads to deception, and deception leads to disobedience. "When lust has conceived, it gives birth to sin" (James 1:15).

James uses the analogy of conception, pregnancy, and birth because the birth process so closely parallels the process he is talking about. When an illegitimate desire is welcomed and acted upon, that act of conception produces a "child" called sin. And once a child has been conceived, its birth is sure to follow.

In other words, committing disobedience is like the act of procreation. The result will always show up after a while. The child of disobedience is sin, and like any other child sin will begin to grow once it has been born.

Part of becoming mature in Christ, as opposed to becoming grown-up children of sin, is learning to submit our feelings to the will of Christ, to operate on the basis of what we know to be true rather than just what we feel. But sin will keep you spiritually immature, a slave to your emotions.

Before we leave this point, let me show you a wonderful promise. Philippians 2:13 tells us, "It is God who is at work in you, both to will and to work for His good pleasure." When your will is combined with God's will, He gives you the power to do what your will is telling you you ought to do. So we are not in this thing alone. We have tremendous power available to us in Christ.

Stage Four: Death

The fourth and final stage in Satan's process is death. James says, "When sin is accomplished, it brings forth death" (1:15).

Sin certainly brings spiritual death. That is one of the fundamental truths we learn from the sin of Adam and Eve. Sin can also produce physical death. We have already mentioned several examples of that.

Satan brings nothing but death and destruction with him, but God is the source of "every perfect gift" (James 1:17). So James says, "Do not be deceived, my beloved brethren" (v. 16). When Satan deceives and leads us into sin, he causes us to miss the goodness of God. Don't ever think you have it better with Satan than you do with God.

Jesus is our perfect example here. When confronted by Satan's temptations in the wilderness, Jesus did not say, "Let Me think about it and I'll get back to you later." He said, "It is written." He dealt with the temptation on the spot, right in Satan's face. He didn't meditate upon the wrong desires Satan suggested and allow them to conceive disobedience.

Satan wants us to roll his ideas over in our minds, to play with them until we start feeling better about them. But that's a process that will lead to death if we follow it.

THE PURPOSE OF SATAN'S STRATEGY

Now that we know the process Satan wants to take us through, we are ready to talk about the purpose behind his strategy. Satan has several major purposes behind his deceptions. Let's go through them.

First Purpose: Prevent Salvation

When it comes to the unsaved, Satan's purpose is to keep them right where he has them, which is on their way to an eternity in hell. So he blinds the minds of nonbelievers to keep them from getting saved and bringing God glory (2 Corinthians 4:3–4). The more people who get saved, the more glory God gets.

Satan doesn't want you witnessing to your unsaved friends. He doesn't want your lost friends to hear the gospel, because when they receive Christ, Satan loses and God gets glory.

Second Purpose: Make Believers Ineffective

When it comes to believers, one of Satan's purposes is to interrupt the process by which God gets glory through our lives. He wants to render us ineffective in terms of any real impact for Christ. That's why he keeps some believers depressed, some discouraged, and others underneath their circumstances.

He wants you there because he knows you can do nothing for God if you're miserable. God won't get glory if you're too miserable to give it to Him. In fact, Satan can twist things so much that he'll get you blaming God for your misery. And if you're not careful, the devil can wind up using you to bring unhappiness and misery to others. He will use us to be his deceivers if we let him.

Third Purpose: Frustrate God's Will

Finally, the devil wants to deflect you and me from accomplishing the will of God by frustrating God's will for our lives.

Satan even tried to frustrate the accomplishment of God's will in Jesus' life. God the Father's will for His Son was the cross, but in the wilderness temptation the devil tried to get Jesus to take the easy way.

Satan also used one of Jesus' own disciples to try to turn Him away from the cross (Matthew 16:21–22). Imagine Peter rebuking Jesus, trying to tell Him where He was wrong. Only Satan could have thought of an attack this bold. Jesus knew who was behind it, because He told Peter, "Get behind Me, Satan!" (Matthew 16:23).

Jesus was saying, "Get behind Me, devil. I have to go to the cross. Peter, Satan is using you, one of My children, to stop Me from doing My Father's will."

If Satan wasn't afraid to try to turn Jesus away from God's will in going to the cross, do you think he will leave us alone? Of course not.

As a matter of fact, Jesus went on to say in this same passage, "If anyone wishes to come after Me, let him deny himself, and take up his cross, and follow Me" (Matthew 16:24). Satan tried to get Jesus to focus on the suffering of the cross and thus to avoid it. Our enemy will do the same to us.

Let's face it. The cross does involve suffering. It's an instrument of death. Bearing my cross means I am willing to identify publicly with Jesus Christ and accept anything that goes with that identification. It means I will bear the scars of being identified with Christ.

You say, "But that can be hard." Only if you don't see the resurrection that follows crucifixion. Ask any Olympic athlete if it's hard preparing for the Games. Ask him or her if there is any pain or suffering involved in four years of training.

But then ask the winner of an Olympic gold medal how it feels to stand on that platform and receive that medal. He or she will tell you all the pain and hardship was worth it. You and I are going to experience some tough times in following Christ. But when we step onto the winner's stand and receive the crown from Jesus Christ, we will say, "It was worth it." Don't let Satan deceive and distract you from accomplishing God's will.

SATAN'S DECOYS

The U.S. Army used to have pneumatic decoys, rubber units that could be inflated and made to look like tanks or trucks or whatever. The army would put these things in strategic locations so that when the enemy flew over doing reconnaissance, it would look like the army had a much larger and more powerful force than was actually the case.

I think you know where I'm going. Satan is busy inflating and placing his "pneumatic decoys" all over the place to make you think he's much stronger than is actually the case.

Since Jesus Christ's death and resurrection left Satan defeated, his only power is the power of deception. His only strategy is to deceive us. So tell him, "I know who you are and how you work, and I don't want any part of you or your works."

11

THE HELPERS OF SATAN

One of the most basic realities of spiritual warfare is that Satan isn't operating alone. He has his own army of spirit beings called demons who obey him and carry out his agenda. A demon is a fallen angel who followed Satan in his rebellion (Revelation 12:4) and now assists Satan's program of opposition to God's purpose, program, and people.

The existence of demons has generally been either denied or caricatured by the world. Hollywood has always been fascinated by the demonic, and many of the popular movies produced over the last few years have featured demon-like forces or aliens bent on destroying the earth.

But the Bible's teaching about the true nature and purpose of demons has been largely rejected by the world and even by many theologians and preachers. Credit Satan with doing a number on the minds of many people. We know that one of his best moves is to camouflage himself so that people don't know he's there.

But the Bible teaches that demons are real, and we need to understand their operation and their purposes. We don't need to fear demons, but because they are active troops in Satan's army we need to know more about them so we can be more alert and experience greater success in spiritual warfare. The Bible says that God created countless hosts of angels. Since one-third of the angels followed Satan in his rebellion and were judged with him, you can imagine the vast array of demons Satan has at his command.

According to Matthew 12:24–26, demons are part of Satan's kingdom—and notice that Jesus says there is no division in that realm. Satan is not about to cast out Satan.

This is very important to understand. One reason that Satan's demonic regime is so successful and so powerful is because it is so unified. There are no "Benedict Arnold" demons. These beings have been forever confirmed in unrighteousness, just as the good angels who did not follow Satan have been forever confirmed in holiness.

No demon gets up in the morning and says, "I don't feel like being a demon today. I want to repent and turn back to God." Demons are loyal to their evil leader, Satan. So let's learn more about these created, fallen angelic beings who help Satan push his agenda on earth and in the heavenly realms.

THE NATURE OF DEMONS

The well-known biblical story of Jesus' encounter with the demon-possessed man in Luke 8:26–39 tells us pretty much all we need to know about the nature of demons:

[Jesus] was met by a certain man from the city who was possessed with demons; and who had not put on any clothing for a long time, and was not living in a house, but in the tombs. And seeing Jesus, he cried out and fell before Him, and said in a loud voice, "What do I have to do with You, Jesus, Son of the Most High God? I beg You, do not torment me." (vv. 27–28)

This man was demon-possessed, or "demonized," which is a better translation of the Greek term used here and throughout the Gospels. When Jesus showed up, this man went into torment. Why? Because Jesus and demons can't be in the same place at the same time and get along. Somebody has to move when Jesus shows up. As we examine this account, we learn some important things about the nature of demons.

Demons Are Personal Beings

The first thing we learn is that demons are personal beings. That is, they display the primary attributes of personality.

For example, demons possess intellect. In the story before us in Luke 8, they recognized Jesus and were able to speak and reason using this man's voice (v. 28).

Demons also have emotions. They begged Jesus not to torment them (v. 28). Since demons do not have bodies of their own, the torment they feel would apparently be in the spiritual or emotional realm.

The third aspect of personality we see in demons is that they have a will. In verses 32–33, they expressed their desire to enter into the herd of pigs that was feeding nearby. We also know that demons have a will because they exercised that will when they chose to follow Satan in his rebellion. So it's not surprising that they were able to make a choice here, but note that they had no power to do what they wanted to do without Christ's permission.

When we see people committing evil, strange, or destructive acts, the usual assumption is that they are insane or mentally unbalanced. The demoniac of Luke 8 certainly appeared to be insane, even dangerously insane. Living among graves without clothes is a crazy thing to do.

But in reality this man was possessed, not just insane. That's why when we are dealing with people who have certain emotional, mental, or spiritual problems, we must consider whether a demonic influence is being exerted on that individual. If we are dealing with a serious spiritual warfare issue and it is not addressed, then we will never be able to fix what is wrong.

The personal nature of demons is important because they are often portrayed on television shows or in films either as some sort of impersonal evil force or as something make-believe to be dismissed. It's part of Satan's deception to cause people not to take him or his henchmen seriously.

Demons Are Spirit Beings

Demons are not only personal beings. They are spirit beings. Paul says specifically that our struggle is "not against flesh and blood" (Ephesians 6:12). Demons do not have bodies of their own, but as we saw above they are able to inhabit the bodies of others.

Jesus revealed more about the nature of demons when He said:

> When the unclean spirit goes out of a man, it passes through waterless places seeking rest, and not finding any, it says, "I will return to my house from which I came."

And when it comes, it finds it swept and put in order. Then it goes and takes along seven other spirits more evil than itself, and they go in and live there; and the last state of that man becomes worse than the first. (Luke 11:24–26)

It was important for a person who faced demonic powers bent on his destruction, as well as the nation of Israel, to make the right decision about Jesus as Messiah, or they would soon be in a worse spiritual condition than when they started.

Notice what Jesus said about demons in the course of His teaching. They are restless when they have no one through whom to express themselves. "Waterless places" are places without life. Like the demons who inhabited the man in Luke 8, this demon became frustrated when it had no way to express itself, so it returned to the place of its former habitation—and it brought the brotherhood!

The demon called this man's body "my house" (Luke 11:24). In Jesus' illustration, the demon returned and had a "family reunion" at the man's expense. Demons often seek a "house" to inhabit in order to find temporary peace and not be sent to the abyss. They are spirit beings who can use the bodies of humans and animals to express themselves.

Demons Are Powerful Beings

The demons of hell are powerful beings. The demons who possessed the man Jesus healed in Luke 8 were forcing him to do violent things, and they gave him superhuman strength. He could break chains as if they were string. No doubt the demons would have eventually killed him, since demons can even drive people to want to commit suicide (Revelation 9:3–6).

Many cases are recorded of people on drugs having so much strength that it takes a small army of people to restrain them. That's not just the chemical in the drug working on them. Drugs and sorcery or witchcraft of any kind are vehicles for demonic activity.

Demons Are Perverted Beings

Demons are also perverted beings. When they rejected God and lined up with Satan, they "earned" a special name. Not only are they called demons, but Jesus called them "unclean spirits." They pervert everything they touch.

As we will see in more detail later, demons pervert the truth of God (1 Timothy 4:1). They want you and me to believe a lie because their leader, Satan, is the father of lies. Paul says they want to pervert God's goodness and make it into something that is all prohibition and denial of the good things God created.

That's why John tells us to "test the spirits" (1 John 4:1). Testing the spirits means knowing which ones are exalting Jesus and which ones are not, because that's always the test. Demons can't handle the presence of Christ. They can't handle the cross or the blood of Christ, or anything that has to do with Him. They leave when Christ is exalted.

Demons are also eager to pervert human sexual relationships (1 Corinthians 7:5; Revelation 18:2–3). Sometimes they have even been able to mix perversion with religious devotion, as in the worship of Aphrodite practiced in Corinth.

Demons are perverted, but the problem is they don't always appear to be so. They want to make their perversion as attractive as possible, even using a twisted version of God's Word against people. That's why you must always measure what you hear by the Word, not by how well it was said or the fact that the person saying it was holding a Bible.

THE ACTIVITIES OF DEMONS

The Bible reveals two basic categories of demons: those who are not yet permanently judged and are free to move about doing Satan's will, and a subclass of demons who were imprisoned for their particular sin.

Demons Who Are Free

The first category of demons is the one we are most familiar with, those demons who are free to move about at Satan's bidding and carry out his purposes.

When I say they are free, I am using that term in a relative sense. Demons are under the ultimate control of heaven, as Jesus made clear on a number of occasions when He told demons what to do and they had to obey. Back in Luke 8, our original text, the demons Christ cast out of the man not only had to leave him when Jesus commanded them to, but they had to ask Jesus' permission to go into the pigs. But since God has chosen to let these "free" demons operate for the time being, they are able to carry out Satan's commands.

Even in this we can see a reminder that Satan is not the equal of God. Satan can't be everywhere at the same time, he doesn't know everything, and he's not all-powerful. So he needs the demons as his agents to carry out his will. The difference is that God uses His angels by choice, not out of necessity.

I want to make one more observation before we leave this category. In Luke 8 the demons inhabiting this man begged Jesus "not to command them to depart into the abyss" (v. 31).

This is the place where all demons that are active now will ultimately be sent (Revelation 9:1). But these demons were worried that Jesus would send them there ahead of their time, we might say, so that they would be out of commission.

Jesus did not send them to the abyss, of course, but allowed them to enter the pigs. There is no record in Scripture of Jesus consigning an active demon to this prison during His earthly ministry. But the demons knew that Jesus had the power to order them into the abyss, and they were worried.

Let me compare this to the children's game of dodgeball. Once you get hit with the ball, you lose and you're out of the game. You're active until you are hit, and then that's it.

The demons knew that anytime Jesus showed up, He had the prerogative to take them out of the game permanently. They didn't want that, but they never doubted Jesus' power to do it. We don't need to doubt Jesus' power over hell either.

Demons Who Are Imprisoned

The Bible refers to a second group of demons who are permanently imprisoned because of the exceptionally gross nature of their sin.

According to Jude 6, these are angels "who did not keep their own domain, but abandoned their proper abode." They are being "kept in eternal bonds under darkness for the judgment of the great day." Peter writes of these demons that "God did not spare angels when they sinned, but cast them into hell and committed them to pits of darkness, reserved for judgment" (2 Peter 2:4).

What is the "proper abode" of angels? Heavenly places,

the spiritual realm. These angels left that sphere when they came down to earth to commit an especially wicked sin.

We referred to that sin earlier, the time when these angels cohabited with women and produced a mutant race of giants (Genesis 6:1–4). This was Satan's race that he hoped would take over. But God found a faithful man in Noah, defeated Satan, and destroyed this evil race of men.

For leaving their proper abode after creation and committing that sin, these angels were cast into eternal fire and eternal judgment, locked up with no possibility of release or parole forever.

THE TARGETS OF DEMON ACTIVITY

Before we turn to another major section of our study, I want to note briefly the four areas that demons target in their activity of carrying out Satan's agenda.

Satan is employing his demons in an attempt to destroy individual lives. "Your adversary, the devil, prowls about like a roaring lion, seeking someone to devour" (1 Peter 5:8). Satan wants you and me and the unsaved world, and he will use any method he can. He wants to keep the unsaved blinded to the truth and the saved ineffective for Christ.

Satan is also using his demons against the family. Satan attempted to destroy Adam's family, and then he tried to create hell's substitute for the family in Genesis 6. Satan and his army will do anything they can to get into a family and break it up (1 Corinthians 7:5).

A third target of Satan and his demons is the church. Satan tries to wipe out the church externally by stirring up persecution, and he goes after the church internally by creating strife and disunity, as we will see later in the chapter. When Ananias and Sapphira sinned, Peter said that Satan filled their hearts to lie to the Holy Spirit (Acts 5:3).

Fourth, Satan wants to destroy society itself. We saw earlier that the nations are controlled by demons (Daniel 10). Some governments are so demonized that the leaders have no conscience about killing their people, and there is no justice in the system.

The culmination of satanic and demonic influence over world government is found in Revelation 18 with the fall of Babylon, the last form of godless government. Satan's influence in world affairs is great, and his goal is total chaos, anarchy, and destruction.

THE FIRST PROGRAM OF DEMONS: TO PROMOTE SATAN

We can state the program of hell in one simple sentence. The program of hell, the demonic agenda, is to promote who Satan is and what Satan does, and to oppose everything that God is and God does. This is the essence of spiritual warfare.

Let's take these two items of the demonic program and study them in some detail, beginning with the promotion of Satan and his agenda.

Demons Promote Satan's Doctrine

We have already alluded to this several times, so let's explore it further. Demons promote the doctrine of Satan. They teach what their master wants taught so that people might live in the darkness of Satan's theology rather than in the light of God's truth.

I want to go back to 1 Timothy 4 and look at the first five verses. Paul identifies what he is going to talk about with the label "deceitful spirits and doctrines of demons"

(v. 1). In the end times, people will pay closer and closer attention to these teachings.

One particular doctrine demons propagate is the idea that God is not good (vv. 3–4). This ought to sound familiar, because this was the argument of the devil back in Eden. Satan was saying to Eve, "If God were good, He wouldn't keep you away from that tree. He would share it with you."

Satan wants you to believe God is holding out on you. But if God is withholding something from you, it's because what you want isn't good for you.

You may say, "But it looks good. It tastes good. It feels good." These are not the proper criteria, however, because things that look and taste and feel good can be bad.

Demonic doctrine hits at things God created to be enjoyed, such as marriage and food (v. 3). To appreciate this, you have to understand that in Paul's day there was a view that divided nature between spirit and matter.

Things that were associated with matter, such as the body, were viewed as evil. Things that were associated with the spirit were viewed as good. This was a false dichotomy and a false view of spirituality.

But those who know the truth know that God has not forbidden marriage or the eating of certain foods. Instead, He has created these things to "be gratefully shared in" by His people.

Then notice what Paul said. "For everything created by God is good, and nothing is to be rejected, if it is received with gratitude" (v. 4).

The problem was that false teachers under the influence of demons were keeping the Christians in Timothy's charge from enjoying what God had provided for them. These teachers were promoting spirituality through asceticism.

If your Christian life is all the negatives, if your spirituality is measured only in can'ts and don'ts, then you have been duped by demons. If you live your Christian life with ingratitude, if you only look at what you don't have or can't have because you're a Christian, then you're missing out on maximizing your spiritual potential.

Paul calls it a doctrine of demons that limits the Christian life to an experience of negatives. Don't get me wrong. There are things we can't do as believers, but these are not the essence of Christianity. God has given us all things to enjoy (1 Timothy 6:17). Satan and his demons want to point out the one tree you can't have rather than the thousand trees you can enjoy.

How do you know whether something is from God? When you can authenticate it by the Word and pray over it legitimately (1 Timothy 4:5). Those are the two criteria to determine whether something is from God.

Here's something else that demonic doctrine wants to undermine: the Son of God. In another familiar passage, Paul warned the Corinthians that the adversary wanted to undermine their devotion to Christ (2 Corinthians 11:3).

Demons want to move Christ out of the center of your life. They know that as long as Christ is at the center, they cannot have dominance over you. Demons want to discredit and steal away the work of Christ in your heart and mine, so that we become distracted and sidetracked by other things.

Demons are also working hard to undermine the gospel of God by blinding people to its truth:

> And even if our gospel is veiled, it is veiled to those who are perishing, in whose case the god of this world has blinded the minds of the unbelieving, that they might

not see the light of the gospel of the glory of Christ, who is the image of God. (2 Corinthians 4:3–4)

The demonic world wants to put blinders on the unrighteous. If you have ever tried to witness to people who simply could not grasp the idea that they cannot earn their salvation, or who refused to believe they were sinners, then you know the truth of what the Scripture is saying.

The Holy Spirit has to break through that spiritual fog in order for people to get a clear picture of the goodness of God in His gospel.

Demons Promote Satan's Destructiveness

Jesus said the devil is in the business of destroying everyone and everything he can (John 10:10). All through the New Testament, we see demonic forces at work to debilitate and destroy people.

I am not saying that all illnesses and other serious problems are demonically orchestrated. However, a lot more physical and emotional illness is demonically orchestrated and influenced than most people are willing to admit.

For example, demons can cause blindness (Matthew 12:22), physical deformity (Luke 13:11), emotional and mental instability (Matthew 17:14–18), and even physical death (Revelation 9:13–15). If it were not for the grace of God, any one of us could have been killed before we came to Christ, because total and eternal destruction is Satan's goal.

Even after we come to Christ and the devil loses us for eternity, his program is to destroy our joy and peace and kill our effectiveness for Christ. And our enemy uses his demons to promote this portion of his evil agenda.

Demons Promote Satan's Domination

Don't forget that Satan is a frustrated ruler. He tried to displace God from the throne of the universe, and he has been out to build his own kingdom ever since. The method he uses is one of seeking to dominate individuals, institutions, and ultimately entire nations. The demons are once again his primary henchmen.

We have already spent time considering the devil's domination of individual people through demons, so I just want to note the reality of demon possession as one means of Satan's attempt to dominate the scene. The demons also seek to dominate organized religion on Satan's behalf. The risen Christ told the church at Smyrna, "I know your tribulation and your poverty (but you are rich), and the blasphemy by those who say they are Jews and are not, but are a synagogue of Satan" (Revelation 2:9).

Did you know that the devil has his own churches? No, I'm not talking about the so-called church of Satan. I'm talking about the church that says it's a church of the Lord Jesus Christ, but is dominated by demonic influence. Satan is in the religion business big-time, and Revelation 17 pictures the last and most wicked form of devil-dominated world religion.

Satan ultimately seeks to dominate nations that he might wage war against God and His people.

When I was in Israel, I went to "Har-Magedon" (Revelation 16:16), or the Mount of Megiddo, which is located in the valley of Jezreel. This is the place where the Bible says the last great battle between the forces of God and the forces of Satan will be fought (Revelation 19:17–21).

God will allow Satan to assemble the leaders of the world's armies at Armageddon in a desperate attempt to wrest control of the universe from Him. But the outcome has already been decided.

However, Satan wants dominion so badly that even after one thousand years in bondage during the Millennium, he will lead one last act of rebellion in his final attempt to gain control (Revelation 20:7–9). That will end in his eternal doom. The enemy will never give up seeking to dominate the world until he is finally judged.

Demons Promote Satan's Distractions

Besides pushing Satan's doctrine, destructiveness, and domination, demons are also effective promoters of the devil's distractions.

In this category I include all the cable television programs and psychic hotlines and newspaper horoscopes that purport to offer people spiritual guidance and advice. I am convinced that far too many Christians are dabbling in these things and are opening themselves up to the evil spirit world.

Satan wants to lure our focus away from Christ by any means possible. I want to be clear about the distractions that demons can bring because the Bible is very clear on this. Let me look at some important passages of Scripture with you.

In Leviticus 19:31, the Mosaic Law warned, "Do not turn to mediums or spiritists; do not seek them out to be defiled by them. I am the Lord your God." In other words, don't visit palm readers or mess with Ouija boards. Don't look to astrology for truth. Don't look into a crystal ball. All that is a denial of the Lord your God. It also makes *you* dirty.

Whenever you appeal to the created order to do what is the prerogative of the Creator, you change gods. You are distracted from the true God—and you invite

His severe judgment. "As for the person who turns to mediums and to spiritists, to play the harlot after them, I will also set My face against that person and will cut him off from among his people" (Leviticus 20:6).

Here's another warning we need to heed. "When you enter the land which the Lord your God gives you, you shall not learn to imitate the detestable things of those nations" (Deuteronomy 18:9). Why? Because "Whoever does these things is detestable to the Lord" (v. 12). When you try to add anything to God and do not allow Him to be supreme, you lose His blessing and invite His curse.

At various times in its history, Israel was plagued by false prophets (see Jeremiah 29:8–9). God always makes a distinction between true and false prophets, because not everybody who uses the name of the Lord is from the Lord (Matthew 7:21–23).

Deceivers have always been out there, but now they are getting more sophisticated. The devil's distractions are looking better and better to the gullible. His demons are hard at work to divert us from faithfulness to Christ. We don't need to help them by playing around with the things of darkness.

In Acts 19:19, the people who got saved in Ephesus brought all their magic books and burned them. Some of us need to do some "burning" in our houses. We need to get rid of some of the stuff we watch and listen to that promotes divination and magic, because these things are compromising God's presence in our homes. We must be able to see through the enemy's distractions.

THE SECOND PROGRAM OF DEMONS: TO OPPOSE GOD

Let's go to the second part of the demons' program,

which is to oppose the Person and work of God. Demons not only promote hell; they oppose heaven.

Demons Oppose God's Position

One of the primary things that demons want to oppose is God's position.

Our God is a jealous God who will not share His glory with any other. He is supreme; we are to have no other gods before Him. So demons seek to oppose God's position primarily through idolatry.

In Deuteronomy 32:17, Moses said of Israel's rebellion, "They sacrificed to demons who were not God, to gods whom they have not known, new gods who came lately, whom your fathers did not dread."

Watch out for "new gods." There aren't any new gods, just old demons behind the mask of new gods. That's why Moses charged the Israelites with sacrificing to demons when they offered their sacrifices to idols.

The people didn't see any demons. They didn't think they were sacrificing to demons. But behind every idol is a demon.

Someone may say, "Well, that's just an Old Testament problem." No, it's a New Testament problem too:

> The things which the Gentiles sacrifice, they sacrifice to demons, and not to God; and I do not want you to become sharers in demons. You cannot drink the cup of the Lord and the cup of demons; you cannot partake of the table of the Lord and the table of demons. Or do we provoke the Lord to jealousy? We are not stronger than He, are we? (1 Corinthians 10:20–22)

Paul was talking about the church at communion, the table of the Lord, which is designed for intimate fellowship with the Lord. Paul says that demons have a table set too, and are enticing believers to sit at it.

How can believers commune at the table of demons? When we partake of an idol that belongs to the godless, unbelieving world and we let its idols become our idols, we enter into communion with demons and provoke the Lord to jealousy.

Some believer may say, "I don't have to worry about that. I share in the Lord's table at church, and I don't bow before any carved images or any stone idols."

But wait a minute. I'm afraid that many American Christians dine at two tables. On Sunday they dine at the Lord's table, then on Monday they dine at the table of demons, because they have idols in their lives.

An idol is anything that takes the place of God in your life. Many Christians in this country are bowing before the idol of materialism. We said above that God has given us all things to enjoy. There's nothing wrong with having things. Materialism is when things have you. That is idolatry.

So the question we need to ask ourselves is, "Am I dining at two tables?" If the answer is yes, you'd better get it fixed if you want the Lord's fellowship and blessing in your life.

Demons Oppose God's Precepts

Demons also oppose God's precepts, the teachings of His Word.

I don't want to spend too much time here, because we have covered this point earlier. Let me just remind you that the devil's opposition to God's precepts started very early when he challenged and denied God's word to Eve.

Eve had to choose whom she was going to believe.

That's the choice we have to make too. God's Word is written plainly for us to know and obey. When the demonic world comes with its lies, we have a clear standard to measure its lies against.

Demons Oppose God's Purity

The opposition of demons extends to God's purity as well as His position and His precepts.

We have talked about the vileness and corruption that Satan and his demons seek to perpetrate. Jude referred to the case of demons who became involved in perverted human sexuality (v. 6), and also referred to *the* biblical epitome of impurity, Sodom and Gomorrah (v. 7). These cities practiced "gross immorality" and "went after strange flesh."

Then Jude turned to the reason for writing his short letter, the false teachers who were plaguing the church. These men "in the same manner . . . defile the flesh" (v. 8). In what manner does Jude mean? In the same manner as the demons and the people of Sodom and Gomorrah.

Demons oppose godly purity. Why? Because the central characteristic of God is His holiness. So demons are really into impurity, and the more vile the impurity, the better they like it. They take what's bad and seek to make it even worse.

How do you think it is possible for drug users to keep coming up with new and more harmful drugs? The demons make sure they keep a new batch brewing all the time. Demons are always coming up with something new to promote ungodliness, because with the ungodliness comes the consequences of ungodliness.

All of us have to battle with sin, which is why 1 John 1:9 is so important. We must confess our sins and cleanse them in the blood, because without the blood of Jesus

Christ we can't get rid of sin's impurity. And if we can't get rid of the impurity, we can't have fellowship with God.

Demons want to keep us defiled and impure, away from the blood. They are unalterably opposed to God's purity.

Demons Oppose God's People

Here is where the spiritual warfare begins to heat up. Demons stand opposed to God's people—and that means you and me.

One way the demonic world opposes us is by slandering us to God. If Satan can use his henchmen to cause us to stumble and fall, then the slanderer has an accusation he can take into heaven's courtroom and fling in God's face. "Did You see what that man just did? Did You hear what that woman said? They claim to be Your children. What are You going to do about it?"

Demons oppose God's people by getting in their way. Paul said he wanted to come to the Thessalonians, but Satan hindered him (1 Thessalonians 2:17–18).

Demons also oppose us by tempting us to sin. Temptation is still the devil's best weapon against us day in and day out. He is constantly dropping the seeds of thoughts that later on can produce a messy harvest if we yield to them.

Here's a method of demonic opposition that you and I need to know about and be alert against. Demons oppose us by sowing division and discord in the body of Christ. James writes:

> Who among you is wise and understanding? Let him show by his good behavior his deeds in the gentleness of wisdom. But if you have bitter jealousy and selfish ambi-

tion in your heart, do not be arrogant and so lie against the truth. This wisdom is not that which comes down from above, but is earthly, natural, *demonic*. For where jealousy and selfish ambition exist, there is disorder and every evil thing. (James 3:13–16, italics added)

The demons know that God is a God of order and unity, which means He will not operate in a context of disorder and disunity. So they are busy sowing jealousy and selfish ambition in the church and in the home.

If you trace most marital breakups, you will find self-ishness lying somewhere at the root. When the church is full of strife and disunity, somewhere in the mess you will usually find someone's ambitions or selfish desires being promoted. Hell loves to see the children of heaven at each other's throats, because the enemy knows that when strife shows up, the Holy Spirit is hindered.

Until we are willing to work harder to keep the unity of the Spirit (Ephesians 4:3) than we do to promote our interests and our preferences, we will continue to suffer discord in the church and in our homes. Until we get to the point where things don't have to go our way all the time, there will be constant divisions and disorder, and God won't show up. He won't help us.

The demons know what they are doing. They are not a house divided. Their strength is in their unity. They operate as one. If we can learn to operate as one with God, as one in the church, and as one in our homes, there will be no room for demons to work. That's why Paul pleaded, "[Be] diligent to preserve the unity of the Spirit in the bond of peace" (Ephesians 4:3).

12

**THE DEFEAT
OF SATAN**

A few years ago in a television sitcom, a man who was unable to watch the Super Bowl football championship game was planning to videotape it and watch it later that night.

His problem was trying to get home and watch the tape without accidentally hearing the final score of the game ahead of time, thus spoiling his fun. He went through all kinds of antics trying to avoid contact with people or the media, and finally he reached his apartment without hearing who had won the game.

But just as he sat down with great delight to enjoy the big game on tape, a friend walked into his apartment, not realizing what was happening. When this other guy saw the game on TV, he casually remarked what an exciting game it had been, and how the winning team had pulled the game out in the final seconds. The poor guy on the couch sank low in dejection as the show ended.

It may not be much fun watching a football game

when you already know the final score. But this is exactly the way we need to approach the subject of Satan and his demons. We already know who wins. If we forget that, we may start reacting to Satan as if he were the ultimate winner instead of the ultimate loser.

Satan was defeated the instant he rebelled against God. That means he has been a loser for all of the ages since that rebellion, and someday he will taste his eternal defeat at the hands of Jesus Christ. As I look at what the Bible says about Satan's defeat, I see four ways in which God's Word declares the devil to be a beaten enemy.

SATAN WAS DEFEATED STRATEGICALLY

The first way that Satan was defeated is what I call his strategic defeat. By this I mean that he devised a strategy—rebellion against God—that failed miserably. There was never a second that God's throne was in danger of toppling.

Creature Versus Creator

Satan made a fatal strategic mistake in that he as a creature rebelled against his Creator, the One on whom he depended to sustain his very life. Satan's "creatureliness" depended on God, yet Satan rose up in defiance of God.

There are two dogs in the Evans house. It would be foolish for either of these dogs to rebel against me, no matter how mad I make them or how little they want me to be their master.

The reason is that I put food in their bowls every day. Every day I pour them water to drink. It is because of me that they can bank on a meal. It is because of me that they can count on having something to drink. It is because of me that they have a place to go when the weather gets bad.

My dogs would be fools to rebel against me. Satan was even more foolish to rebel against God, and his strategy suffered a decisive defeat.

A Temporary Illusion

Even though the devil is defeated, he can work an optical illusion against us to get us to think he's bigger and more powerful than he really is. Here's what I mean.

Let's pretend for a minute that it's OK to look directly at the sun. So you're looking at the sun, which is 865,000 miles in diameter. But hold a quarter up close to your eye, and you can block out the sun.

That's what Satan wants us to do, focus on his "quarter"-sized power rather than on the awesome power of God. If you focus too much on the devil, he can block you from seeing God. Then you get a bigger view of Satan than you ought to have and he keeps you defeated, instead of your defeating him in the strength God provides.

God's Glory Seen Through Satan

For His own sovereign reasons, God did not simply obliterate Satan when He defeated him. Instead, God decided to turn Satan's rebellion against him in a way that would bring God more glory.

In other words, God is using Satan's rebellion and defeat to display His great glory and accomplish His good plan. In fact, God is using Satan to bring Himself more glory than He would have had if Satan's rebellion had not occurred.

You might need to think about all of this for a few minutes. Let me help you with a real-life illustration.

God invited Satan to consider His faithful servant Job. Satan wanted to put Job's faith to the test, but he had to get God's permission. We must never forget that. Satan cannot bring anything into your life that God has not reviewed and permitted. Never forget who is in control here.

The first two chapters of the book of Job show that God took Satan up on the proposal to test Job. But God knew that Job would hold firm and honor Him despite severe testing, and in so doing, Job's life brought God more glory than it would have brought had Satan's testing not come.

I realize there are some heavy issues of theology and divine sovereignty involved in Job's case. But we can't deny the stated fact that God permitted Satan to test Job.

God will permit Satan to test us too. And if, when that happens, we look at what the devil is trying to do instead of what God wants to do, we let the quarter block out the sun.

It's not always easy to keep your focus on God. But when you are ready to make the kind of declarations Job made, you are ready to allow God to use Satan's work against him.

What did Job say? "The Lord gave and the Lord has taken away. Blessed be the name of the Lord" (Job 1:21). "Shall we indeed accept good from God and not accept adversity?" (Job 2:10). "Though He slay me, I will hope in Him" (Job 13:15).

If Job can say this, we can say it. I doubt if any of our problems will come close to matching Job's. If you can't bless the name of the Lord even in the middle of a trial, then that trial is having more power over you than God wants it to have. He allows it that He might get more glory from your life.

By the way, did you notice the subject of Job's statements? He was focusing on God, not the devil. God is the subject all the way through the book of Job. The issue in Job's trials was not what Satan did, but what God could do.

Look at the way God used Satan's intentions to bring about His purpose and glory in the life of a prideful, independent Peter. God hates pride more than any other sin because it reminds Him of the devil's rebellion. So He had to deal with the pride in Peter's heart.

Just before Jesus' crucifixion, the Lord stunned Peter by telling him: "Simon, Simon, behold, Satan has demanded permission to sift you like wheat; but I have prayed for you, that your faith may not fail; and you, when once you have turned again, strengthen your brothers" (Luke 22:31–32).

Notice first that Satan had to get God's permission to go after Peter, just as he did with Job. God granted him that permission because Peter was proud and needed to be humbled.

So Satan went right to work. First, he tempted Peter to brag about his faithfulness in response to Jesus' declaration (Luke 22:33). Then Satan got Peter to fail when the moment of truth came, and he denied Jesus three times. The only thing that kept Peter from falling apart completely was that Jesus was praying for him.

If Satan is making your life miserable, the question you need to ask is, "God, why did You give Satan permission to sift me?" That's where you'll find the answer and the way to fix the problem. God gave Satan permission to test Peter severely because He knew that when Peter "turned again" and repented, he was going to be a greater minister on God's behalf than he would have been as a prideful, self-confident disciple.

Does that mean we invite Satan's sifting? Of course not. But the moment you say, "That will never happen to me," that's when God gives the devil permission to sift you, because that's pride speaking.

We're spending extra time on this issue, but it's important. Remember, we're talking about Satan's defeat here, not his victory. Satan doesn't have any ultimate strategic advantage over you, because he has already been beaten strategically.

And God not only defeated Satan, He turns Satan's strategy against him. The only thing the devil knows how to do is get us to do what he did, to turn against God in rejection and rebellion. But God will not be outmaneuvered by the enemy.

I can't leave this section without dealing with another classic case of how God uses Satan for His own purposes: Paul's "thorn in the flesh" (2 Corinthians 12:7).

Paul said that this problem, which apparently was some kind of intense physical pain, was "given" to him, yet it was also "a messenger of Satan [sent] to buffet [him]." Paul tells us why: "To keep me from exalting myself!" (v. 7).

Paul struggled with pride. He was a proud man before he got saved, and that pride evidently came over into his Christian experience.

Now he really had something to be proud of, because God had put him at the top of the heap in the church. Paul had received more revelation than any of the other apostles. He was going to write more books of the Bible than any other apostle. He was the only apostle who was transported to heaven and came back to talk about it. He was uniquely blessed, and he had to battle pride.

So God said to Paul, "I am going to help you with your struggle. I am giving Satan permission to bring a problem into your life that is far too big for you to handle."

Paul said that because the trial was so great, he asked God three times to take it away (2 Corinthians 12:8). But God said, "My grace is sufficient for you, for [My] power is perfected in [your] weakness" (v. 9). And Paul made the right response. "Most gladly, therefore, I will rather boast about my weaknesses, that the power of Christ may dwell in me."

If Paul were here today, somebody would advise him to go to a meeting and get deliverance from his thorn. But God did not want Paul delivered. He wanted him empowered. This "messenger of Satan" was given to Paul to keep him humble and to keep God's power flowing through him. And Paul himself said he was a more effective servant for Christ with the weakness than he would have been in his own strength (v. 10).

God's Judgment Using Satan

Before we move on to the next way in which Satan has been defeated, we need to see one other way in which God uses Satan's rebellion in the lives of His people —in the matter of discipline and judgment.

One person whose life reveals this is King Saul of Israel. When Saul first became king, the Bible says that God changed his heart (1 Samuel 10:9). But as time went on, Saul proved to be disobedient and rebellious.

Things got so bad that God finally sent Samuel to anoint David as the next king (1 Samuel 16:1–13). Then we read this statement in verse 14: "Now the Spirit of the Lord departed from Saul, and an evil spirit *from the Lord* terrorized him" (italics added). So the king's attendants brought in David to play his harp for Saul and soothe him (vv. 15–23).

But the evil spirit began to drive Saul into madness, and in 1 Samuel 18:10–11, while David was playing for Saul, the king threw a spear at David to kill him.

Someone watching Saul might say he was just insane and needed to be put on medication or put away. But what Saul needed was to turn back to God and ask Him to lift His hand of judgment, because God was using Satan's kingdom to terrorize Saul.

A lot of people may not believe God would do that to a person. That's because a lot of people are mixed up on God's relationship to the evil in this world. God never touches evil Himself, because He is perfectly holy. But God will permit evil forces to do evil. He will give Satan and his demons permission to make someone miserable if that person, like Saul, is living in spiritual rebellion.

Remember, Satan has temporary control over this world. He is the ruler of this planet. He can cause all sorts of havoc, and he can bring evil in people's lives when God gives him permission. Satan is defeated, but God can still use him to discipline and judge a rebellious person like Saul or us.

In Saul's case, the discipline of God did not bring repentance as Satan drove Saul finally to destroy himself (1 Samuel 31). But even though Satan won a temporary victory in Saul's life, there was never any moment when God was not in sovereign control of the situation.

God even used the betrayal of Judas, which took place under Satan's influence (John 13:2, 27), as a means of fulfilling His plan of redemption (Acts 2:23–24).

SATAN WAS DEFEATED PROPHETICALLY

A second way that Satan has been defeated is

through the prophecy that God spoke back in Genesis 3:15 when He was pronouncing judgment on Adam, Eve, and the serpent for their sin.

God's "I Wills"

At the beginning of this book we saw Satan's five "I will" statements in Isaiah 14. The devil declared what he was going to do, but he failed. In Genesis 3:15 God declares an "I will" of His own, and no one can stop Him.

Five times the devil had said, "I will." Here God said, in effect, "Let's put your 'I will' statements against My 'I will' statements." God said He would put enmity or strife between the woman's seed and the serpent's seed.

This is the continuation of the struggle begun in heaven with Satan's fall. Satan produces his evil seed, and God produces His righteous seed. These two lines began their conflict with Adam's two sons, and the battle has been on ever since. God's righteous seed will win out, because no one can frustrate God's "I will."

The second part of God's "I will" declaration in Genesis 3:15 is implied rather than spoken, but it is no less powerful. It is the prophecy of the righteous Seed, Jesus Christ, who will crush Satan. We could state the middle phrase of the verse this way, "[I will see to it that] He shall bruise you on the head."

Genesis 3:15 also indicates that God's victory would not come without suffering. The bruising of God's righteous Seed on the heel is a cryptic, prophetic way of referring to Jesus' sufferings at His crucifixion. But even though Jesus died, it was Satan who received the fatal blow.

Why? Jesus rose again. A bruise on the heel is not fatal. But Satan got bruised or crushed on the head, which was a death blow. Satan's defeat was announced prophetically in Eden, and it was accomplished at Calvary and with the empty tomb of Jesus Christ.

Satan's Attack

The strife between the woman's seed and the serpent's seed is unfolded throughout the rest of the Bible. Beginning immediately in Genesis 4, the followers of God and the followers of the devil are engaged in conflict.

When Abel was born, Satan probably thought he was looking at the fulfillment of God's prophecy, the one who would crush his head. Remember, Satan is not all-knowing. He can't see the future, and he can't know God's plan until it is revealed.

So when Satan saw Abel bringing offerings that God accepted, he knew he had to do something to get rid of this seed. So he put murder in the heart of Cain, and Cain killed his brother Abel (1 John 3:12).

But let me tell you something about rebelling against God. You can't possibly win—not only because God is infinitely greater in power, but because He doesn't tell everything. "The secret things belong to the Lord our God" (Deuteronomy 29:29). God always has the last word because He has His secrets.

So even though Satan got Cain to kill Abel in an attempt to get rid of God's righteous seed, God had something Satan hadn't counted on. And in that part of His plan, God maintained His victorious edge.

God's Victory

What Satan didn't count on was the birth of Seth (Genesis 4:25–26). When Seth was born, Eve herself spoke of the significance of his birth: "God has appointed me another offspring in place of Abel; for Cain killed him" (v. 25). Seth was God's substitute for Abel.

Now you see what this has to do with the angelic conflict that began in heaven and was continued on earth. It was in the days of Seth's son Enosh that "men began to call upon the name of the Lord" (Genesis 4:26). God had someone else ready to take Abel's place. God always has someone prepared to make sure His will is accomplished.

Satan didn't know that God had a plan. All he knew was that when Seth was born, he got a divine curveball thrown at him. He decided that since he couldn't be sure which son was the righteous seed, he would do the job right and corrupt the whole human race. That brings us right back to Genesis 6 and Satan's grotesque plan to produce a demonic seed.

We've read verses 1–4 of this chapter, but let's read on. In verses 5–7 it sounds like the devil's plan has worked, because God says He intends to wipe out the human race. But God knows something Satan didn't plan on. "Noah found favor in the eyes of the Lord" (Genesis 6:8). The righteous seed would be preserved through Noah.

There's a lesson here. Even when it looks like the devil has the upper hand, God always has a Seth or a Noah. He always provides a way out (see 1 Corinthians 10:13). If you are rebelling against God, He may let you think you're winning for a little while. Satan thought he had wiped out God's seed. But he didn't know that God had a righteous man named Noah tucked away. And through Noah, the righteous seed was preserved.

Much later, Satan used the same strategy against the baby Jesus by driving Herod to kill all the boy babies in Bethlehem (Matthew 2:16–18). But our enemy didn't count on God sending His angels to lead Jesus and His family to Egypt.

SATAN WAS DEFEATED HISTORICALLY

We can thank God that Satan was defeated prophetically in Eden. Now here's the next stage in God's victory. Satan was also defeated historically at the cross.

Looking ahead to the cross, Jesus said, "Now judgment is upon this world; now the ruler of this world shall be cast out. And I, if I be lifted up from the earth, will draw all men to Myself" (John 12:31–32). The Cross was the ultimate defeat that Satan did not anticipate.

The Judgment of the Cross

When Jesus Christ was on earth, He let the devil know there was one Man he couldn't mess with. Jesus tied up the "strong man," the devil, so He could plunder the devil's house (Matthew 12:29). As we have already seen, Jesus had total control over Satan's demons. They had to do what He said, because He was and is infinitely stronger than the devil.

But it was in His death that Jesus really crushed the head of Satan. Satan was judged at the Cross (John 12:31; 16:7–11). How was Satan judged? On the Cross, God removed the curse of sin that Satan caused to be laid on mankind in the Garden of Eden.

When Satan tempted Eve, he was banking on a fact he knew about God because he had experienced it himself: When you sin, you come under God's curse. There is nowhere to run from it. You don't have to like it or even believe it, but sin brings a curse.

The Bible says that anyone who does not keep God's law perfectly is under a curse (Galatians 3:10). Sin is the failure to keep God's law. It is falling short of His standard, which is perfection. The reason unbelievers will spend eternity in hell is that sin puts men and women under the curse of God's broken law.

But Jesus removed the curse of sin, which was the curse of the Law (Galatians 3:13). Let's stop here for a minute and talk about a biblical principle that relates directly to spiritual warfare.

If Satan can't tempt us to go off into a life of overt sin, he will tempt us to go the other direction, that of trying to please God and earn His favor by our goodness. Satan doesn't care what it takes to distract us from Christ, just so we arrive in hell.

Satan has a lot of people believing they are good enough to get into heaven. But you need to understand that God's law, embodied in the Ten Commandments, is the source of sin's curse. We wouldn't know what sin was if we didn't have God's perfect standard to measure it against.

People go around reciting the Ten Commandments, but God didn't give them to be recited or memorized. He gave them to be obeyed. When we fail to keep God's commandments, we fall under His curse.

The Ten Commandments are good laws, but they are bad news for sinners like us, because the only thing the Law can do is condemn us when we violate it. It has no power built into it to help us obey.

For instance, God's law says, "You shall not steal." How many times have you stolen? Someone might say, "Oh, I've never stolen money from a bank or anything like that. I just took some pencils home from work."

But God's question is, "Were they yours?" God doesn't make the kinds of fine distinctions we make.

The Ten Commandments also forbid lying. How many times have you lied? How many times have you chosen to do something else besides worshiping God?

That's idolatry, which is also condemned in the Ten Commandments.

Do you see how the commands of God are bad news for sinners?

One of my favorite analogies for the law of God is the speed limit law.

The speed limit law only tells you how fast you can go. It doesn't help you drive at that speed. Even when you are obeying the law, the police officer doesn't pull you over and say, "I just want to congratulate you on obeying the speed limit. All these other people are speeding, but I want to write you a ticket of congratulations because you are keeping the law."

Why doesn't the officer do that? Because the law can only condemn you when you break it. It doesn't praise you when you keep it. The law gives the basis of condemnation, not the basis of congratulations. God's law brings a curse, and Satan loves to put people under the same curse he is under. But on the cross Jesus lifted the curse.

The Blessing of the Cross

Satan and his curse were judged and defeated at the cross. Jesus' cross turned what was our judgment into our blessing. That's reason enough for us to praise God, but let me give you more reasons that the Cross has become a blessing for us.

One reason is that once we have been freed from the curse of sin, we cannot sin our way back under it. Satan has been defeated so royally and completely that he no longer has any claim on us once we belong to Christ. The writer of Hebrews says, "But [Jesus], having offered one sacrifice for sins *for all time,* sat down at the right hand of God. . . . For by one offering He has perfected *for all time* those who are sanctified" (10:12, 14, italics added).

This is good news because it means you don't have to worry that a year from now you will commit a sin that will put you back under the curse. Jesus provided not only for the sins you have committed, but also for those you will commit. Jesus has removed the curse of sin forever. That's why we can't lose our salvation.

God judged and defeated Satan at the Cross, so Satan can no longer make sin an issue to separate us from God.

Here's a second blessing of the Cross, also found in the book of Hebrews:

> Since then the children share in flesh and blood, He Himself likewise also partook of the same, that through death He might render powerless him who had the power of death, that is, the devil; and might deliver those who through fear of death were subject to slavery all their lives. (2:14–15)

The Cross has removed the fear of death for those of us who know Jesus Christ.

One way Satan holds people hostage is through the fear of death. You say, "But isn't it normal and natural to fear death?" Only if you don't understand the Cross. If you know Jesus, you don't have any reason to be afraid to die.

The reason is simple. Once you know Jesus, you're never going to experience the thing you are afraid of. You're never really going to die, because one millisecond after you close your eyes in death, you will be ushered into the presence of the Lord and your eyes will open on heaven.

You won't even be at your own funeral! Everybody else will be there, but not you. You're never going to cease to exist. If the doctor says your disease is terminal and you have twenty-four hours to live, you have only just begun to live. To be absent from the body is to be "at home" with the Lord (2 Corinthians 5:8).

How can you be afraid of something that is just a vapor? The fear of death should not hold us in bondage. That's what the Cross did for you. So if you're afraid of death, Satan has you looking at the quarter instead of at the sun.

A little girl who always took a shortcut through a cemetery on her way home from school was asked why she wasn't afraid to walk through a graveyard. She answered, "Because my home is on the other side." For the believer, death is just the shortest route home.

SATAN WILL BE DEFEATED ETERNALLY

Here's a fourth and final way in which Satan is defeated. It is still future in terms of history, but it is as good as done from God's viewpoint. Someday, Satan will be eternally defeated.

Temporary Access to God's Presence

The beautiful thing about Satan's eternal defeat is that when his eternal sentence is executed, our enemy will be put away forever. The devil, who has led countless millions to hell and has harassed and hurt God's people for eons, will be banished to hell. This is the final stage of his judgment.

Satan went from living in God's presence to having temporary access to God's presence after his sin. At the Cross, Satan suffered another defeat because he was rendered powerless. His weapons were taken away from him.

Then in Revelation 12:7–12 we see the final war in

which Satan will be "thrown down" (v. 9). No wonder this elicits great rejoicing on the part of God's saints. Finally, Satan will no longer have even temporary access to heaven.

Eternal Banishment

The last we hear of Satan is in Revelation 20, which describes the devil's confinement during the millennial reign of Christ, his last gasp of rebellion, and his eternal judgment:

> And I saw an angel coming down from heaven, having the key of the abyss and a great chain in his hand. And he laid hold of the dragon, the serpent of old, who is the devil and Satan, and bound him for a thousand years . . . ; after these things he must be released for a short time. . . . And when the thousand years are completed, Satan will be released from his prison, and will come out to deceive the nations which are in the four corners of the earth, Gog and Magog, to gather them together for the war. (vv. 1–3, 7–8)

At the end of the Millennium, those who didn't want Jesus to rule over them will get a final opportunity to rebel. Satan will be released to bring out the rebellion that they harbored in their hearts for the thousand years in which Christ reigned.

But the battle will be over quickly, because fire will come down from God and devour them (v. 9). Then will come the moment that God's people have been waiting for: "The devil who deceived them was thrown into the lake of fire and brimstone, where the beast and the false prophet are also; and they will be tormented day and night forever and ever" (v. 10).

The Bible calls this "the second death" (Revelation

20:14). Earlier in this verse it says that "death and Hades" are also thrown into the lake of fire. So not only is the devil sent there for eternity, so are Hades and the people in it.

The *New American Standard* translation is helpful here because it renders the word used here as "Hades." This is the place of torment for people who have died without Jesus Christ, such as the rich man Jesus talked about in Luke 16:19–31. These people are awaiting the final judgment, described in Revelation 20:15. Hades is the place of punishment today.

But Hades is not the final judgment. The holding cell for a death-row prisoner is not the final step. Execution is that prisoner's final judgment. And eternal hell is the final judgment for the devil and his demons and his human followers.

Satan was judged a long time ago, and hell was prepared for him and his angelic rebels (Matthew 25:41). Jesus said He saw Satan fall from heaven like lightning (Luke 10:18). We can use the analogy of lightning and thunder to understand what is happening in Revelation 20.

Lightning and thunder occur at the same time, but we see the lightning before we hear the thunder because light travels faster than sound. Satan's judgment was pronounced in heaven in eternity past, and now in Revelation 20 we hear the "thunderclap" that follows the lightning as he is thrown into the eternal lake of fire. The point is that there is no question about Satan's defeat and eternal destiny.

But the truly tragic thing is that the devil will not be alone in the lake of fire. "If anyone's name was not found written in the book of life, he was thrown into the lake of fire" (Revelation 20:15). Mankind is judged because of this connectedness to Satan.

Let me make something very clear. God is in charge of hell, not the devil. The devil will be the most tormented being in hell, not its ruler. He will suffer torment as the judgment of a holy and righteous God, and in the midst of his punishment Satan will have to acknowledge God's holiness and justice. Satan is already defeated.

PART FOUR

YOUR
AUTHORITY

13

THE PURCHASE
OF AUTHORITY

Now that we have reviewed the angelic world, both the holy and the evil angels, and have come to understand something of what they are like and what they do, we are ready to move on.

With this chapter we begin a new section of our study. We have learned that this world is Satan's domain. For now, he is "the ruler of this world" (John 12:31). And because Adam turned the world over to the evil one, Satan exercises a certain amount of authority.

But God in His grace thwarted Satan's attempt to take over completely. God's plan would be fulfilled even in Adam's failure, because God promised that one day His seed would come through the woman to crush Satan (Genesis 3:15).

But in the meantime, we are right in the middle of this battle called spiritual warfare. And because we are engaged in this angelic conflict, what we need is the power, the authority, to wage victorious warfare.

We need to keep Satan from destroying our families, breaking up our marriages, owning our children, controlling our minds, and inflaming our passions. We need to get the devil off our backs.

But where does the authority for successful spiritual warfare come from? We are introduced to the source in Hebrews 2, where we discover that the answer is a person. The author of Hebrews says that God has another person in the spiritual battle, and he tells us that we need to see this person: "We do see Him who has been made for a little while lower than the angels, namely, Jesus, because of the suffering of death crowned with glory and honor, that by the grace of God He might taste death for everyone" (Hebrews 2:9).

If we are going to be winners in spiritual battle day in and day out, week after week, we need to see Jesus. The key to having authority in spiritual warfare is to "see Jesus"—to understand and put into practice all that He has purchased for us by His death, resurrection, and ascension.

If we could only see Jesus, we would see Someone who has already won the battle for us. It is our inability to see Jesus that has limited our authority in the realm of the angelic conflict and spiritual warfare. When we can see Jesus in the sense I described above, we will be introduced to authority we never knew possible.

Therefore, I want us to see and understand three important things about Jesus and His purchase of authority for us: the person of Jesus, the payment of Jesus, and your position in Jesus.

THE PERSON OF JESUS CHRIST

When Adam sinned, God's promise of a seed from the woman who would crush the serpent's head was also a warning to Satan that the battle was not over. It appeared that Satan had won a big round, but someday a descendant of Eve would give birth to a baby who would crush Satan. Why did God decide that the ultimate victory over the devil would come through the human line?

God could have crushed Satan at any moment in a blast of sovereign power. But God wanted to demonstrate His power over Satan through another plan, using the weakness and frailty of human flesh to defeat the powerful ruler of the evil spirit world. Again, it's the lesser overcoming the greater.

The Right Time for Jesus

The promise of Genesis 3:15 was made in the ancient past. But God made good on it one night in a stable in Bethlehem. Paul put it this way: "When the fulness of the time came, God sent forth His Son, born of a woman, born under the Law" (Galatians 4:4).

Between the time of God's promise and its fulfillment in Jesus Christ, God had put in place the sacrificial system of the Mosaic Law to cover sin until the Savior would come.

The Law provided temporary relief for sin until it was time for the Savior. The Israelites brought bulls and goats to offer on the altar to cover their sin. And every time an animal was sacrificed, it was a way of affirming, "One day a woman is going to have a baby who is going to crush Satan's head."

When it was just the right time, when all the conditions God wanted were in place, Jesus was born of a woman. Jesus was born while the Law was still in effect. He lived under the Law, but He came to make the final payment for sin and fulfill the Law.

Don't read Galatians 4:4 too fast, or you will miss something very significant about Jesus. The One who purchased our authority over the devil is not just another spiritual warrior. He is God in the flesh. The Scripture is precise here. Paul said the Son was "sent," but the baby was "born." The Son existed before the baby was born. Isaiah said the same thing. "A child will be born to us, a son will be given to us" (Isaiah 9:6). The child had to come through the birth canal, but the Son already existed.

In the person of Jesus we have what theologians call the hypostatic union of deity and humanity, the two natures of Christ. The Son, the second person of the holy Trinity, was poured into humanity, the seed of the woman. The baby forming in Mary's womb was God in the flesh.

God had to have a man to fulfill the promise of Genesis 3:15—but this Man had to be the kind of man who would not do what Adam did. He had to be the kind of Man who could face the devil one-on-one and never yield.

What God needed was the God-man, Jesus Christ. So God sent His Son, born of a woman, to reclaim the dominion that Adam had handed over to Satan.

Satan's Attack on Jesus

Satan knew he was in trouble when the time came for Jesus to be born. So the enemy pulled out all the stops in his warfare against the Savior.

Satan tried to foul things up before Jesus was born by subjecting Mary to humiliation and causing Joseph to divorce her.

But the fullness of God's time had come, and Jesus was born. Then the devil turned to King Herod for help, stirring him up to kill the babies in and around Bethlehem. Satan was doing everything he could because he had a big problem on his hands.

Remember, Satan does not possess all knowledge. He is not God's equal. In the birth of Jesus, God threw Satan the proverbial curveball. The devil had been rolling along, defeating person after person because he knew there was no man who could handle him.

But Satan didn't count on God becoming a man. That was part of the plan he didn't calculate. He had been saying to God, "Give me another Adam. I can take care of him. Give me 'Adam Jr.' No problem. Just keep those Adams coming, because there is not a man You can create who can stand against my angelic power. Who do You have to handle me?"

God said, "Try this one. I am going to send My Son to earth to become a Man and defeat you."

So the eternal God entered time and space as a Man. Satan tried to destroy Jesus, but none of his ideas worked. Please note, by the way, that God used the angels to thwart Satan at every turn.

As we saw earlier, the birth account of Jesus is filled with angelic visitations. It was an angel who told the wise men to go back home another way so Herod wouldn't find out where Jesus was.

It was an angel who led Joseph and Mary to take their baby to Egypt, out of Herod's reach.

When killing Jesus didn't work, Satan tried to overthrow Him by the temptation in the wilderness. The devil tried to get Jesus to do the same thing Adam did, act independently of God.

And at one point Satan used the same tactic, food. Satan must be big on food. Satan told Adam and Eve, "Eat this fruit." He told Jesus, "Why don't You turn these stones into bread?" (see Matthew 4:3). Adam ate apart from God's will and failed. Jesus refused to eat outside of God's will and won the battle.

Jesus' Conquest of Satan

Why did Jesus have to go to all the trouble and suffering of fasting for forty days in the wilderness and then facing Satan head-on in intense spiritual combat? Why didn't Jesus just exercise His deity and destroy Satan right there in the wilderness?

For the same reason God did not crush Satan the moment he rebelled or in the Garden of Eden. He had a different plan, one that would display His power and grace. Jesus had to win the battle as a Man, as the seed of the woman.

In fact, Jesus lived His whole life on earth with the limitations of humanity. Don't get me wrong. Jesus was fully God in His flesh, but He voluntarily submitted to the limits of humanity. Even when Jesus performed a miracle, He did it in dependence on His Father.

Jesus lived as a Man to demonstrate that He had the right to rule and to challenge Satan based on His obedience and dependence on God. Satan knew what Jesus was all about. So instead of just pulling out His deity, Jesus fasted in the wilderness for spiritual power, then pulled out God's Word and shut Satan down.

If only the first Adam had used the word of God when Satan tempted him and his wife. If only Adam had reminded Eve, "God said we can't eat from this tree." Adam didn't use the word, but Jesus did—and He emerged victorious.

Satan wasn't finished, though. He had one more strategy to defeat Jesus—the cross. So according to Luke

22:3, Satan entered into Judas Iscariot, motivating him to betray Jesus Christ into the hands of His crucifiers.

Things looked bad for Jesus at the cross. But the cross did not catch God by surprise. He already had a plan in place that would turn what Satan thought was his finest moment into his worst defeat!

Jesus came "that He might destroy the works of the devil" (1 John 3:8). God would use the cross, an instrument of death and destruction, to destroy Satan's power and purchase for us all the authority we would ever need for spiritual victory.

THE PAYMENT OF JESUS CHRIST

In order to conquer Satan, Jesus had to conquer death, because death is Satan's weapon.

But to conquer death, Jesus had to pay for sin, since death is the consequence of sin. It was sin that brought death into the world, because God has decreed, "The soul who sins will die" (Ezekiel 18:4).

There's only one way to pay for sin, and that's through death. And there's only one way to conquer death, and that's through resurrection. You need resurrection power to conquer death. Somebody has to get up from the dead if death is going to be defeated.

This is what Jesus did in His payment for sin. He entered the realm of death, which is Satan's domain, and beat the devil in his own territory. You know a person is powerful when he beats you on your own turf! Jesus said, "I will meet Satan at the place he owns, which is death."

A cemetery is Satan's work (Ephesians 2:1–3), and that's why people fear death. They know it is the last enemy (1 Corinthians 15:26) and that it's an enemy none of us has ever been able to beat. So anyone who can beat death has broken the power of the biggest, "baddest" weapon Satan has. Enter Jesus Christ into the battle.

Canceling Our Debt

Paul describes our problem and the payment Jesus made for sin in this classic passage:

> When you were dead in your transgressions and the uncircumcision of your flesh, He made you alive together with Him, having forgiven us all our transgressions, having canceled out the certificate of debt consisting of decrees against us and which was hostile to us; and He has taken it out of the way, having nailed it to the cross. (Colossians 2:13–14)

We were dead in sin and without hope, because we had a "certificate of decrees" posted against us. This is a very significant phrase.

In Roman law, when a person was convicted of a crime and sent to prison, a list of his offenses was drawn up and posted on his cell door. This was his certificate of decrees, showing why he was in prison. Anybody who walked by his cell could see why a person was in prison because of the certificate of decrees.

Jesus Christ had a certificate like this posted over His cross. Remember that after Pilate had tried Jesus, he went out to the crowd and said, "I find no guilt in this man" (Luke 23:4). But the people shouted, "If you release this Man, you are no friend of Caesar" (John 19:12), because Jesus had claimed to be King of the Jews.

Pilate yielded and condemned Jesus, but in order to crucify the Lord he needed a certificate of decrees to show why this Man was being executed. So Pilate had a sign posted on the top of Jesus' cross, written in Hebrew, Greek, and Latin: "Jesus of Nazareth, King of the Jews."

As far as the crowd was concerned, Jesus was being crucified for treason against Rome. The Jewish nation wanted Him put to death for blasphemy because He called Himself God. And as far as Satan was concerned, he was eliminating the Seed of the woman who was going to crush him.

But little did Satan know there was another certificate of decrees posted above Jesus' cross. This was a divine certificate, drawn up by God, bearing the name of Tony Evans and every other person who has ever lived or who will ever live.

This certificate contained every sin of every person, and every charge on that certificate was valid. We were hopelessly guilty—and the sentence for those sins was death.

But Jesus bore the punishment for all of those sins. He took our guilt. The Bible says that Jesus Christ did not die as innocent, but as guilty. "[God] made Him who knew no sin to be sin on our behalf, that we might become the righteousness of God in Him" (2 Corinthians 5:21).

Now we get to the good part. When a criminal had finished his sentence and paid his debt to society, his certificate of decrees was taken off his cell door and stamped with one Greek word: *tetelestai*, "paid in full." The certificate was canceled (Colossians 2:14) and handed to the former criminal, so he could prove to anyone who asked that he was now free. Those charges could never be brought against him again.

What were Jesus' last words on the cross? "It is finished!" (John 19:30). This was actually just one word: *"Tetelestai!"* The debt that you and I owed to God was paid by Jesus Christ, completely.

Why were the charges against us "hostile to us"

(Colossians 2:14)? Because they carried the death penalty, for one thing. But also because Satan could always bring them up against us.

Satan knows that God in His holiness cannot tolerate sin, so Satan delights to bring up the charges against us. He loves to accuse people. He tells God, "Look at what this person has done. I have the certificate right here. Look at the charges against him."

But let me tell you something. When Satan goes before God and brings up Tony Evans, Jesus Christ steps in and says, "Look at the stamp on his certificate. His debt has been paid in full. I have paid for sins he has not even committed yet."

That's why once you are saved, you can never be lost again. Jesus paid the full price for your sins before you were even born. He satisfied the demands of God against sin.

Announcing the Victory

Jesus' death took care of the sin problem. God's wrath against sin has been satisfied, and He is now free to declare us forgiven because the debt has been paid.

But there was still an authority problem. Jesus had to deal with the question of who is in charge in the universe. That brings us to what happened between the time of Jesus' death and His resurrection. This is "the rest of the story."

Jesus not only purchased the forgiveness for our sins by His death, but He also reclaimed the authority of the universe that Adam had relinquished by his sin (Matthew 28:18).

Satan and his demons in the underworld needed to hear the announcement of Jesus' victory. So did the saints who had died before Calvary and were in a place called "paradise" or Abraham's bosom (Luke 16:23). So while Jesus' body was lying in the tomb, Jesus in His spirit went to Hades.

In the Bible, Hades is not the same as the lake of fire, or eternal hell. Hades was the temporary abode of those who died before the coming of Christ. Everyone who died before Calvary went to Hades, because Hades had two compartments in it.

Jesus' story of the rich man and Lazarus in Luke 16 is the clearest picture we have of this temporary arrangement. Lazarus died and went to paradise, but the rich man died and woke up in torment (Luke 16:23). The two could see each other, but they were separated by "a great chasm" (v. 26).

Why didn't Lazarus go to heaven as we know it, and the rich man to the eternal lake of fire? Because God was still operating on the "layaway" plan—the Old Testament system that provided only a temporary holding place. It was not until the death of Christ that the final matters relating to eternal destiny were settled.

But Jesus made the final payment on the layaway plan. What happens when you make the last payment on a layaway? You get to take the merchandise home with you.

That's exactly what Jesus did, according to Ephesians 4:8. "When He ascended on high, He led captive a host of captives." Jesus went in spirit to the paradise compartment of Hades and announced to those Old Testament saints, "I have paid the price. It's time to go home."

Then He led those saints in a great march to heaven in the greatest "shuttle service" in history. This is why Jesus could tell the thief on the cross, "Today you shall be with Me in Paradise" (Luke 23:43).

But that was not all. Jesus also visited the torment

side of Hades, where He announced His victory to the lost souls in Hades and the devil and his crew (1 Peter 3:18–20). Jesus' proclamation was, "Satan, I declare total victory over you."

See, Satan didn't count on the fact that the death of Christ would satisfy God's justice in such a way that God could show His love to sinners without compromising His holiness. To put it another way, Satan was aced by grace.

Getting God's "Receipt"

You may say, "But how do we really know God did all of this?" When you pay the price for something, you get a receipt to show that the purchase was made and the full price was paid. You don't want any doubt. You don't want anyone to think that you did not really pay for the merchandise. Your receipt is your proof. God gave us a receipt to prove that Jesus paid the price for sin, and to show that His payment was accepted. That receipt is the Resurrection.

Early on Easter Sunday morning, when Mary Magdalene came to anoint the body of Jesus, she discovered that He had risen. And then she met Him in the garden and ran to tell the disciples that the Lord had risen.

The Resurrection was proof that God was satisfied with Jesus' death and payment for sin. Several times in the book of Acts, the apostles appealed to the fact that God raised Jesus from the dead to prove that He was the Christ. Peter said there were many witnesses who saw the resurrected Christ (Acts 2:32).

Disarming Satan

So what did Jesus' victory do to Satan? Go back to Colossians 2:15, where Paul writes: "When He had disarmed the rulers and authorities, He made a public display of them, having triumphed over them through Him [Christ]."

When Jesus rose from the dead, Satan was disarmed. He was stripped of his weapons (the literal meaning of "disarmed"). He lost all of his ammunition, and he was rendered powerless (Hebrews 2:14).

Jesus Christ went into Satan's territory of death and took away the captives of death who were waiting in paradise. Then Jesus beat death Himself by rising from the dead. And he took away the fear and the pain of death for all of those who believe in Him.

Satan's best weapon was deactivated. The roaring lion (1 Peter 5:8) had his teeth pulled out. The devouring lion was overcome by the Lion of the tribe of Judah, and now Satan is on a leash. We now have authority over Satan, not in and of ourselves, but because we belong to Christ.

Our Position in Christ

So we understand the person of Christ, that He had to be a Man empowered by God to defeat Satan. We understand the payment of Christ, that He died to pay for sin and to triumph over the devil.

But if we are going to be victorious in our conflict with Satan, we also need to understand our position in Christ.

Because we don't know who we are in Christ, we don't know how to relate to our enemy the devil. We have powerful Christians living powerless lives because they keep looking to Satan for permission to live as Christians. But Satan is only powerful in our lives when we allow him to be powerful.

This is why Jesus' triumph did not end with the

Resurrection. Jesus told His disciples He had to leave them. He was ascending back to heaven as a High Priest to take His blood and apply it to the mercy seat in heaven. And He was ascending as a triumphant King to be enthroned at the Father's right hand, from where He rules all of creation today. "All authority has been given to Me in heaven and on earth" (Matthew 28:18).

Sharing in Christ's Triumph

Jesus Christ was enthroned by God the Father, and all powers came under His authority, including the power of Satan and his demons. Earlier in Colossians 2, Paul had written: "In [Christ] all the fulness of Deity dwells in bodily form, and in Him you have been made complete, and He is the head over all rule and authority" (vv. 9–10).

According to Ephesians 1:20–22, when God raised Christ from the dead, He "seated Him at His right hand in the heavenly places, far above all rule and authority and power and dominion. . . . And He put all things in subjection under His feet."

Jesus Christ rules over all from His throne in the heavenlies. And he has "render[ed] powerless him who had the power of death, that is, the devil" (Hebrews 2:14). But the beautiful thing is that we have been raised up with Christ and are seated with Him "in the heavenly places" (Ephesians 2:6). Jesus Christ not only sits enthroned, but we sit enthroned with Him. He has partnered with us to share His victory with us.

The word *triumphed* in Colossians 2:15 pictures the parade given to a victorious Roman general, who would bring his spoils and his captives in chains back to Rome and put them on display. Jesus triumphed so completely over Satan that He is marching the devil around in chains, displaying him as a whipped foe. And because we are in Christ, we share in His victory.

Jesus Christ triumphed over the devil through His blood. It was the blood of Jesus that paid for our sin and secured for us a place of authority with Him in the heavenly places. That's why we see the saints overcoming the devil by the blood of the Lamb (Revelation 12:11).

Exercising Christ's Authority

Do you see why I say you must understand your position in Christ? You must know who you are in Christ and begin exercising your authority under His authority.

You can't beat Satan in your own authority, because you don't have any. The key is that you have been raised and seated with Christ. Satan knows he can handle you, but he knows he can't handle Christ.

The devil's strategy is to keep you from living your life in the power of Christ, claiming the authority that is yours because you are under His blood.

When a police officer directing traffic signals for you to stop, you stop. Why? Because that officer is wearing a uniform and a badge as symbols of authority.

That officer standing in traffic doesn't have the power to make you stop. You can drive right on by. But because the officer is wearing the symbols of his or her authority, and because you know that officer has been delegated authority from the local police department to stop traffic, you honor that authority and obey the officer. The uniform says it all.

But what happens if you don't honor the officer's authority and keep on driving? You will soon discover that the officer has real power to back up his or her authority, because there will be cars with flashing lights coming after you to arrest you.

As a believer you are clothed in a red "uniform," the precious blood of Jesus Christ. When Satan sees that uniform, he has to stop.

Satan won't stop when he sees you trying to use the power of positive thinking. He won't stop because you are making New Year's resolutions to try to beat him. He's not impressed by your efforts, because he knows there is no authority behind them. In other words, he can run through your stop signal because he knows there is nobody there to back you up.

But when you claim your authority through the blood of Christ, that's another story. Satan has to stop for that.

Some of us believers are praying, "God, please give me victory over the devil."

God is saying in response, "You already have the victory. Put on your red uniform." When you step out under the blood and the authority of Jesus Christ, when Satan comes after you he has to pull up short. He can't handle the blood.

Fighting *from* Victory

Here's the point. In your Christian life, you don't fight for victory, you fight *from* a position of victory. You don't say, "I am going to try to be victorious over Satan today."

Instead, you say, "Jesus Christ has already been victorious over Satan. So today, by faith, I am going to live in Christ's authority, trusting His blood to give me power over any attacks of the evil one." That's authority.

NOTHING TO FEAR

One day a butterfly was fluttering in great fright, because it was being pursued by a sparrow. The sparrow kept pecking at the butterfly, eager to devour it. But the butterfly was on the inside of a window, the glass separating it from the sparrow.

The sparrow kept pecking, trying to get at the butterfly. And the butterfly kept fluttering around in terror at the presence of the sparrow. The butterfly couldn't understand that the pane of glass between him and the sparrow kept the sparrow from doing what it wanted to do.

What scared the butterfly was that the sparrow was so close, right in his face. If only the butterfly could have understood that the pane of glass was all he needed for protection, no matter how close the sparrow seemed to be.

Tomorrow morning, Satan is going to be in your face again. He's going to be trying to devour you, to ruin your testimony and capture your children. But remember that Jesus Christ has slid a pane of glass in between you and Satan. This glass is red, stained with His blood.

Satan can peck at you, and he may seem close, but he can't touch you without God's permission, because you are protected by the blood of Jesus Christ. So you don't have to be afraid anymore.

And one day, according to Revelation 20:1–3, you won't have to worry about Satan anymore. Because on that day an angel from God will be sent down with a chain to wrap around Satan. And this one who deceived the nations will be thrown into the abyss for one thousand years.

Jesus Christ will order an angel, perhaps Michael or Gabriel, to tie Satan up. And then like a conquering Roman general, Jesus will put the devil on display, parading him through the streets on the way to the abyss.

I can hear Michael or Gabriel leading Satan in his chains and shouting out, "Move out of the way. Dead man walking."

So when you get up tomorrow, get up in the authority of Jesus Christ. Overcome Satan by the blood of Christ, because He has purchased that authority for you. Live under Christ's authority, and you get Christ's authority.

Then you can fight from a position of victory instead of fighting for victory. Jesus has already won the victory for you by His person, His payment, and His position. Tell Him you want His authority.

14

THE AGENCY
OF AUTHORITY

As a pastor, I get to perform marriage ceremonies. During the ceremony, there is one crucial moment when a transfer of identity and authority takes place.

The father of the bride walks the bride down the center aisle. He stands at the front, waiting for his cue. And then at the appropriate time in the service, I ask, "Who gives this woman to be married to this man?"

The father says, "I do." Then a young man steps up, and the father gives his daughter to the young man and steps aside.

Here is this man who has loved, taken care of, and provided for this woman for twenty or twenty-five years. He has been the male authority in her life.

But a year or two earlier, some smooth-talking dude came out of nowhere and captured this young lady's heart. And now at the wedding, this young man takes over. In fact, the father is invited to sit down and be quiet.

We no longer need Dad, and he is no longer the focus of attention. His daughter, beaming with joy, makes a commitment to the new love in her life. And the groom commits to love and cherish and provide for his bride. In essence, he replaces the father.

I've had occasion to bump into fathers who didn't go for the replacement. I've known fathers who still wanted to tell their married daughters what to do. And sometimes, a daughter is so used to having her daddy direct her life that she has a hard time adjusting to her new husband's authority.

The problem with all of this is that a married woman's loyalty doesn't belong to her father anymore. Any demands he makes on her life are now illegitimate. And the woman must give her allegiance to her husband, not her daddy. She is under a new authority because she has a new identity.

Let me tell you something. Before we knew Jesus Christ, we were the devil's children. He dominated our lives, told us what to do. But then one day we met Jesus, and there was a marriage. We transferred our identity to Him through salvation and came under His authority. Hell no longer had a claim on us.

But Satan is like a domineering parent who doesn't want to give up his ownership. He wants to maintain dominance in your life, even though you are now someone else's bride and you belong to Jesus Christ.

The problem with some believers is that they have been in Satan's house and under his dominance for so long, they don't know how to live with their new love, Jesus Christ. They don't know how to respond to this new identity and this new authority in their lives.

By now I hope you have gotten the point that we are in a spiritual battle. And in this battle, the degree to which we become identified with Christ, come under

His authority, and learn to use His authority is the degree to which we will experience victory.

The reason is that our battle is not against flesh and blood. It is against evil powers in the spiritual realm, the heavenly places. We have learned that the death, resurrection, and ascension of Jesus Christ have purchased all the authority we will ever need.

Now I want to consider what I call the agency of our authority. I'm talking about the church, the body of people that Christ formed and has left on earth to be the means by which He will defeat and dethrone the Evil One. Let's consider some key truths about the church as our agency of spiritual authority.

CHRIST HAS DELEGATED HIS AUTHORITY TO THE CHURCH

The first thing we need to understand is that Jesus Christ has delegated great spiritual authority to the church. In fact, let me say it in a stronger way. The church, *and only the church,* has been delegated spiritual authority by Christ.

I say that because we live in a world of "freelance" Christians who are off doing their own thing in isolation from the body of Christ. To say that this is not the way God intended believers to function is an understatement. We need to be vitally connected to the church to experience Christ's delegated power and authority over the devil.

The passage in which Jesus delegated His authority to the church is also the earliest mention of the church in the New Testament:

[Jesus] began asking His disciples, saying, "Who do people say that the Son of Man is?" And they said, "Some say

John the Baptist; and others, Elijah; but still others, Jeremiah, or one of the prophets." He said to them, "But who do you say that I am?" And Simon Peter answered and said, "Thou art the Christ, the Son of the living God." And Jesus answered and said to him, "Blessed are you, Simon Barjona, because flesh and blood did not reveal this to you, but My Father who is in heaven." (Matthew 16:13b–17)

The Delegator of Authority

Notice first who it is that is delegating this authority. The people were guessing that Jesus was one of the great prophets of the past.

You and I would be flattered if someone compared us to John the Baptist, Elijah, or Jeremiah. But for Jesus, comparison to any human being, even the greatest leaders who ever lived, is an insult. Jesus is in a class by Himself because He's the eternal Son of God, second person of the Trinity.

It was important that all the disciples realize and confess this, because they were to be the first and primary recipients of Jesus' delegated authority. Even though Peter was the spokesman, he was speaking for all of them, because Jesus asked the question this way: "Who do you [plural] say that I am?"

Peter was saying to Jesus, "We've already discussed this issue, and let me tell You what we have concluded. You are the Messiah, the Christ, Son of the living God."

Jesus then told Peter and the other disciples, in effect, "You are right. Now let Me show you what I am going to do as the Messiah and Son of God." This is where we get to the church: "And I also say to you that you are Peter, and upon this rock I will build My church; and the gates of Hades shall not overpower it" (Matthew 16:18).

The Builder of the Church

This is the first occurrence of the word *church* in the New Testament. This Greek word, *ekklesia,* was used of an assembly of citizens who gathered together to make governmental decisions in a city or district. It was also used of a congregation gathered for religious purposes in Israel, such as in a synagogue.

Here Jesus declares that He is going to build something so awesome that even hell won't be able to stop His building program. Since Peter was the one to confess Jesus as Lord and Savior, Jesus used a wordplay on Peter's name to specify the foundation on which He would build His church. Stay with me for a few paragraphs, because this is important.

The church was not built on Peter. In the Greek text, Peter's name is *Petros.* The rock on which Jesus promised to build His church is the word *petra.*

The word *Petros* means "stone." *Petra* is a feminine form of the word for rock or stone, so it couldn't refer to Peter. The classical Greek word *petra* meant a group of stones that had become connected to form a rocky cleft or a large slab. So this word has to do with the coming together of many stones.

Jesus was saying, "Peter, I am going to build My church on your confession of Me as Lord." The church is made up of people who confess the Lord Jesus as Savior, a group of individual stones who come together to form a solid rock that will roll over hell! Peter later described the church as "living stones [who] are being built up as a spiritual house" (1 Peter 2:5).

The first thing we need to notice in Matthew 16:18

is that Jesus said, "I will build *My* church" (italics added). Don't think for one minute that we are building the church using Christ's name.

The only church that can overcome the onslaughts of hell is the church that Jesus is building—a community of believers who cross racial, cultural, and class lines (Ephesians 2:14). If you and I have our own agenda, call it what you want, but it is not a church. The church is Jesus' church. That means He sets the agenda. He must be the authority.

The one thing that hell can't stop is the church. It can stop anything and everything else, but it can't stop the church because it's what Christ is building.

This means if you are detached from the church, you are not in a position to keep the forces of hell from overrunning your life. The reason is that you are like a finger detached from its hand, or a hand without an arm. We have too many Christians today who want to live isolated lives, not understanding that it is the community of saints that God has ordained to stop hell.

When you can't break through to God on your own, if you're part of the community of believers they can join forces and help you break through to God together. The devil isn't too afraid of one isolated believer. But he trembles when the church goes into action.

On the Offensive

I also want you to see that the church is on the offensive, not the defensive.

The reason so many Christians are defeated is that they are defensive Christians. They are always backpedaling, trying to stop the devil from overpowering them. They are fussing about the temptations the devil puts in their path, wishing he would stop it.

It would be great if Satan would stop tempting us. But that isn't going to happen, because the devil isn't going to stop being what he is. He is always going to be the devil.

But Jesus makes clear in Matthew 16 that it is hell, not the church, that is on the defensive. The church is moving out, on the offensive. It is hell's job to stop the church, not vice versa.

So instead of looking at what Satan is doing, we need to take a close look at what Christ has done in building His church. When you understand what Christ has done, you can be on the offensive. When you gather with other believers at church, you come to a place of victory, not a place of defeat.

Assaulting the Gates

The church has the authority of Jesus to assault "the gates of Hades." What does Jesus mean by the imagery of gates?

In the ancient world, the gates of a city were the place of authority. The elders of the city met at the gates to make decisions. It was like our city hall. So the gates of Hades are the place where Satan and his demons have met together to try to set hell's agenda for your life. Satan wants to usurp God's authority in your life and replace it with his authority. And he has a plan by which he is seeking to accomplish that.

He may try to use your mate, your children, your boss, or your circumstances. But whatever the method, the devil and his demons have met to map out their strategy to steal, kill, and destroy (John 10:10).

Jesus called this strategic place the gates of Hades, which we saw in the previous chapter is not the same as the lake of fire, eternal hell. Hades is the realm of spiritual death, the "prison house" where the dead went before Jesus Christ rose from the dead.

Whenever Satan moves against you, he always moves in the realm of death, because "the wages of sin is death" (Romans 6:23). And even if Satan doesn't kill you physically, he wants to ruin you spiritually because it's the same thing in his book. He wants you to live in the sphere of death.

Too many believers are living in the sphere of death, even though Jesus has already given us victory over the grave. They do not understand the authority the church has to assault and overpower the gates of Hades.

The Keys of the Kingdom

Now we're ready for another important part of Jesus' teaching concerning the authority that Christ has delegated to the church.

Jesus said, "I will give you the keys of the kingdom of heaven; and whatever you shall bind on earth shall be bound in heaven, and whatever you shall loose on earth shall be loosed in heaven" (Matthew 16:19).

Keys are a symbol of authority in the Bible (see Isaiah 22:22; Luke 11:52). The one who has the keys has access, which translates to authority.

The keys Jesus was talking about belong to the kingdom of heaven. Why is the word *keys* plural? Because the gates of Hades are plural. Keys can open locked gates. Jesus is saying that for every hellish gate, there is a corresponding heavenly key.

For everything Satan throws at you, there is always a divine response. There is no problem in your life to which God does not have a response. That's why you need to quit messing with the gates of hell and start learning how to use the keys of the kingdom that Jesus has given the church. The keys of the kingdom are tied to a concept that Jesus called binding and loosing. What does that mean? It has to do with allowing or forbidding, with access or lack of access.

The church of Jesus Christ has been given the keys of the kingdom of God. It has been given access to heaven, so that whatever the church declares on earth, if it agrees with the kingdom of God, has already been determined in heaven.

In other words, there is a backup for the things you do on earth that are in concert with the kingdom. If you are doing kingdom business, if you are a kingdom Christian living a kingdom life, then you can have kingdom victory.

There's a good example of what it means to be on a kingdom agenda in Matthew 16. After Peter's confession, Jesus told His disciples that He was going to the cross.

Peter rebuked Jesus for saying this, but Jesus turned and said to Peter, "Get behind Me, Satan!" (v. 23). Jesus called Peter the devil because Peter was trying to stop Jesus from carrying out God's agenda.

Jesus let Peter know that he was operating on Satan's agenda, not on God's kingdom agenda. Peter thought he was helping God by trying to stop Jesus from going to the cross. But in reality, to try to turn Jesus away from the cross was to cooperate with the devil, since Satan's goal was to keep Jesus from accomplishing what He came to do.

A lot of us don't have the authority of the keys because we're following the wrong agenda. We need to make sure we are on God's kingdom program. Jesus tells us how to get on that program in Matthew 16:24 when He says, "If anyone wishes to come after Me, let him deny himself, and take up his cross, and follow Me."

Living on a kingdom agenda means giving up the rights to your life. There's only one reason to take up a cross, and that's to die on it. Our problem in the church today is that we have too many Christians who are still in charge of their lives. But if you are running your own existence, you can't have God's victory and God's authority.

When you die, you relinquish all rights to yourself. We are to die each day in the sense of giving up our rights and our plans. As Paul put it, "I have been crucified with Christ; and it is no longer I who live, but Christ lives in me; and the life which I now live in the flesh I live by faith in the Son of God, who loved me, and delivered Himself up for me" (Galatians 2:20).

See, there is no authority in your plans or mine. There is no authority in what we want to do. Our only authority is when we take the keys of the kingdom. The keys overcome the gates of hell, but you must die to yourself.

In Matthew 16, Jesus went on to say, "Whoever wishes to save his life shall lose it" (v. 25). If you're still trying to save your life—still trying to work your own plan—God won't help you do that.

But if you are a functioning part of His church, when you're ready to lose your life for His sake, He's ready to release His authority in your life.

Authority and Responsibility

There is one other thing I want you to know about the keys of the kingdom before we move on. We have talked about this before, but I want you to see it in this context. The principle is that God has given you the keys, but He won't use them for you.

What I am saying is that authority demands responsibility. The power to overcome the gates of hell only works if you are doing what God has asked you to do. If you're not fulfilling your spiritual responsibility, don't expect authority. If you're sitting back waiting for God to do it when He has already handed you the keys, you're going to be waiting a really long time.

Let me show you an example of what I mean. In Exodus 14, the children of Israel were trying to leave Egypt when they came to the Red Sea. The Egyptian army was bearing down on them, and the sea was in front of them. As far as the people were concerned, they were trapped. They cried out in fear to God.

> But Moses said to the people, "Do not fear! Stand by and see the salvation of the Lord which He will accomplish for you today; for the Egyptians whom you have seen today, you will never see them again forever. The Lord will fight for you while you keep silent." (Exodus 14:13–14)

Then in verses 15–16, God said, "Why are you crying out to Me? Tell the sons of Israel to go forward. And as for you, lift up your staff and stretch out your hand over the sea and divide it, and the sons of Israel shall go through the midst of the sea on dry land."

God was telling the people to get with it and go. They had cried out to Him, they knew what He had decided to do, and now it was time for them to move. But they were just standing there, so God asked them, "Why haven't you done anything? Why aren't you moving? Get going."

See, just saying "amen" is not enough. Amen only works when you are willing to step out on what you just amened. Some believers have been saying amen for years, but they don't have any authority or any victory.

To get the power, you have to get up and start moving toward the Red Sea.

That takes faith, because the water hasn't parted yet. The sea didn't part until the people were ready to act on God's word. Until you act, you won't have the power of the keys to unlock doors, because authority always demands responsibility.

THE CHURCH HAS BEEN EXALTED TO A POSITION OF AUTHORITY WITH CHRIST

Here's a second principle you need to understand about the church. Jesus Christ has not only delegated His authority to the church, but He has elevated the church to a position of authority that takes us far above all other powers, including Satan.

Jesus Is in Charge

The reason Jesus can raise the church to such an exalted position of authority is that He Himself was raised triumphantly from the dead and enthroned in heaven over all principalities and powers. In other words, Jesus is firmly in charge.

Paul wanted the church at Ephesus to understand this, so he prayed this prayer for the church:

> I pray that the eyes of your heart may be enlightened, so that you may know what is the hope of His calling, what are the riches of the glory of His inheritance in the saints, and what is the surpassing greatness of His power toward us who believe. These are in accordance with the working of the strength of His might which He brought about in Christ, when He raised Him from the dead, and seated Him at His right hand in the heavenly places. (Ephesians 1:18–20)

Paul was praying that the church at Ephesus would understand what they had and who they were associated with. He was praying that the church would understand what took place when Jesus Christ was raised from the dead.

What happened is that the risen and ascended Christ now possesses all authority in heaven and on earth (Matthew 28:18). He is in charge of the universe. Paul goes on to say that Christ is exalted "far above all rule and authority and power and dominion, and every name that is named, not only in this age, but also in the one to come. And He put all things in subjection under His feet" (Ephesians 1:21–22a).

Like a conquering general, Jesus has His foot on the neck of His enemies. Everything and everyone on earth and under the earth is subject to Him.

God the Father raised Jesus and seated His Son at His right hand, the place of ultimate authority. He runs the show.

Many say that the United States is the only superpower left in the world today. That makes the president the most powerful man in the world.

But the reality is that there is only one superpower in this universe, and it's the kingdom of God. And since Jesus Christ is sitting in the position of authority in this kingdom, let me say it again. He is in charge.

We Are Raised with Jesus

You may be saying, "That's great that Jesus is exalted in heaven. It's great to know He is in charge. But I'm still stuck here on earth."

If you think that, somebody has been lying to you! According to Ephesians 2:6, believers have been raised up and exalted with Christ. God did not just give you new life when He saved you. God brought the church along when He raised Jesus from the dead and seated Him in the place of authority in the heavenly places.

So if Jesus Christ is in charge, and we are exalted with Him, then we ought to be exercising His power and His authority. If we aren't, something is wrong. Something is out of whack, because Ephesians 2:6 says that where Jesus is, you and I are. The church has been raised with Christ.

Jesus Has the Keys

And just for your encouragement, you need to know that by virtue of His death, resurrection, and ascension, Jesus Christ has gained possession of another important set of keys.

These are called "the keys of death and of Hades" (Revelation 1:18). They are possessed by the One who was dead, and is now "alive forevermore."

Who had the keys of death and Hades before Jesus died and rose again? Satan had them. We saw in the previous chapter that death is Satan's domain. Hades was his prison house for the spirits of the dead.

So how did Jesus take the keys of death and Hades from Satan? While Jesus' body was in the tomb, He went in spirit into Hades itself, as we learned earlier, and freed Satan's captives. Jesus conquered death, and then He conquered him who had the power of death, the devil (Hebrews 2:14).

No wonder Paul asks, "O death, where is your victory? O death, where is your sting?" (1 Corinthians 15:55). It's all gone, because Jesus Christ went into Satan's house and took that bad boy's keys away from him!

Jesus has all the keys, and all the authority. And He is sharing that authority with believers like you and me through the church, which is seated with Him in the position of authority.

Satan can't lock you up anymore, because Jesus took his keys. So if you feel like you are locked up right now, you need to know that Jesus can let you out. He can set you free.

Satan Is Powerless

If the church has been exalted with Christ above all authorities and powers, where does that leave Satan and His demons?

It leaves them defeated, disarmed, and totally powerless, that's where. Hebrews 2:14 says that although Satan once had the power of death, he has been "render[ed] powerless" by the death and resurrection of Jesus Christ.

This is why Satan must function largely by deception. Of course, Satan can still hurt us while we are on this earth, but ultimately his real weapons have been taken away from him. All the lion has left is his roar. With the resurrection of Christ, Satan's spiritual graveyard was robbed (Ephesians 2:4–6).

The tragedy is that Satan's lies and deceptions work so often, even with believers. Satan can get us to believing that we have no authority, that we are the helpless prisoners of our past or our present.

Of course, if you were the victim of an abusive parent, a broken home, or some other tragedy, I'm not minimizing that. Those kinds of things are horrible, and they certainly leave their scars.

But to allow something from your past, or even your present, to own you as a Christian means that you're believing a lie. If you are in Jesus Christ, you have already been raised and exalted with Him. You occupy a position of tremendous authority. And you can draw on that authority to allow Christ to take charge of your life in the power of the Holy Spirit.

THE CHURCH IS TO EXHIBIT THE AUTHORITY OF CHRIST

Here's the third and last point I want to make in this chapter. As the agency of God's authority in this age or dispensation, the church is being called to put His authority and power on display to the world, to the angels, and to the devil.

The Mystery of the Church

Paul says in Ephesians 3:9 that the church is "the mystery which for ages has been hidden in God."

For all the ages of history, God had a secret He wasn't telling anyone. A mystery in the Bible isn't something that's hard to figure out. A biblical mystery is something previously hidden that has now been revealed.

Paul says the church was God's mystery, kept hidden until His time to reveal it. And why was the mystery of the church revealed? Paul answers that in verse 10: "In order that the manifold wisdom of God might now be made known through the church to the rulers and the authorities in the heavenly places."

God demonstrated His "multicolored" wisdom through the church. That's what the word *manifold* means. God's wisdom is multicolored.

What a tremendous statement! God has unveiled His great mystery—which is that by His grace, He would save unworthy sinners of every race and language and bring them together into a brand-new community called the church.

Grace was the "curveball" God threw at Satan. The devil didn't count on grace. All Satan knew was that all of us had sinned and rebelled against God the way he had sinned and rebelled. And Satan knew that a holy God could not tolerate sin, but had to judge it—the way He judged Satan.

But God had a surprise for Satan: His grace. God demonstrated something marvelous to the entire angelic realm. He sent His Son to redeem lost people and bring them into a new relationship with Him through a new entity called the church.

Only the "manifold wisdom of God" could pull off a program like that. But God did it, and in so doing He exhibited the church to all of creation as evidence of His wisdom. The devil and his demons—and the holy angels too—were left staring in amazement.

Peter says the angels are looking at the church, trying to figure out how God's grace works (1 Peter 1:12). They had never seen grace before, and now they are looking at us in wonder.

Good Exhibitors

If the church is Exhibit A of God's grace and power and authority, guess what? We should be good exhibitors of His, showing off His power and authority over the world, the flesh, and the devil. We should be exercising Christ's authority, because we are seated with Him above the "principalities and powers" that are causing our problems in the first place.

At the beginning of this book, we learned from Psalm 8 and Hebrews 2 that man was created a little lower than the angels. We are the lesser; angels are the greater.

But hold on. When Jesus Christ rose from the dead and seated us with Him in the heavenly places, we took a giant step upward. The angels are now watching the church in order to understand the manifold wisdom of God.

But I think the angels are doing more than just watching us. Now that we have been raised with Christ far above all principalities and powers, the angels are under our authority. That is a principle we have run into before. When you respond to God, and your response is consistent with His kingdom agenda, the angels may act on your behalf.

Put very simply, many of us don't get angelic help because we don't understand that the angels are waiting on us to respond to God. We're in the driver's seat, so to speak, when it comes to exercising God's authority in spiritual warfare.

We have been raised with Christ. Therefore, the church should be demanding its territory back from Satan. He's like a squatter who is illegally occupying ground he shouldn't be occupying. But Jesus Christ has issued Satan an eviction notice. It's time for the devil to get off the property.

Jesus has sent the church to deliver the notice and evict the squatter. Jesus provided all the legal authority we need to overcome Satan. Our job is to exercise that authority—to invade Satan's territory, declare to him what the eviction notice says, and put his furniture out on the street.

The law has a provision called a restraining order, an order forbidding a person to get too close to you. The cross of Jesus Christ is your restraining order to keep Satan off your back so you can live in light of who Christ is and who you are in Him.

But that means you are going to have to declare, "God, I am going to demonstrate, not just talk about, what it means to follow You. I am going to act on what

You said, calling on Your authority to set me free from whatever binds me and exhibiting Your power in the world."

Power Versus Performance

If you have ever seen a circus arrive in town, you have seen the elephants standing out in a parking lot or somewhere, tethered around one leg with a chain attached to a peg in the ground.

These elephants are huge, powerful beasts. Any of them could rip that peg out of the ground anytime they feel like it. They certainly have the power.

But the elephants don't budge. Do you know why? Because since they were little baby elephants, they have been taught that when the trainer puts that chain around their leg, they have no power to do anything. Why are the elephants chained up? Because they are in town to perform, not to demonstrate their power.

Do you see where I'm going? As Christians, we are in town to demonstrate the power and authority of God. We are not here to perform for the devil like his circus animals or spiritual puppets.

But Satan has fooled a lot of us. He has put his puny little chain around our leg, and we are convinced we can't do anything.

We go around dragging that chain on our leg, even while we're saying, "Oh yes, I know He's able." We are all chained up, even while we're singing about a God who is so high we can't get over Him, and so wide we can't get around Him. And all the while, that chain is rattling, and Satan and his demons are eating cotton candy and enjoying the show.

But the church is not in town to perform. Christ has delegated His incomparable authority to us. He has exalted the church with Himself, and put us on display as Exhibit A of His grace and power. It's time for you and me to pull that peg out of the ground and begin walking, talking, and acting like who we are in Christ. He has set us free (John 8:32)!

15

THE WEAPONS
OF AUTHORITY

I'm told that many years ago, when the staff of a mental hospital wanted to evaluate patients for possible release, one of the tests they gave was to take a patient to a janitor's closet. There the patient found the water running and overflowing the sink because the sink had been plugged up.

The person was given a mop and told to clean up the mess. The staff wanted to see whether the patient would simply try to mop up the overflowing water, or deal with the root problem by turning off the spigot. The patient's response told the staff whether this person was in touch with reality or not, and therefore was or was not ready to be released.

Anyone who is in touch with reality knows that you can't mop up a mess when the source of the mess has not been dealt with. What I have been trying to do throughout this book is put you in touch with the reality of spiritual warfare.

My purpose is that you won't waste your time trying to mop up your circumstances, when God has given you all the spiritual authority you need to address the root cause of the circumstances. If you want to change the fruit, you must first address the root.

In the language of our illustration, I want to help you quit simply mopping up the overflow. I want to show you how to turn off the spigot and start getting things cleaned up.

Or to change the imagery, I want to help equip you with the weapons of your authority, "the full armor of God." To do that, we are going to unfold Ephesians 6:10–17, one of *the* foundational passages on spiritual warfare that we have referred to and alluded to many times already. In exploring these great verses, I want to talk about the nature of your armor, the need for your armor, and the names of the pieces of your armor.

THE NATURE OF YOUR ARMOR

Paul doesn't waste any time in spelling out the nature of the armor you have for spiritual warfare. It's "the full armor of God" (Ephesians 6:11). The armor is something God gives us, not something we put together on our own.

But before Paul gets to the armor, he gives us an important exhortation: "Be strong in the Lord, and in the strength of His might" (v. 10).

Do you know what this says? This says the battle is the Lord's, not yours. That's what this entire book is designed to communicate to you.

"Be strong in the Lord" is a passive command. That means God supplies the strength, not you. It's His battle. Your job is to put on the armor He supplies, to "dress for success."

Many big corporations like IBM used to have pretty strict dress codes because the company wanted its employees to have a certain look the company believed was critical for business success. Seminars teach business people how to dress for success, how to wear the kind of clothes that make the right impression and get the job done.

Well, if you want to get the job done in spiritual warfare, you have to dress for spiritual success. You must put on the armor of God (Ephesians 6:11).

The armor is all from God. Our job is to "dress up" in Jesus every day.

That's exactly what Paul says in Romans 13:11–14. He tells us to wake up from our spiritual sleep and put on "the armor of light" (vv. 11–12).

What is armor of light? Paul explains it in verse 14 when he says, "Put on the Lord Jesus Christ." So if you want to dress for success in spiritual warfare, put on Jesus when you get up every morning.

One reason children love Halloween is that they get to dress up like somebody else, usually somebody famous or powerful or scary or someone they have dreamed of being. Kids enjoy the idea of looking like someone else because it gives them the chance to feel and act like the person they are portraying.

Paul says that we are to dress up to look like Jesus every day of our lives. But this isn't a children's masquerade. This is reality; this is spiritual war. We need to dress up in Jesus because the devil isn't one bit scared of you and me. The only person who has ever scared the devil is Jesus Christ.

So put on your Jesus outfit, and the devil won't be able to hang with you.

THE NEED FOR YOUR ARMOR

You may be saying, "Tony, I already know why I need my armor. It's because I'm in a war against a tough enemy."

You've got it. You need your armor because you are fighting a spiritual enemy, the devil and his fallen angels (Ephesians 6:12).

And while I'm on reminders, let me go ahead and finish verse 12 by reminding you that you are not fighting people. The worst person in your life is not your problem. That person is only the vehicle through which Satan is getting at you. So don't get sidetracked fighting people.

Let's talk about our need for the armor of God as Paul explains it in Ephesians 6. He writes, "Put on the full armor of God, that you may be able to stand firm against the schemes of the devil" (v. 11).

The key phrase here is "stand firm," which Paul repeats in verses 13 and 14. The reason you need to put on your armor is because of your enemy, because of Christ's victory, and because of the coming "evil day" (v. 13).

Because of Your Enemy

The first reason you need God's armor is because of your enemy.

Satan's attacks come from the unseen realm of the spirit. Therefore, if you don't use God's spiritual weapons to fight your spiritual battle, you are going to war with a cap pistol.

What are some of the cap pistols we use to try to defeat Satan? For some of us, it's our anger. We get mad and tell people off. But anger is a human weapon that doesn't work against a spiritual enemy.

Others of us have tried to use human weapons like positive thinking or "positive confession," naming and claiming this and that. Or we make New Year's resolutions. But these "cap pistols" don't work in the war against Satan.

You can't use human weapons to win a spiritual war. The devil is far too crafty for us. He has schemes and plans we can't even see. We need the armor of God because of the enemy we are up against.

Because of Your Victory

The second reason you need God's armor is because of the nature of the victory Christ has won for us. Let me explain.

Three times here in Ephesians 6, Paul tells us that our goal in spiritual warfare is to stand firm. That means to hold the ground Jesus has already won for us.

This does not negate what we said earlier about the church assaulting the gates of hell with the keys of the kingdom. But the assault is led by the risen Christ. That's a lot different than us going out looking for demons to whip.

You have probably listened to the television preachers who are always talking about attacking the devil. But the Bible doesn't tell us to attack Satan. It tells us to stand firm.

Why? Because Jesus has already invaded Satan's domain and won back all the territory Adam lost, and then some. So our job is to hold the ground Jesus has won, not to fight to win. Remember that we are fighting *from* victory, not *for* victory.

One reason the church has so many defeated Christians on its hands is that they are still trying to whip Satan. That means they're fighting the wrong battle. We saw in Colossians 2:15 that Jesus has already beaten and embarrassed Satan. So all we have to do is stand firm.

We as believers are like a football team that's ahead 72-0 late in the game. When your team is up by that many points, winning is no longer the issue. You don't need to score any more points. You're only on the field to hold your ground and keep the other team from scoring.

You need to understand that Satan is trying to rob you of spiritual victory and spiritual blessings *you already possess.* Ephesians 1:3 says God has already blessed us with every spiritual blessing it was possible to give us.

Would you go out and borrow money if you already had a million dollars sitting in your bank account? Would you go out on the streets like a pauper and ask, "Buddy, can you spare a dime?" if your daddy owned it all?

Some of us are walking around like spiritual paupers when Jesus Christ has credited to our account all of His power and authority. Our weapons are weapons of authority, because of the decisive victory Jesus has won for us.

Because of the Evil Day

A third reason you need your armor is found in an interesting phrase in Ephesians 6:13. Paul says we need to stand firm and resist Satan "in the evil day."

What is the evil day? That's the day when your number comes up, so to speak. One translation puts it, "when things are at their worst" (NEB). That pretty well says it.

Are you having it pretty easy right now? Enjoy it, because an evil day is coming. That's not pessimism, just reality. There are days when Satan is going to unleash the forces of hell on you. When those times come, you need to have your armor on.

Ask Job about the evil day, when Satan unleashes everything he has against you. Job couldn't do anything about his horrible losses, but he stood firm by saying, "Though He slay me, I will hope in Him" (Job 13:15).

You need the armor of God to stand firm when the evil day comes. In 1 Corinthians 16:13 Paul writes, "Stand firm in the faith." That's the key. You can stand firm because your faith is in the One who provides you with the armor.

He has surrounded you with protection, so you don't have to worry about the enemy's attacks. God wants us to hold our ground and not budge when the evil day comes.

THE NAMES OF THE ARMOR

For the rest of the chapter, I want to do a detailed study of each piece of the armor God has provided for us. These are important weapons you must know how to wear and how to wield if you are going to make the most of the spiritual authority you have in Christ.

The Belt of Truth

The first piece of armor Paul names is the belt of truth. "Stand firm therefore, having girded your loins with truth" (Ephesians 6:14a).

The spiritual armor Paul describes in this chapter is patterned after the armor and weapons of a Roman soldier of the day. For instance, these soldiers wore a long tunic that flowed down to the ground. But when it came time to fight, the soldier picked up that tunic and tucked it in his belt so he would have mobility for battle.

A Roman soldier also carried his sword on his belt, and his breastplate connected to the belt too. So the belt was fundamental, because everything else connected to it. Without his belt, a soldier couldn't keep himself together.

We men use our belts today to hold up our pants and keep our shirts tucked in. It gives us the look we want, keeps us neat, and holds everything together.

That's what the truth is designed to do for us spiritually. The truth is an objective standard of reality that stands outside our experiences and above our opinions. That standard of truth is the Word of God.

When you're up against a foe who is trying to take away your joy, your meaning, your future, your family, and even your life, you'd better not go out to battle without your belt of truth on.

The belt of truth is becoming more and more important because we live in a world that no longer accepts objective truth. Our children are not taught objective truth in school anymore. We live in a day of "I think" or "That's just your opinion." Everybody has an opinion, everybody has an idea.

Truth today is totally relative, and "tolerance" is the current buzzword. That's why you'll hear people say, "What's true for you is not necessarily true for me." The devil will whip you if he finds you without your belt of truth.

We need to know God's truth because the devil is a liar. He thrives on lies, so if he can get you in an environment where there is no objective standard of truth, he will milk it for all it's worth.

People say, "I don't want anybody telling me how to live my life." They don't want objective truth when it comes to the spiritual world. But the amazing thing to me is that when it comes to other things that really matter, people suddenly want objective standards.

For example, nobody wants a surgeon who says in the operating room, "You know, I *think* this is where I need to cut on you. Other doctors have a different opinion about this operation. No one can really say who is right, so all of us surgeons just cut wherever we think best. Let's try an incision here and see if I'm right."

Is that the kind of doctor you want? I don't either!

Suppose you went to a pharmacist who said, "I can't say for sure, but I think this is the medicine you should take. The pharmacist down the street thinks these pills could kill you, but who knows? What's right for him isn't necessarily right for me. Try them and let's see what happens."

When you're up in a plane, you want your pilot to be *very* narrow-minded and very sure about his standard of truth. You don't want him guessing which button to push or which lever to pull.

When we're in the operating room, we demand an objective standard of truth. When we go to the pharmacist, we want precise standards. And in an airplane at 35,000 feet, we sure enough want truth!

Truth is the beginning point of authority. The belt of truth holds your life together and protects you from the lies of the evil one. The belt of truth also keeps us from replacing God's Word with our feelings.

If you want real weapons of spiritual authority, you have to be ready to say that when God's Word contradicts how you feel, then your feelings are wrong and God's Word is right.

Satan gets nervous when he sees that you are committed to God's truth, because you haven't left him any loopholes he can get through. Satan is getting at a lot of believers because how they feel is more important than what God says.

The belt of truth goes around the "loins," the midsection. This is the area that provides strength to the body, but it is also a vulnerable area that needs protection. When your midsection is protected by truth, you are off to a good start, for Jesus Christ is truth (John 14:6).

The Breastplate of Righteousness

The second piece of armor is also found in Ephesians 6:14. "Stand firm therefore . . . having put on the breastplate of righteousness."

The Roman soldier's breastplate protected his chest, his heart. What is the best protection for your heart in spiritual warfare? The best protection is to be covered in Christ's righteousness.

This is talking about our salvation. A lot of Christians don't understand all that happened to them when they got saved. A lot of Christians only know that Christ forgave their sins.

But that's not all that happened. If you know Jesus Christ as your Savior, not only were your sins forgiven, but Christ gave you His perfect righteousness. That is, God credited the righteousness of Christ to your spiritual account. You are righteous today as a Christian because of this transfer.

The theological term for this transaction is imputation. Christ's righteousness was put on your account. As a Christian, you are not simply a forgiven sinner. You stand as righteous in God's sight as Jesus Himself, because Jesus' righteousness is wrapped around you like a robe. When Satan accuses you, you can point to your righteous standing before God.

So you don't get up in the morning determined to try to be righteous. That's human effort. Instead, you get up in the morning and say, "Because of Christ, I am righteous today." The breastplate of righteousness is part of the armor you wear all the time, because every day you are dressed in Christ's righteousness.

One reason so many Christians exercise so little authority in spiritual warfare is that they don't really know who they are. That's why in his writings, Paul always starts with who you are in Christ before he gets to what you are to do for Christ.

The book of Ephesians is a good example. Paul outlines our Christian identity in chapters 1 to 3, then he spends chapters 4 to 6 telling us how to act.

If you don't get those two things in the right order, you are going to wind up with a lot of human effort without much divine power. You can't act with authority against Satan until you know what authority you possess.

In other words, we act like turkeys sometimes because we forget we are eagles. Instead of soaring spiritually, we waddle.

The breastplate of righteousness speaks of our exalted position in Christ. As we put it on each day, we have protection against Satan and his demons, because they can't hang out in an environment of righteousness.

Of course we fail at times and act unrighteously. But that's when we confess our sin (1 John 1:9) and keep on going.

You don't lose your breastplate just because you blow it. Righteousness isn't just something you practice. It's your identity. You *are* righteous in Jesus Christ.

Let me tell you one more thing before we move on. Because you are a righteous person, God is going to help you pursue things that enable you to act like who you are and help you avoid things that do not enhance your righteousness. This means He will have to discipline you on occasion.

One day my granddaughter, Kariss, was running around the house with scissors. I told her to give them to me because I was afraid she would fall with them and get hurt.

But Kariss didn't want to give me the scissors. She wanted to run around with them and do her own thing because she wanted to cut some paper. So I had to catch her and take the scissors away from her.

God will do the same for us, not because He doesn't want us to have any fun. He doesn't want us falling on the things we grasp and hurting ourselves. He's after our long-term blessing. So our prayer each day as we put on the breastplate should be, "Lord, I thank You that You have already made me righteous. Help me today to live up to what I already am."

The Gospel of Peace

The third piece of spiritual armor we need to wear are the shoes of "the gospel of peace" (Ephesians 6:15). If you are going to stand firm, you definitely need reliable footwear.

Earlier in Ephesians, Paul had said that Jesus is our peace (Ephesians 2:14). So we're still talking about getting dressed up in Jesus. The "gospel of peace," the good news of Jesus Christ, not only brings us truth and righteousness, it brings us peace of heart.

The Roman soldier wore shoes with cleats on them for surefootedness in battle. A soldier had to be able to stand and fight without slipping and sliding around, because lost footing could be fatal.

Do you ever feel like your life is slipping and sliding all over the place? You're doing your "James Brown" thing, just slipping and sliding. That's when you especially need to have the peace of God anchoring your feet and guarding your heart.

We need to distinguish between the peace *of* God and peace *with* God. Peace with God only comes when you place your faith in Christ and become a Christian.

Once you know Christ, you are in position to enjoy the peace of God, which He gives to His children each day as they prepare for spiritual warfare. But it's peace *with* God that is listed as the bit of equipment here.

Paul says we need to be prepared with peace because the world we are going to face is not always peaceful. In fact, since we are engaged in spiritual battle we should expect turmoil.

But when we are wearing peace with God like shoes on our feet, we can handle whatever Satan brings against us—problems on the job, trouble with family—without stumbling. We don't need to pop a pill in the morning or do anything else like that to deal with life. God's peace is on duty.

Our national ministry, The Urban Alternative, took a group of friends on a cruise not long ago. During the cruise we hit a terrible storm. There were thirty-foot waves. It was horrific.

The captain sent us this message: "This is a bad storm, the worst we've ever been in, but don't worry. This ship was built with these kinds of storms in mind." He was reassuring us the ship was seaworthy.

The storms in your life may be bad, but the peace of God is seaworthy. It can handle whatever storm you face. Or in the imagery of spiritual warfare, the peace of God can keep you calm even when the battle is raging all around you.

Is the devil attacking hard right now? The peace of God can help you stand firm while Jesus deals with the enemy through you. When you get dressed each day, check to make sure you are wearing God's peace.

The Shield of Faith

The fourth piece of armor Paul tells us to take up is

the shield of faith, which allows us to "extinguish all the flaming missiles of the evil one" (Ephesians 6:16b).

The shield that a Roman soldier carried into battle was about four-and-a-half feet square. It was a huge shield that would even cover part of the body of the soldier fighting beside the shield-holder. So Roman soldiers lined up side by side in close formation with their shields together, and all of them were covered as they advanced.

What is this shield of faith that is able to protect you from anything Satan could ever fire at you? It is acting on the truth that you say you believe. You take up the shield of faith when you take the truth that you "amened" on Sunday and live it out on Monday.

One of the best examples of what I'm talking about is Joshua at the battle of Jericho (Joshua 6). God told Joshua to have the Israelites march around the city once a day for seven days, and then march around seven times on the seventh day.

That must have seemed like a foolish thing to do. It didn't make sense militarily. It certainly wasn't accepted strategy for warfare. But God commanded Joshua to do it, and He promised to fight Israel's battle.

So no matter how it looked to anyone else, Joshua took up the shield of faith and obeyed God. And God delivered Jericho into Joshua's lap.

I'm also reminded of Naaman, the Syrian commander who was covered with leprosy (2 Kings 5). Elisha told Naaman to go and dip seven times in the Jordan River to be cleansed.

Naaman got insulted, because the Jordan is a dirty, muddy river. He didn't want to be embarrassed in front of his servants by having to dip in the Jordan. But his servants convinced him to do it, and Naaman did what

God's prophet told him to do. He was healed because he chose to believe God.

See, obeying God can sometimes seem foolish, difficult, or downright embarrassing. But God wants us to trust Him even when it doesn't make sense to trust Him. At times like these, we need to pick up our shield of faith and obey.

I was once counseling a couple having marital problems. I gave the husband some things to work on and told him, "These things may be hard to do right now. But because they are based on the Word of God, I believe if you'll do them your marriage will improve." He came back later and asked for some more things he could do!

What God asks us to do may be hard at the time, but our response of faith can extinguish the enemy's flaming arrows.

If you remember those old TV westerns, you know the damage that flaming arrows can do. The wagon train would be fighting off the Indians, with the wagons in a circle.

But then a few Indians would set fire to their arrows and shoot them. Those arrows weren't aimed at the settlers behind the wagons. They were aimed at the canvas tops of the wagons, which would burst into flame.

Why did the Indians want to set the wagons on fire? First to distract the settlers and get them fighting the fires, because they couldn't fight the fires and the Indians at the same time.

But the main reason for setting the wagons on fire was to get rid of the settlers' protection. With the wagons burned down, they wouldn't have anything to hide behind.

Satan wants to hit us with as many flaming arrows as he can. That way, while we're fighting one fire he can hit us with another.

Ever had days like that? Sure you have. So have I. The flaming arrows are hitting all over the place. And if we don't get all the fires put out, Satan will burn down our protection.

The question is, how can you put out Satan's fires? Answer: you can't. But the shield of faith can. If you will act on God's Word and believe Him, God will send His angelic host to snuff out Satan's fiery arrows as they come in.

The Helmet of Salvation

The helmet of salvation (Ephesians 6:17a) is the next piece of armor that can give you authority over the enemy.

The helmet protects the head, the control center of the body. So the helmet of salvation covers a very key part. The purpose of a soldier's helmet was to absorb blows without causing damage to the head, much like a football player's helmet absorbs the shock of blows to his head.

Paul's reference to the helmet may imply our protection in a current spiritual battle, the way our salvation protects us from Satan's claim on our lives.

Paul may also be thinking of the ultimate deliverance that salvation will bring, our hope for the future when our salvation is consummated. He uses the term *helmet* in this sense in 1 Thessalonians 5:8.

But in the context of spiritual warfare, we're talking about the battles you and I face every day. With the helmet of salvation protecting us, we have the authority we need to get on top of our circumstances, instead of letting our circumstances bury us.

When you ask people how they are, they will often reply "Oh, I'm all right, under the circumstances."

For the Christian, the response needs to be, "What are you doing under there?" When you pick up the helmet of salvation and put it on, you are saying to the devil that because of your salvation, God has given you victory over your circumstances. The helmet helps you fight from a position of victory.

We have let our circumstances become God. And when circumstances become God, we can't be in proper relation to God. So put on your helmet. Sure, Satan is trying to deliver a blow to your head. He knows where to strike. But the helmet of salvation can absorb the blow.

The helmet allows you to say to Satan when he hits you with his best shot, "I can do all things through Him who strengthens me" (Philippians 4:13). The helmet reminds you that God "is able to keep you from stumbling" (Jude 24). The helmet's visor allows you to see Jesus (Hebrews 2:9) and focus on Him. You won't get very far in spiritual warfare without your helmet.

The Sword of the Spirit

Now we're ready to complete the full armor of God. We do that when we take up "the sword of the Spirit, which is the word of God" (Ephesians 6:17b). The sword mentioned here is not the soldier's long sword, but a short, dagger-like weapon about ten inches long.

This sword had a needle-like point and it was sharp on both sides. It was used for close-in fighting and could do some serious damage. It could cut an opponent coming and going. "The word of God is living and active and sharper than any two-edged sword," Hebrews 4:12 says.

What's interesting is that the term Paul uses for *word* here does not refer to the Bible as a written book of truth, the way we normally think of the Word of God. This is not the Bible sitting on your coffee table or bookshelf.

Instead, this is *rhema,* the utterance of God, the Word as it is spoken. Paul is talking about the use of the Word, not just its existence. Many of us go to church every Sunday with our Bible under our arm, but we don't always know how to wield it like a sword to slice the devil in half in spiritual battle.

The best example of wielding the Word was the temptation of Jesus. Satan attacked Jesus, but Jesus answered, "It is written," and then defeated Satan with the Word. Jesus didn't argue or dialogue with the devil. Jesus simply hit him with the Word, and the battle was over.

See, Satan loves to hear you and me talk to him and argue with him, because he knows our word doesn't have any authority from God to cut him in half. If we don't know the Word of God well enough to use it against the devil, no wonder we get defeated. No wonder we have no authority. The authority is in the Word.

That's the armor of God, the weapons of your authority. Is your armor in good shape? Are your belt, breastplate, and gospel shoes laid out when you go to bed, ready to be put on tomorrow? Are your shield, helmet, and sword close by, ready to be grabbed when needed? Then you're ready for the battle.

And if you can't remember all the individual pieces of your spiritual armor, then just remember Christ. For if you have an intimate relationship with Him, you also have the armor!

16

THE ACCESS
TO AUTHORITY

We're ready for the last chapter in this section on spiritual authority. Since we have talked about how it was purchased, where it is found, and what it consists of, we are ready to talk about how to access the authority God has for us in spiritual warfare.

The weapons of your warfare won't do you a lot of good if you don't know how to put them into action. Remember, you need to know how to use your weapons, because we are not in a parade, we are in a war.

Too many believers parade into church every Sunday and then march home, and the truth of God never really gets into their lives. People like this are no threat to Satan, because he knows they will never use their spiritual weapons against him. The weapons are for show and entertainment only.

In the previous chapter we studied the believer's spiritual armor, the six pieces of offensive and defensive weaponry God has equipped us with (Ephesians 6:10–17).

THE BATTLE IS THE LORD'S

But the apostle Paul doesn't stop writing there, because in the very next verse he gives us the secret to using this great authority God has made available. We might say that after describing the Christian's battle dress, Paul tells us *how to get dressed,* how to access the authority we possess: "With all prayer and petition pray at all times in the Spirit, and with this in view, be on the alert with all perseverance and petition for all the saints" (Ephesians 6:18).

It is prayer that gains you access to the authority you need for victorious warfare. Prayer is the way you get dressed for battle. So let's talk about the vital place of prayer in spiritual warfare.

THE SIGNIFICANCE OF PRAYER

Remember the story of the emperor who had no clothes? That's the way a lot of us go around spiritually. We're basically naked, unclothed, because prayer is not a dynamic, vital, potent, consistent, controlling, and all-encompassing reality in our Christian lives.

Because we don't have our spiritual clothes on, because we don't know how to put on our armor, we wind up being spiritually embarrassed. Worse than that, we are getting mopped up by Satan when God has given us everything we need to defeat our enemy.

One of the first things a commander tries to do in warfare is to establish superiority in the air. Whoever controls the air war usually controls the war. If you establish air superiority, you'll suffer fewer casualties on the ground.

One of our problems is that the church is suffering a lot of casualties on the ground because we haven't established superiority in the air—in the heavenly places where the real warfare is taking place.

There's one big difference between an earthly army and the church. An earthly army has to go out and win the air war to establish superiority. But Jesus Christ has already won the spiritual war and established air superiority for all eternity.

Our task is to take the superiority we have and use it to win our battles. That's important, because it's possible to lose a battle even when you have superior weapons.

The Authority of Prayer

The significance of prayer to spiritual warfare is evident in the very first word of Ephesians 6:18: "*With* all prayer" (italics added).

With is a connecting word. Paul is saying that prayer is vitally connected to his discussion of spiritual warfare and the Christian's armor that has just preceded this verse.

Prayer is the atmosphere in which you are to fight. It's the way you stay in vital daily contact with your Commander. In other words, the way you activate the authority and use the armor described in Ephesians 6:10–17 is by prayer.

Remember, three times in this section (vv. 11, 13–14) the apostle has told us to stand firm. That means to hold the territory Jesus Christ has won for us and not let the devil take any territory back.

But the problem is that the devil has already taken back a lot of territory from many of us believers. He has taken back the territory of peace from some of us. From others, he has taken back the territory of our homes, our families, or our businesses. From still others, the devil has taken back the authoritative position that God has given us.

Satan is always looking to take back territory that Christ has won. So if we are going to stand firm, we must know how to put our armor on and how to use it. And that authority is activated through prayer.

The kind of prayer Paul has in mind here is intense, fervent, knowledgeable prayer that enables you to reach into heaven and make withdrawals on your spiritual account.

Our job in the Christian life is not to add to what Christ has done. He has made all the deposits necessary for every spiritual need we will ever have. When God says we need to pray, He is inviting us to draw on the accomplishments of Christ.

So Paul says, "In light of the blessings God has already blessed you with, in light of His provision for your armor, go ahead and claim your authority through prayer."

To put it another way, without prayer you don't get to use the things God has granted you. But when you access the armor of God through prayer, Satan can't really hurt you.

The Protective Power of Prayer

Prayer is so potent because it provides us with spiritual protection even when the battle is at its hottest. It's in prayer that we locate the ground on which we can stand firm.

Prayer is like the pioneer father and his son who were trying to outrun a prairie fire in their wagon. The windswept flames were moving so fast that the father realized they couldn't outrun the fire. They would have to make a stand and fight it.

So the father stopped the wagon and jumped out. He quickly dug a shallow trench around a large circular area, then set the grass in that area on fire. When it had burned off, the man and his son stepped inside the circle.

As the raging fire approached, the boy became afraid and said, "Dad, we've got to get out of here."

But the father replied, "No, Son. We need to stand right here."

"But, Dad, the fire is coming!"

"Trust me, Son. Stand still. The fire is going to go around us. It won't touch us, because this area has already been burned once."

Jesus Christ was "burned" once for all on the cross. When you stand in Him, Satan's fire can't reach you. But we want to try to outrun the fire. We want to run away when God says, "Stand firm." Prayer helps us to take that stand. It gives us protection from the flames.

It is reported that the emperor Napoleon once looked at a map and said, "If it were not for that one red dot, I could rule the world." That red dot was the British empire, the one place on the map Napoleon couldn't conquer.

Satan is a lot like Napoleon. He looks at the cross and says, "If it were not for that one red-stained cross, I could have conquered the human race." If God had not become a Man and entered time and space in the person of Jesus Christ, Satan could have had his victory. He could have had us.

But we escaped Satan's clutches because of that one red-stained cross! Now what we need to do is stand on what Christ has done, protected from the enemy by the power of prayer.

For a lot of us, however, prayer is like the singing of the national anthem before a ball game. It gets things started, but it has nothing to do with what follows on the field. We need to learn what warfare praying is all about so that prayer becomes vital to what is happening on the "field" of our lives.

The Essence of Prayer

Of course, the essence or heart of prayer is communication with God. As we all know, good communication involves both talking and listening.

You may be saying, "Tony, that's too simple. Give me something complex." I think that's part of our problem sometimes. We are looking for some deep mystery about prayer, when the reality of it is right in front of us.

If prayer is communication with God, then in order to communicate with God effectively, we need to know something about Him. We need to understand His greatness.

Many believers pray to a God who is too small. By their lack of understanding about God and their failure to appropriate His power, they reduce God to a microforce in their lives. And let me tell you, if your God is small, your prayers are going to be small. And if your prayers are small, you're a big target for the enemy.

Some of us spend hours talking to other people and only a minute talking with God. There's nothing wrong with talking to people. But people aren't the source of our spiritual authority. It's through prayer that we access our great God.

Knowing the God we are praying to also involves the understanding that prayer is not some magical formula by which we make God appear to do our bidding. We are not Aladdin, and God is not our genie.

Some people have the idea that prayer is persuading God to do what we want Him to do. But prayer is not getting God to conform to us. Prayer is conforming ourselves to God.

It's fine to make our requests known to God. But we had better be sure that what we want God to do for us is what *He* wants to do for us. Otherwise, we will waste a lot of time and energy in prayer.

Do you know people whose prayer life hasn't advanced for all the years they have been Christians? People like this say the same thing every time, every day. You could say their prayers with them because you have them memorized.

Do you know why some believers' prayer lives haven't changed for all those years? Because their knowledge of God hasn't changed for all those years.

If our knowledge of God is anemic, our prayers won't get beyond, "Now I lay me down to sleep. . . ." Prayers like that will not enable us to stand against Satan. But if our knowledge of God is deepening by the time we spend in His Word and on our knees, when those deep problems come we can go even deeper with God.

The Necessity of Prayer

Prayer is necessary because the battle we are fighting is spiritual. Prayer is necessary because it is through prayer that we engage the spiritual realm. When we pray, things happen in the heavenly places.

I am often asked the question, "If God is going to do what He wants to do anyway, why do I need to pray?" Answer: Because Scripture tells us that there are certain things God will not do apart from our prayers.

Don't ask me to explain why God chose to do things this way. I just know that He did.

We do somewhat the same thing with our children. We want them to ask us for things that they need, because asking teaches them dependence. It teaches them that the good things of life don't just materialize out of thin air, but are provided by someone who loves them.

Asking also teaches our children gratitude, because they need to learn to say "Thank you" when they receive something. And asking gives our kids access to the good things we have for them.

One of the best examples of a believer approaching God in prayer is the prayer of the prophet Daniel (Daniel 9:1–19), which we referred to earlier. Daniel knew from his knowledge of Jeremiah's prophecy (v. 2) that the seventy years of Israel's captivity were about to end.

So Daniel proceeded to pray a great prayer in which he confessed his people's sins and called on God to remember His covenant with Israel and end His people's humiliation in exile from Jerusalem.

In other words, Daniel prayed God's own Word back to Him and called on Him to honor it.

One of the great things about prayer, especially if you know the Word of God, is that in prayer you can hold God to His Word. I don't mean you can coerce Him, but you can pray like Daniel, "O Lord, hear! O Lord, forgive! O Lord, listen and take action! For Thine own sake, O my God, do not delay, because Thy city and Thy people are called by Thy name" (v. 19).

Daniel was reminding God of what He had said about Jerusalem and its people. He was holding God to His Word. Moses did the same thing when God announced He wanted to destroy Israel and start over with Moses (Exodus 32:10).

Moses went before the Lord and reminded Him of three things (vv. 11–13). He reminded God that these were the people He had rescued from Egypt. Moses reminded God that if He destroyed the nation, the Egyptians would accuse God of doing evil.

And finally, Moses reminded God of His great

promises to Abraham and his descendants. Then verse 14 says, "The Lord changed His mind." God was still sovereign in this situation, but from our human standpoint the intercession of Moses caused God to change His plans.

Moses knew how to pray. He basically said, "God, if You do this, Your name is going to look bad, and You will be embarrassed among the gods. God, it is in Your best interest to preserve Your people. You need to forgive Your people."

I call this putting God on the spot. Moses was able to do this in his prayer because he understood God's nature. Moses appealed to God's grace, knowing that His grace could overrule His wrath.

But Moses had to pray before God would relent. In His sovereignty, God decided that He would allow Moses' prayer to "change His mind."

We have the same privilege as Moses to hold God to His Word in prayer. It's not a matter of His reluctance to fulfill His Word, but a test of our faith to believe and act on His Word. That fact has some tremendous implications for our spiritual warfare.

For example, if the devil has been holding you in bondage to a habit you don't believe you can break, you need to hit him with the truth of Philippians 4:13: "I can do all things through Him who strengthens me." When you act in Christ, you have power.

Do you see what I'm saying? The enemy has got us believing lies. "I can't overcome this habit." "There is no saving this marriage." "I can't be the spouse God wants me to be."

Those are bold-faced lies. If these things are really true, then God is a liar. We would never call God a liar, but that's what we do by our actions when we don't claim His Word and His power in prayer. In prayer we can hold God to His Word.

Prayer is also necessary because of spiritual resistance in the heavenly realm. In Daniel 10, a passage we have turned to several times, Daniel is told that the answer to his prayer was delayed three weeks by a demon called "the prince of Persia."

Daniel's prayer was heard and answered the first day he prayed. But it took three weeks of intercessory prayer and activity on the part of the angels, especially the archangel Michael, to break the demonic blockade and get the answer through.

So let me say it again. Prayer is necessary because the battle is spiritual. When we pray properly, God puts out a restraining order against the powers of darkness.

THE SCOPE OF PRAYER

Prayer gives you access to your authority and your spiritual weapons. The scope of prayer is also included in Ephesians 6:18. We are to pray "at all times" and "with all perseverance and petition for all the saints."

A Full Agenda of Prayer

The key word here is pretty obvious, isn't it? Prayer is to be made *all* the time, with *all* kinds of prayers, for *all* the saints.

So the scope of prayer is as wide as the world and as full as the hours in our day. God wants us to bombard the heavenlies with our prayers. In a war, an army doesn't fire just one shell or launch one missile at the enemy. An army pounds the enemy with repeated fire.

Paul tells us to pray with all kinds of prayer. In the Bible, we see people praying in all kinds of postures: standing, kneeling, lying prostrate, walking. They used all kinds of prayers: thanksgiving, praise, supplication, intercession. Whatever the prayer need is, there is a kind of prayer to meet it.

Paul also says to pray all the time, with perseverance. Don't "hang up" on God too soon. As Paul put it in 1 Thessalonians 5:17, "Pray without ceasing." If you and I are going to see this thing work, prayer cannot be an addendum to our day or week. It must be the controlling agenda of our lives. We need to pray when we feel like it and when we don't.

Anybody who's serious about prayer can tell you that real prayer is hard work. Why is that? Because this is war. Satan doesn't want you to do any praying at all.

That's why sometimes when you get on your face before God, your mind goes every which way. You can't even focus on what you're doing. Satan will distract you if he can.

He will also make you too tired to pray. Have you ever knelt by your bed and woke up twenty minutes later, wondering what happened? We've all done that.

But probably the best method Satan has for keeping you from praying is keeping you too busy to get around to praying. So many times we tell ourselves, "I'm going to get around to praying one of these days."

Some of us have been trying to get around to prayer for years and haven't made it yet. That's fine with Satan, because he understands that if you ever bombard the heavenlies with prayer, you're going to knock him back.

Let me give you a word of encouragement here. The more intimate your relationship with God is, the easier the work of prayer is. It still takes work, but it's enjoyable work when you're communing with someone you love.

Anybody who's married knows this. In the early days

of a courtship and marriage, a couple wants to be together and communicating all the time. A new believer often feels that same sense of excitement about his relationship with God.

The challenge in marriage, and in prayer, is to maintain that level of intimacy and desire in the communication. Just as marital communication can degenerate into one- or two-word "conversations" grunted over a newspaper or a TV show, so our prayer life can degenerate into a few quick words tossed in God's direction.

Maybe that's why we don't see more answered prayers and miracles in our lives. James says, "You do not have because you do not ask" (James 4:2). Ephesians 6:18 also says we need to pray for "all the saints." In other words, I'm not in this by myself. We are in this together. If you only pray for yourself, you won't see many answers to prayer. God won't help you to become a more selfish Christian.

Remember that the Lord's Prayer is not, "My Father who art in heaven," but "*Our* Father who art in heaven" (italics added). The Christian life is a family affair. The church, as the agency of God's authority for spiritual warfare, needs to be praying together for each other.

The Perspective of Prayer

When you pray, you enter into a whole other realm. You enter into the heavenlies. It gives you a different perspective.

Do you know how things look from the window of an airplane? When you're up that high, everything looks orderly. The fields all look perfectly laid out. No matter how chaotic things actually are on the ground, from high up everything looks great.

That's what prayer does for you. Our problem is that

we've been on the ground too long. We've lost the divine perspective. When that happens, we begin operating according to the wisdom from below, not the wisdom from above.

Interestingly, James calls the wisdom from below "demonic" (James 3:15). That means Satan gets you thinking and acting the way he wants. The only way you can find the wisdom from above, the heavenly wisdom, is by communicating with heaven.

THE SPHERE OF PRAYER

The last thing I want us to see about prayer is the sphere of prayer.

Let's go back to Ephesians 6:18 one more time and notice that Paul instructs us to pray "in the Spirit." This is the Holy Spirit, of course. We are to pray in His power, in the strength and spiritual insight He provides.

But this sounds rather ethereal. How do you know when you are praying in the Holy Spirit?

Praying in the Spirit

Let me answer that by first pointing out that in the Scriptures, being in the Spirit is always contrasted with being in the flesh. So Paul is talking about the spiritual environment in which we live. If we are going to pray in the Spirit, we must be immersed in the environment of the Spirit.

In 1 Corinthians 2, Paul shows us what it means to be in a Holy Spirit environment. This is an important passage, so I want to quote at length:

> "Things which eye has not seen and ear has not heard, and which have not entered the heart of man, all that God has prepared for those who love Him." For to us God re-

vealed them through the Spirit; for the Spirit searches all things, even the depths of God. For who among men knows the thoughts of a man except the spirit of the man, which is in him? Even so the thoughts of God no one knows except the Spirit of God. Now we have received, not the spirit of the world, but the Spirit who is from God, that we might know the things freely given to us by God, which things we also speak, not in words taught by human wisdom, but in those taught by the Spirit, combining spiritual thoughts with spiritual words. (vv. 9–13)

Notice that those who live in a Spirit-dominated sphere or environment are the ones to whom the things of God, even the deep things, are revealed. If we are going to pray in the Spirit and find authority and power for spiritual warfare, we will need the revealing work of the Spirit to our hearts.

Why is this so important? Because often we don't even know what to pray for, so the Spirit has to intercede for us (Romans 8:26).

Notice also that to pray in the Spirit, we must have "spiritual thoughts." If you and I think like the world, we'll pray like the world. If we learn to think like the Spirit, we'll pray in the Spirit. To pray in the Spirit requires a mind-set that comes from God.

We have too many Christians who are getting their thought patterns from the world. When Christians think like the world, they start defining deviancy down.

By that I mean that Christians start doing the things the world is doing, and then they start saying in effect, "Well, I haven't sunk as low as the other people out there. As long as I stay one notch above the world, I'm OK." That's what happens when our thinking patterns are formed by the world. But God wants us to think spiritually.

Knowing the Word

How do believers get Spirit-directed thoughts? Paul says they come from being combined with "spiritual words" (1 Corinthians 2:13). In other words, the only place you're going to find spiritual thinking is in a spiritual book. And there's only one perfect spiritual book.

This means you can't pray like you ought to pray unless you know the Word of God. We touched on this earlier in the chapter, but let me make a few more observations about its importance.

I hate to say it, but I'm afraid a good portion of our prayers can basically be trashed because they have nothing to do with God's revealed Word. They don't reflect His thinking at all. God is only going to answer prayer that is consistent with His Word.

So you and I must allow ourselves to be captivated by the mind of Christ, which comes as the Spirit of God combines the spiritual thoughts of God with the spiritual words of God. Then we will be addressing the Spirit's concerns in the Spirit's way.

A Biblical Example

As we close this chapter and this section on your authority for spiritual warfare, I want us to see a biblical example of praying in the Spirit. The example is in Acts 4:23–31, and it's right on target for what we're talking about because the context of this prayer is intense spiritual warfare.

Earlier in Acts 4, Peter and John had been arrested for preaching Jesus. The Jewish authorities threatened them not to preach in that name anymore and let them

go. Peter and John went back to the church and reported the threat they had received (v. 23). That's the setting
for the prayer in verses 24–30.

I won't try to quote the whole prayer, because you
can read it for yourself. What I want to do is point out
some of its features.

The first thing you need to see about this prayer is
that the disciples don't start right off praying about their
problem. They start off talking about the greatness of
God and quoting His Word back to Him (vv. 24–26).

In other words, this prayer begins with theology and
the Word of God. The disciples were saying, "Lord, we're
in a mess. But You are a big God. God, before we talk
about the mess we are in, let us remind You what You
have written in Your Word."

Only after the disciples had set the situation in its
proper spiritual context did they get around to talking
about their immediate problem (vv. 27–30). Here is their
actual request: "And now, Lord, take note of their threats,
and grant that Thy bond-servants may speak Thy word
with all confidence" (v. 29). Notice that they didn't pray
that they wouldn't be persecuted, but that they wouldn't
let the fear of persecution hinder their witness.

Verse 31 tells what happened when they had finished praying. "The place where they had gathered
together was shaken, and they were all filled with the
Holy Spirit, and began to speak the word of God with
boldness." When God's people pray in the Spirit, something is going to shake!

Why don't we see more places shaking today? Why
don't we see more impossible marriages and unhappy
homes being shaken, and people falling back in love
again? Why don't we see more people being shaken
loose from their addictions? Why aren't more believers

being shaken free of depression and all manner of mental and emotional prisons?

I'll tell you one reason. It's because we don't talk to God the way the believers in Acts 4 talked to God. They were able to combine spiritual thoughts with spiritual words. They went to the Word and reminded God of what He had promised. And because they had that confidence, they could pray boldly in the Spirit, "Lord, because You said it, we believe You will do it."

ACCESSING GOD'S AUTHORITY

I recently heard of an incident from the early days of my alma mater, Dallas Theological Seminary. The school needed ten thousand dollars, which was a lot of money in the early 1920s. The money was needed by nine o'clock on a certain morning.

The day before the money was due, Dr. Lewis Sperry Chafer, the seminary's founder and president, and others prayed that God would supply the need. Dr. Chafer prayed that the money might come from a totally unexpected source, as a way of knowing that the answer was from God and not just the result of some previous contact. Dr. Chafer asked that it might happen that way so that God alone would get the credit.

At eight-thirty the next morning, a check arrived from a banker, who wrote, "God woke me up at three o'clock this morning with Dallas Seminary on my mind. Something compelled me to write you this check." The check was for exactly ten thousand dollars.

See, when you know who God is, you can go to Him with authority. What we need to do is stop complaining or worrying about our circumstances and start accessing our spiritual authority in prayer.

The story is told of a boy who went to an amusement park with his father for a day of fun. The father went to the ticket booth and bought some tickets so his son could go on the rides.

Then Dad told him, "Son, I'll hang on to the tickets. You go and ride the rides. Whenever you need more tickets, just come back and I'll give them to you. That way, you won't lose them."

Later, a young boy whom the father had never seen before came over to him and said, "Sir, I'd like to have four tickets."

The father looked at him and said, "I'm sorry, but I don't know you. These tickets are for my son." The other boy was about ready to turn away disappointed when the man's son came running up.

"Dad, it's OK. This is my friend John from school. I told him you had tickets, and that he could come over and ask you for as many as he needed. It's OK, because I sent him."

The illustration isn't perfect, but you get the idea. Some of us are broke and need God to give us tickets so we can enjoy this ride called life. We can't afford to ride the roller coaster. We don't have a ticket to get on the Ferris wheel.

In other words, we don't know what victory in spiritual battle feels like. We don't know how it feels to fight from a position of spiritual strength.

But when we know the Son, we can pray in His name and His authority. And Jesus will say, "Father, I know him. I know her. They are My friends. They're with Me. You can give them all the tickets they need."

Do you want to ride the rides? Do you want victory in your spiritual battles? Start accessing your authority in prayer, and Jesus Christ will let you ride. He'll give you victory, because He has already won the victory for you in the heavenly places.

PART FIVE

YOUR ACTIONS

17

TEARING DOWN STRONGHOLDS IN YOUR PERSONAL LIFE

We have covered a lot of ground, studied a lot of Scripture, and unfolded a lot of theology on our way to this final section of the book.

Now that we have done all this in an attempt to understand spiritual warfare, let's take up some of the weapons God has given us and start assaulting the gates of hell. Let's start attacking and tearing down the strongholds that Satan has erected against us in our personal, family, church, and community lives.

Let's begin by defining a satanic stronghold. A stronghold is a mind-set that accepts a situation as unchangeable, even though that situation is contrary to the will of God.

I think it's safe to say that many people in the body of Christ are in bondage to satanic strongholds. They have yielded ground to Satan in their lives, and he has used that ground to build an outpost from which he wages war and makes that person his prisoner of war.

Strongholds are like fortresses. Once they get built, they are difficult to attack and take out. Some of those who have Satan's strongholds in their lives have tried everything to escape, but nothing has worked.

Some strongholds are pretty obvious. Drug addiction is a satanic stronghold in which the flesh develops such a strong craving for chemicals that, no matter how hard the person tries, he cannot let it go.

Other people are imprisoned by a stronghold of relationships. Other people have captured them emotionally, and they are being held prisoner. For some, it could even be parents who have long since died, but whose damaging influence will not allow the imprisoned person to go free.

Past abuse is another stronghold. Many believers are being held captive by abusive relationships that have left scars on their souls as well as their bodies. Satan has been able to use this history to capture many and hold them spiritually and emotionally captive.

For still other believers, the strongholds are not so obvious. They are private strongholds, fortresses of the mind and spirit that can often be hidden from others. Sexual addictions such as pornography are a good example of this type of stronghold. Illicit thoughts and activities capture the mind, and people are unable to get themselves free.

No matter how many times they promise themselves they won't buy that magazine, watch that show, or log on to that pornographic Internet site, they keep going back because they have been captured by a stronghold of the mind.

Attitudes like anger, bitterness, and unforgiveness are also strongholds that we can allow Satan to construct in our hearts and minds if we are not vigilant against him.

It's unfortunate that Christians allow the devil to build his strongholds in their lives. It's even more unfortunate when they come to believe that this is the way they are doomed to live the rest of their lives.

Some of us blame other people for our strongholds. But people cannot cause us to surrender ground to Satan. They can certainly have an influence on us and help set us up for a stronghold. But strongholds get built when we fail to deal with sin and the devil in our own lives.

Sometimes we blame our strongholds on circumstances. A husband might say, "I wouldn't have hit my wife if she hadn't made me angry." No, all the wife did was provide an excuse for her husband's lack of control to express itself.

Someone else might say, "If they didn't have all that junk on cable television and in the movies and on the magazine racks, I wouldn't have a problem." No, all that junk does is help reveal how messed up the person with the problem really is.

Strongholds are ultimately spiritual problems, so until we attack them with our spiritual armor, they won't be torn down (2 Corinthians 10:4).

Jesus said, "That which is born of the flesh is flesh, and that which is born of the Spirit is spirit" (John 3:6). Too often we fight problems of the spirit with weapons of the flesh. My task in this chapter is to help you tear down strongholds in your personal life—or help a brother or sister in Christ do the same.

REMEMBER YOUR POSITION IN CHRIST

The first thing you must do if you want to see spiritual strongholds topple is to remember your position in Christ.

Your Connection to the Winner

We have seen that as believers, we have an exalted position—raised from the dead with Christ and seated with Him in the heavenly places (Ephesians 2:6).

And we have seen the corollary action that should follow this knowledge: "If then you have been raised up with Christ, keep seeking the things above, where Christ is, seated at the right hand of God. Set your mind on the things above, not on the things that are on earth" (Colossians 3:1–2).

This means if your mind is set on an earthly solution to your spiritual struggles, then you won't see a heavenly response. The solution to the strongholds Satan builds in our lives is found in Christ, "for in Him all the fulness of Deity dwells in bodily form, and in Him you have been made complete, and He is the head over all rule and authority" (Colossians 2:9–10).

Christ has all the spiritual authority you will ever need, because He is in charge in the universe. He has already beaten Satan and made a public spectacle of him (Colossians 2:15). Therefore, if you are going to beat the evil one, you need to connect to Jesus, the One who won the victory over Satan.

Your Legal Authority over Satan

Your exalted position in Christ not only gives you a vital connection to Him. It also gives you legal authority over Satan so that when he attacks you, you can announce, "Satan no longer has any rights or jurisdiction in my life."

I have a suspicion that there aren't many believers who understand their position in Christ well enough to realize when they are under attack, "This is an illegitimate attempt by Satan to place me under his authority. He has no rights or claim in my life, because I have been legally set free by Jesus Christ."

That simple statement can pack a lot of power, because Satan does not want you to understand the legal authority you have in Christ. He wants you to forget who you are, because he knows that then you will never exercise your legal spiritual rights conferred on you by the Lord of heaven!

Let me illustrate it this way. I was watching a football game when a player got upset at a referee's call. In the process of angrily protesting the call, this player did a sports no-no. He bumped the referee.

All sports have become very strict about players touching the officials in any way. When an athlete bumps an official, that official can call on definite rights that have been conferred on him by the league's rules and by virtue of his position as a game official. So you can guess what happened next.

When the referee got bumped, he reached into his back pocket, pulled out a yellow penalty flag, and threw the flag up in the air. He called time, waved his hands to stop play, and booted the offender out of the game.

It didn't matter that the player was twice the size of the ref and probably ten times as strong. It didn't matter that the player was protected by pounds and pounds of equipment, while the ref wore only a striped shirt and white pants.

How was that referee able to throw a penalty flag in the face of a three-hundred-pounder, and then send him to the locker room? Where did the ref get that kind of authority? From the rules of the league. His authority was all legal. It had nothing to do with the size or strength or padding of the participants.

My friend, Satan is a lot bigger and stronger than you. He's been lifting weights longer than you have. But in your spiritual back pocket you have a flag that represents the legal rights Christ has given you. When Satan starts bumping you, pull out that flag and send him to the showers. The rights you have in Jesus Christ give you more power than Satan has.

When the enemy starts bringing up your past, for instance, and telling you that you can't overcome it, you have the legal right to flag him and say, "You're a liar. I have legal papers here. Jesus has triumphed over you, and I'm with Him."

So remember—and use—your position in Christ. You are seated with Him in heaven. You have rights against Satan. He has to retreat before authority that comes from Christ.

RELY ON GOD'S PROVISION

Here is a second component in the process of tearing down personal strongholds. You must rely on God's provision.

The apostle James writes, "[God] gives a greater grace. Therefore it says, 'God is opposed to the proud, but gives grace to the humble'" (James 4:6).

Rely on God's Greater Grace

What is this "greater grace" that God gives us? James is not talking about salvation here, so the issue isn't saving grace. This is the grace we need to live victorious lives as believers.

James is talking about grace that is greater than the mess you may be in right now. It doesn't matter how big the mess is or what you've been through, the grace that is available to you in Christ is bigger than your mess.

In other words, the grace God gives you to tear down personal strongholds is far greater than the power keeping those strongholds propped up.

You may say, "But I was abused." That's terrible. You don't have to pretend it didn't happen. But God has greater grace for you.

You say, "But you don't understand. I've been addicted to _____ (fill in the blank in your life) for years." What James says is that even when you add up all the years of your addiction, God still gives greater grace. God has an inexhaustible supply of grace to overcome whatever junk we have accumulated in our lives.

A lot of us have accumulated more junk than we can even remember. But take all the mess you remember, add it to all the mess you forgot, and God still has grace that is greater than all your sin. There is no reason to leave satanic strongholds standing in our lives when God has made provision for us to tear them down.

Surrender to God

If all this grace is available, the natural question is, How do we get it? James lines out the answer in the following verses. He begins by saying, "Submit therefore to God" (James 4:7a).

What does it mean to submit to God? We'll get to that, but first James gives us a great picture of what submission does not mean (James 4:1–5). You're not submitted to God if your life is marked by things like illicit pleasure, strife, lust, envying, and friendship with the world.

The reason I titled this section "surrender" instead of "submission" is that surrender is the forgotten element in submission. You don't often hear the full story when the concept of submission is taught. If you want to submit to God so you can receive His greater grace, you need to understand all that is involved in submission.

Submission is usually presented as the process of making a commitment to Christ. That's important, but it's possible to make a commitment to the Lord without really surrendering our wills to Him.

Here's what I mean. Someone who is struggling with a stronghold can say, "I've made a commitment to the Lord, and I'm going to stop doing what I've been doing."

That sounds fine, but many people who make that kind of commitment promptly go out and fall flat on their faces. Why? Because commitment doesn't work unless it is preceded by surrender. A commitment may simply be another way of saying, "I'm going to do this myself. I'm going to beat this problem. I promised God I was going to do it, and I'm going to do it."

But we already know that we can't beat Satan on our own. So while commitment often says, "I can," surrender says, "Lord, I can't do this in my power. I'm too weak. I cannot live up to Your standards in my own strength."

When a soldier surrenders in a war, he is saying, "I quit. I can't fight any longer." If you want greater grace from God, you must surrender yourself and your own efforts to win the battle and tear down your strongholds. That's a different kind of surrender, because you are surrendering to your Commander rather than to the enemy!

You may be thinking, *Wait a minute, Tony. Just a few chapters ago you said believers needed to quit going around saying, "I can't." Now you're saying we need to say, "I can't."*

What I'm talking about here is the attitude that says, "I can lick this thing myself." There's a big difference between that and realizing that we need Christ's strength to do what we need to do (Philippians 4:13).

When it comes to what Christ can empower us to do, there's no reason to say we can't do something. But Christ's power doesn't kick in until we let go of our delusions of self-power. And that comes through surrender.

Commit to God

But there is still a place for commitment. Having said to God, "I can't do this on my own," you are now ready to say, "But through Your provision of that which I lack, I can go out and tear down the strongholds that are defeating me. In Your strength, I *can* fulfill Your expectations for me." You have now invited God to do for you what you can't do for yourself.

Philippians 2:12–13 explains how this spiritual paradox works. Paul writes, "Work out your salvation with fear and trembling; for it is God who is at work in you, both to will and to work for His good pleasure."

God has a work for us to do in spiritual warfare, but the only reason our efforts produce anything is that He is powerfully at work in us. What we often want to do is try it ourselves and ask God to bless our best shot.

We are too self-sufficient, and that's why we haven't been able to tear down the strongholds. It's not that we don't try. I'm not saying that we set out to let problems and sins and failures take hold in our lives and become strongholds.

How many times have believers promised themselves and God on New Year's Day, "I'm going to stop doing this or that this year." And they really mean it. They just don't have the power to carry through with their intentions.

But God has something infinitely better for us than self-effort. It's called greater grace.

Draw Near to God

James continues his instruction to us when he says, "Draw near to God and He will draw near to you" (James 4:8).

How do we draw near to God? We draw near to Him when we enter His presence and spend time in prayer and worship before Him. If the only worship and the only praise God gets out of you is on Sunday morning, you're not drawing near to Him. You're just visiting Him occasionally.

Let me tell you something wonderful that happens when you draw near to God in praise and worship. It gives the devil an allergy. He's allergic to the praise of God. Satan is hypersensitive to prayer. When the air is filled with prayer and praise, it chokes Satan up and makes it hard for him to function—just like pollen in the air aggravates a physical allergy.

When prayer starts filling the air, Satan can't hang around because the environment is too uncomfortable for him. Satan can't handle it when you draw near to God. He can't function when you turn Sunday morning worship into a way of life. He's got to vacate the premises because he gets allergic.

In other words, Satan ought to start sneezing and choking every time he comes near us because the atmosphere around us is full of praise.

REPENT OF SIN

Along with remembering our position and relying on God's provision, tearing down our personal strongholds also involves repentance for sin.

The apostle James continues in James 4:8–9, "Cleanse your hands, you sinners; and purify your hearts, you double-minded. Be miserable and mourn and weep; let your laughter be turned into mourning, and your joy to gloom."

Admit Your Sin

James could not have been much clearer about our need to call sin what it is and deal with it ruthlessly and completely. The reason God can't help some people is that they never sin. They just "make mistakes." But Jesus didn't die for our mistakes. He died for our sins.

Admitting our sin simply means taking personal responsibility for it. You cannot pass the buck when it comes to your sin.

We live in a society where everybody else is to blame for the bad stuff people do. But what happened years ago or what wrongs people may have suffered do not exonerate them from what they do in the present.

It's easy for us as believers to deny our sin too. If you don't see a stronghold as any big deal, you aren't going to be motivated to cleanse your hands and purify your heart of it. It takes humility to admit your sin, but when you humble yourself in this way you get God's greater grace (James 4:6).

Give Up Pride

The opposite of humility is pride, and James 4:6 goes on to say that "God is opposed to the proud." Instead of getting God's greater grace, the proud person gets God's hand in his face, resisting him and pushing him away.

Why does God push proud people away from Him? When you and I are too proud to come to God and admit to Him where we messed up, we remind Him of

Satan. When we are too proud to submit to God, we remind Him of the angel who said, "I'm tired of submitting to God. I'm tired of humbling myself before Him. I want to do this God thing myself and have creation bowing to me."

You can't be proud and come to God seeking His greater grace. Why? When you come needing grace, you don't have anything to brag about. When you need God's mercy, you can't be talking about who you are and what you have done. God wants to talk about your sin and you want to talk about your goodness. It doesn't work. Pride and humility don't mix.

God hates pride, and you are proud when you refuse to come to Him and call sin what it is. You must repent of sin if the strongholds in your life are going to fall.

RESIST THE DEVIL

I've saved this one for last even though it appears earlier in James 4. "Resist the devil and he will flee from you" (v. 7).

We have talked about resisting the devil before, but I want you to see it in the context of tearing down strongholds. The important thing here is the order in which James puts his exhortations. Notice that submitting yourself to God must come before resisting the devil.

Peter helps us here because he says the same thing. In 1 Peter 5 he says, "Humble yourselves, therefore, under the mighty hand of God, that He may exalt you at the proper time" (v. 6).

This is the difference between your trying to take down those strongholds in your own strength and surrendering to God so He can empower you to do it. When

God exalts you, you can rise above any problem, addiction, attachment, or anything else holding you captive.

Why do you need to humble yourself before God? Because, Peter says, you have an enemy who is like "a roaring lion, seeking someone to devour" (1 Peter 5:8). The devil wants to eat up your mind, chew up your circumstances, devour your joy, shred your dignity, and digest your marriage and your family.

That sounds bad, but Peter goes on. You don't need to flee in fear before this lion. Instead, "resist him, firm in your faith" (v. 9). Here is the same order of events as in James. Submit to God, and you're ready to resist the devil.

You say, "Tony, I know I need to resist Satan. But how?" There is only one way to resist Satan successfully. We've seen it before, but it's important to restate it here. The only way you will be able to resist Satan is by knowing and using the Word of God. It's your answer to Satan's lies when he says, "You'll never change," "You're hooked," "You can't help yourself, go ahead," "It's useless to fight it. Just give in."

Know and Use the Word

We know what successful resistance looks like because we have the perfect example in the temptation of Jesus Christ (Matthew 4:1–11).

Satan told Jesus, "You're hungry. A body has to eat. Go ahead and make Yourself some bread." "You deserve to win the attention of the people. Go ahead and jump." "You can have these kingdoms right now. Just bow down to me."

I can guarantee you that nothing you and I will ever face will compare with the temptations Jesus faced. And He answered every one of them with the Word of God:

"It is written." After Jesus used the Word on Satan, the Bible says Satan left Him (Matthew 4:11). When you resist the devil with the Word of God, you pull out the lion's teeth.

So when Satan comes and tells you, "You'll never really change," you can tell him, "I am a new creation in Christ Jesus. I have been raised with Christ. I am setting my mind on things above, not on things below" (see 2 Corinthians 5:17; Ephesians 2:6; Colossians 3:1).

The next time Satan lies to you and says, "You'll never be free of your problem," tell him, "You're a liar, because God said anyone whom Jesus has set free is free indeed" (see John 8:36). Remind the devil that God's Word is truth (John 17:17), and that the truth sets people free (John 8:32). Satan will leave you alone, because he can't stand up to the Word.

Put God's Word to the Test

I want to ask you a question. If we have all the authority and power we need to defeat Satan and tear down the strongholds he has built in our lives, why don't more of us believers put God's Word to the test more often? What are we waiting for? Why should we pull back and cower in fear?

I know one person who put the Word to the test. His name was David, and his story is found in 1 Samuel 17.

David had an enemy who was much bigger than he was. Goliath the Philistine giant had everybody in Israel scared. King Saul was scared. The whole Israelite army was scared. But David was indignant, because this Philistine was defying the army of the living God.

So David volunteered to fight Goliath. Saul tried to give David his armor, but all it did was weigh David down. He had his spiritual armor on, and that was all he needed. God had empowered David to kill a lion and a bear, so a nine-foot pagan would be no problem. David said, "Because I've seen God work yesterday, I am not afraid of what I might confront today."

Goliath laughed at David and taunted him, but David had an answer. This is the key to the story. David said, "You come to me with a sword, a spear, and a javelin, but I come to you in the name of the Lord of hosts, the God of the armies of Israel, whom you have taunted. This day the Lord will deliver you up into my hands" (vv. 45–46a). Then David proceeded to kill Goliath and take off his head.

Since you and I will probably never have a satanic stronghold bigger than Goliath, there's no reason we can't tear them down. We have the Word of God, and we have a High Priest, Jesus Christ, whom the Bible says faced every temptation you and I will ever face (Hebrews 4:14–16). We can go to Him anytime we need.

God's Word says you are a new person in Christ. It says you are free indeed if Jesus Christ has made you free. It's time to claim your new identity in Christ and act on it. It's time to draw on His inexhaustible provisions. It's time to deal with the sin that keeps those strongholds propped up. And it's time to send Satan packing.

Will we still struggle if we do all of this? Of course we will. We will have to battle as long as we are in the flesh. But we have every weapon we need to defeat Satan. Let's take them and go out to meet the giant. God is waiting to topple him if we will confront him in Christ's name.

18

TEARING DOWN STRONGHOLDS IN YOUR FAMILY LIFE

It's probably safe to say that you know at least one family that either has fallen apart, is falling apart, or is functioning far below what God intended the family to be. The family you know may even be yours.

Some families suffer because the relationship between the husband and wife has become paralyzed. Other families are hurting because rebellious children are causing grief. Still other families are suffering because some members are reaping a harvest of trouble from the sins committed by an earlier generation.

All of these problems and more can easily become strongholds that Satan builds to get a grip on a family and keep it from being everything God intended the family to be. The tragedy is that many families battling satanic strongholds decide that the fight is no longer worth the grief, so they want to throw in the towel and give up. Spouses head for divorce court because they don't see any solution to their dilemma.

Satan is definitely in a "building boom" today in erecting family strongholds. He knows what he is doing, because he has been at it for a long time. He built his first stronghold in the first family in history. And he did it right in the middle of the Garden of Eden, God's paradise. Let's look at the method Satan used to drive a wedge into the family of Adam and Eve.

THE FIRST FAMILY STRONGHOLD

It should not surprise us that the first family stronghold in history came about as a result of the first recorded case of earthly spiritual warfare—the temptation of Eve and its aftermath in Genesis 3.

The fall of Adam and Eve, and the subsequent problems in their family, were caused by an attack from the fallen spirit world. Satan infiltrated the first home and disrupted it. His attack caused spiritual deterioration in the lives of Adam and Eve, which led to relational deterioration in their family.

We know that this sin resulted in a family stronghold because it carried over to the next generation when Cain killed Abel. This wasn't just a one-time thing. Satan's infiltration of Adam's family became the foundation for family murder.

So we can trace the first family breakup and the first family stronghold to the work of the fallen angel world. And we could say that every family breakup can be traced to the same source, because Satan's premier goal, next to destroying you, is the destruction of your family.

Reversal of Roles

What was the methodology Satan used to infiltrate the family of Adam and Eve and build his stronghold?

Satan's method was simple. He got Adam and Eve to

reverse their biblical roles and responsibilities. We could summarize what Satan told Eve in the first five verses of Genesis 3 with two statements: "You don't need God. And you don't need Adam."

Satan got Eve to act independently of God. He tempted her to use her own reasoning and her own logic to reverse God's order and to think in terms of independence. Satan then influenced Adam to become a passive male and stand on the sidelines. Eve took over the leadership. Adam became the submissive responder, the roles were reversed, and Satan had an open door.

Whenever roles are reversed in marriage, a context is created whereby Satan can infiltrate the home. Marriage conflict was the result of the role reversal in the first family. The failure of Eve to remain in her role, and the failure of Adam to take his rightful role of leadership, opened the door for the devil to take over both roles, and it was a disaster for the family.

According to Genesis 3:7, Adam and Eve had to sew fig leaves together to cover themselves, for they became ashamed of each other and of themselves. Now, instead of openness and authenticity, there was hiddenness and secrets.

In the encounter with God and the judgment that followed, both parties passed the blame to someone else. Adam, who had been so excited about Eve just a few verses earlier, now said to God, "It's her fault." And Eve fingered the serpent.

The Resulting Curse

The curse God pronounced in Genesis 3:14–19 was staggering. Notice that there would be conflict in the home. God said to Eve, "Your husband . . . shall rule over you" (v. 16).

In other words, men would seek to control women by domination. As evil as it is, as wrong as it is, men would seek to dominate women and not to lead lovingly. And the desire of the woman for relationship and for partnership would become a battle rather than a blessing.

God cursed the ground for the man so that from then on, he would come home tired from a day of trying to wrestle a living out of a stubborn earth. Instead of coming home to serve his wife, he would come home expecting to be served by her, and that would produce conflict. And after all this, Adam and Eve had to endure the murder of one son by another son.

Satan's infiltration of the family allowed him to build strongholds, some of which have been passed down through families for generations. He will use any means he can to worm his way into a family and wreak havoc.

Three Causes of Family Strongholds

How does Satan work his way into a family and build his strongholds? I'm not just talking about a family having an occasional argument or some other conflict. I'm talking about a situation in which a family is imprisoned by a problem it can't break free of.

Satan uses a number of means to bring about family breakdown and the building of strongholds. Let's discuss a few of the most important and most common so we can learn how to tear down what Satan has constructed.

Unresolved Anger

One of the ways Satan can build a stronghold in your family is through unresolved anger.

You may know the familiar passage of Scripture I am about to quote. But when you read it in the context of satanic strongholds, it takes on a new level of meaning.

The passage I'm referring to is Ephesians 4:26–27: "Be angry, and yet do not sin; do not let the sun go down on your anger, and do not give the devil an opportunity."

There are a lot of angry people out there—angry at parents, mates, children, or even themselves, for things that have happened. If a wrong has been committed against you, you have a right to be angry. The Bible says that the Lord is angry with the wicked every day (Psalm 7:11 KJV).

Anger at sin is valid. But prolonged anger violates the scriptural command to resolve it quickly, and it provides the ground Satan needs to build that unresolved anger into a stronghold. Paul says it clearly in Ephesians 4:27. Lingering anger becomes an opportunity for Satan. It gives the enemy the unlocked door he needs to break into your home and do his destructive work.

For some of us, not only has the sun gone down on our anger, but the moon has gone down as well. In other cases, the week has passed and we are still angry. And the saddest of all are those situations where decades have passed and the anger in the family is still unresolved. Some people even take their anger to the grave.

This kind of anger makes everyone else in the family pay for what one or two people have done. Suppose you were eating with your family at a restaurant, and when you were finished the waiter brought you your bill and the bills for everyone else who was eating in the restaurant at that time.

Your argument would be, "It's not fair to make me pay for what everybody else ate." In the same way, it's not fair for your family members to pay for what someone else did.

And yet, there are Christian parents making their

children pay for the anger Mom and Dad have toward each other. There are wives making their husbands pay for the failures of those wives' fathers when they were girls. And on it goes.

It's easy to say that we need to resolve our anger quickly, but it's another thing to do it. How can we put a stop to this cycle of destructive family anger that allows Satan to have a "building boom" in putting up his strongholds?

An analogy that I think helps a lot is to treat unresolved anger the way we do a videotape in our VCR. When a particular videotape has finished playing, we push the eject button and take it out.

The advantage of a VCR is that it allows you to play a tape over and over again, as many times as you want. But even when you get a new tape, you can't play it until you eject the old tape.

Unresolved anger is like that old videotape. You play it and relive what it was that made you angry. But instead of ejecting the tape when it's finished, you keep rewinding it and watching it again. And every time you watch it, you get mad all over again.

You have to quit playing that anger tape. The only way I know to do that is by hitting the eject button of forgiveness and releasing the offender. Otherwise, Satan will continue using your anger to defeat you in spiritual warfare and infect your family with his poison.

Releasing the offender and dealing with sin may require that you sit down and write or call a family member to say, "You hurt me deeply, but I cannot let your hurt control the rest of my life. And so, for my sake and for yours, I forgive you and release you of any emotional obligation to me." If the other person doesn't know the incident you're talking about or sees no need for forgiveness, you need to be very careful about this approach. Ask the Holy Spirit for guidance.

That's one way to tear down an anger stronghold in your family. Another way is to seek forgiveness from others if you are the offender. Then when Satan tries to get you to play that old anger videotape, serve notice on him that in the name of Jesus Christ, that tape has been ejected.

Of course, Satan will come back more than once, trying to play that tape on the VCR of your heart and mind. But all you have to do is push the eject button each time by claiming your position in Christ and reminding the devil that the anger has been forgiven and laid to rest.

Rebellion

Rebellion is another powerful weapon Satan uses to disrupt families and build strongholds.

Rebellion simply means to go against God's established order of authority. Satan was the original rebel, so it's not surprising that he would attempt to foment rebellion in the family. Rebellious children can tear a family apart as quickly as anything. So can adults who refuse to submit themselves to God's legitimate chain of command.

In fact, I want to spend most of my time here dealing with the adults, because God said in Exodus 20:5 that He would pass the results of disobedience on to the third and fourth generation. Parents can hand their children and grandchildren a real mess when they rebel against God's authority. Some Christians are setting in motion a pattern of rebellion that will have generational consequences if the pattern is not reversed.

Before we talk about specific examples of rebellion,

I want us to see how seriously God takes the sin of rebellion. The apostle Peter has some strong words about rebellion as it relates to the angelic conflict and then to people who have joined in that rebellion against God.

Peter writes, "God did not spare angels when they sinned, but cast them into hell and committed them to pits of darkness, reserved for judgment" (2 Peter 2:4).

The sin of these angels was that they joined Satan in his rebellion. The people of Noah's day, and the citizens of Sodom and Gomorrah, can also be classified as rebels.

Peter reminds us that God also brought judgment against the world of Noah's day, and against Sodom and Gomorrah (vv. 5–6). Then Peter says, "The Lord knows how . . . to keep the unrighteous under punishment for the day of judgment" (v. 9).

But then in verses 10–12, Peter applies the principle of God's judgment to the false teachers of his day. Notice a few traits of these people. They "indulge the flesh in its corrupt desires," "despise authority," and are "self-willed." They are also not afraid to "revile angelic majesties" (v. 10).

What is the fate of these rebels? They are like wild, unreasoning animals, "born as creatures of instinct to be captured and killed" (v. 12).

That's strong talk. These false teachers had no respect for God or His holy angels. They refused to place themselves under divine or angelic authority, and therefore they placed themselves under God's severe judgment.

My point is that wherever you see rebellion against God's legitimate chain of command, you find God's judgment and not God's help.

One of the most common examples of family rebellion that can lead to a stronghold is the rebellion of children. God takes this sin so seriously that the Mosaic Law made provision for the stoning of an older, rebellious child who refused to obey his parents (Deuteronomy 21:18–21).

There is no record that this was ever carried out, but it was on the statute books of Israel. Rebellious children must be brought under authority, or they will eventually shred your family life. In more extreme cases, this may require removing the rebellious child from the home for a period rather than allow him or her to destroy the family.

But spiritually, rebellion goes far beyond unruly children. If a husband and father is rebelling against the authority of Christ in his life and home, he can't blame God if his family is falling apart. To get things back on track, he must line himself up under God's established chain of authority.

A woman who has bought into the lie of radical feminism and refuses to respect her husband's position of authority is allowing Satan to build a stronghold of rebellion in her family. She too must begin to operate according to God's chain if she wants God's help to break this stronghold.

In connection with this, let me remind you again of a seminal passage, 1 Corinthians 11:3–10. Verse 3 outlines God's chain of authority: "I want you to understand that Christ is the head of every man, and the man is the head of a woman, and God is the head of Christ."

This issue of obedience to proper authority even applies to Jesus Christ, because He is under the authority of His Father. Every Christian man is under the authority of Christ, and every wife is under the authority of her husband. This is the way God intended things to be in the church and in the home.

After establishing the pattern, Paul went on to discuss the specific place of women in the church. I want to review this briefly because it touches on the issue of rebellion and makes an important point.

If a woman in that day wanted to display an attitude of rebellion against her husband or the male leadership of the church, she would remove the head covering that God said she needed to wear (v. 5).

This act of rebellion, however, was not just against God-ordained human authority. It was rebellion carried out in the presence of angels (v. 10). And anyone who showed the angels that she was rebelling against God's authority could not count on angelic assistance in her life or home. The holy angels function under proper authority, and rebellion takes a person out of the sphere in which angels can minister to them on God's behalf.

Rebellion is a serious sin in God's sight. It can lead to the presence of satanic strongholds. There's only one way to deal with rebellion, and that's to remove it like a cancer, no matter how radical the procedure required to get it out.

Selfishness

A third sin that can lead to family strongholds is the sin of selfishness.

This is a big one in our day because so many people are after "personal fulfillment," no matter what the cost to their marriages or families. We expect children to be selfish because they are born in sin and they haven't yet learned socially acceptable ways of dealing with selfishness. But it's a lot easier to deal with selfishness in a child than in an adult.

Paul addresses selfishness in the area of sexual intimacy in marriage (1 Corinthians 7:1–5), but the principle has a wider application. The principle is this: "Let the husband fulfill his duty to his wife, and likewise also the wife to her husband" (v. 3).

This applies to a couple's sexual life, but also to other areas of marriage and family life. Marriage involves duties and privileges. Each partner has authority over the other partner's body (v. 4).

But when people become selfish, they can begin withholding from their partner the self-giving love that should mark marriage. So Paul told the married couple, "Stop depriving one another" (v. 5).

Whenever husbands and wives become so selfish that they refuse to meet each other's needs, the problem can go far beyond the bedroom. And when selfishness becomes a problem in a marriage, guess who shows up?

Satan looks for situations of selfishness in a home so he can exploit them for his purposes. Displaying selfishness is like saying, "Satan, you are welcome into our home." And the devil is always looking for that invitation.

You don't even have to open the door for the devil yourself. Just unlock the door through things such as unresolved anger, rebellion, and selfishness, and he'll open it himself.

The Wrong Kind of Effort

As you read this, you may be saying, "I'm trying to do this family thing right, but it just isn't working."

Well, the problem may be that you're trying the wrong thing. The issue is not just that you're trying, but *what* you are trying. Are you using your spiritual weapons to attack family strongholds, or are you using the world's methods and simply sprinkling a little Jesus on top?

It's like the couple who wanted to start doing things together, so they decided to go duck hunting. (Don't ask me why duck hunting; it's not my story!)

The couple inquired what they needed, and they were told, "The main thing you need for duck hunting is a good dog." So they bought a hunting dog and headed out. The man and woman hunted all day long, but didn't bag one duck. Finally the husband looked at his wife and said, "Honey, we've got to be doing something wrong here. We haven't caught a duck yet."

His wife answered, "Well, I'm not sure, but maybe if we throw the dog up a little higher, he can catch a duck."

That's what a lot of Christian families are doing. They're trying, but they're using a dog to do what a shotgun was designed to do! And they wonder why they aren't getting anywhere.

It's OK to have a dog, but it takes firepower to bring down a duck. And it takes spiritual firepower to bring down Satan and his strongholds. It takes the firepower of our spiritual weapons.

THREE WEAPONS FOR TEARING DOWN STRONGHOLDS

With that in mind, let me give you three potent weapons you can use to tear down satanic strongholds in your family.

Proper Marital Roles

There's not a lot of introduction needed for this one. The strength of the family begins with the strength of the marriage bond. And God has a lot to say about that.

"Wives, be subject to your husbands, as is fitting in the Lord" (Colossians 3:18). To put it another way, "Wives, honor your husband's position of headship."

A wife may say, "But I don't like my husband right now." You don't have to like him to honor the position

God has put him in. A lot of people don't like their bosses, but they honor their bosses' position.

God calls a wife to honor her husband, whether she agrees with him all the time or not. Sarah is the model of this honor, because she called Abraham lord (1 Peter 3:6).

And what did Sarah get? She got a miracle, a baby when she was ninety years old. God miraculously intervened in Sarah's life and gave her Isaac, a miracle child. Peter says that when a woman operates this way, it is precious in the sight of God.

Some Christian wives need to repent of their rebellious attitudes toward their husband's authority. If a wife wants God to change her husband, she needs to honor his position. That gets her out of the way so God can deal with the man.

Why is this a big deal with God? First, because it reflects the order He has established. And second, because we are talking about spiritual warfare and satanic strongholds. Satan is so potent that even the archangel Michael didn't rebuke him. We need the weapons of God to defeat the devil.

The Bible also addresses husbands. "Husbands, love your wives, and do not be embittered against them" (Colossians 3:19).

Some of us men have attitude problems too. Some of us think our wives are genies that appear magically out of a lamp, bow to us, and say, "Your wish is my command."

Our wives are our partners, not our servants. How can you know, Christian husband, if you are loving your wife? It's simple. What are you sacrificing for her? Loving your wife like Christ loved the church (Ephesians 5:25) involves sacrifice.

Let me put it this way. Make sure that at the end of the day, you have made more deposits than withdrawals in your wife's emotional and spiritual account.

We men have the propensity to come home and want to know what's for dinner and why it isn't ready yet. We want our wives to do this and that and meet our needs, and we are constantly making withdrawals from their accounts. Then we wonder why the account is empty at night.

Our wives need emotional and spiritual nourishment. They need our love, our attention, our help with the kids. They need us to listen to them and care about the things that are affecting them.

It would revolutionize a lot of Christian marriages if the husband would simply ask himself this question: "What deposits can I make in my wife's account today?" If he will make an effort to make those deposits, a husband will find that they accumulate interest. And Satan will have one less door of access into the home.

Proper Parenting

A second weapon we can wield to attack Satan's strongholds is in our own hands as parents. "Fathers, do not exasperate your children, that they may not lose heart" (Colossians 3:21). A similar command appears in Ephesians 6:4. Although both verses are addressed to fathers, mothers need to heed this warning as well.

In other words, encourage your children, don't discourage them. Don't put them down. Tell them what their possibilities are under God. Teach them His Word and model it before them. And give them all the love and support they need to find God's will and His calling for their lives.

Obedient Children

Colossians 3 also addresses the children in the home: "Be obedient to your parents in all things, for this is well-pleasing to the Lord" (v. 20). Paul reminds us in Ephesians 6:2–3 that this is the first commandment with a promise attached to it.

The best antidote to rebellion is obedience. This isn't something parents can begin teaching when their kids are teenagers. Children need to be taught early the importance of honoring and obeying their parents.

Sometimes this requires that children be reminded who is in charge. Kids need to understand that obedience is crucial to their well-being as well as the well-being of the home. Don't let Satan use your children to build a stronghold.

FIGHTING FOR YOUR FAMILY

In Nehemiah 4:14 this great leader told the people of Jerusalem, who were being threatened by their enemies, "Fight for your brothers, your sons, your daughters, your wives, and your houses."

That's what we have been talking about all along. We're in a spiritual war, although some of us haven't started fighting with God's weapons yet. When you're at war, you can't afford to let the enemy build strongholds in your backyard.

In the first heavyweight championship fight between Mike Tyson and Evander Holyfield, Tyson won the first round, but Holyfield took it from there.

In the Garden of Eden, Satan won the first round. But Jesus has taken it from there. So fight for your family. Don't give up just because Satan won the first round.

In the eighth round of their first championship fight,

Holyfield and Tyson butted heads, and Tyson was not the same after the blow to his head. Genesis 3:15 says that Jesus Christ would give Satan a blow to his head, and Satan would never be the same again.

That blow was delivered on the cross of Calvary, so keep on fighting for your family. Satan does not have any right to build his strongholds in your family if you are under the blood of Jesus Christ. Let me tell you two more things about that championship fight. Tyson didn't know what had happened to him when he was knocked to the canvas. He told reporters he needed to look at the video to tell what hit him.

If you will use the weapons of God on Satan, he won't know what hit him. He'll have to look at the video to see how he lost the battle for your family.

One more thing. Even though Mike Tyson lost that fight, he still left the arena a rich man. He had a lot of spoil to take with him because he was guaranteed a purse worth millions of dollars. Tyson had a lot of money to show for a losing fight.

Satan has lost the fight, but he's still taking prisoners and hauling in the booty. Don't let him add your family to his account. Don't let him take you and your family as spoils when he's the loser and you're the winner in Jesus Christ.

I want to close this chapter with a word of encouragement for you. After Adam and Eve let Satan wreck their lives through sin, God did a gracious thing. He drove the man and woman He had created out of Eden and put cherubim at the entrance to guard it lest they return (Genesis 3:22–24).

God acted kindly by driving Adam and Eve out. Why? Because God didn't want them to eat of the Tree of Life and live forever in their sinful state with no hope of redemption. He evicted them from Eden, but they left with the promise of a coming Redeemer ringing in their ears. That Redeemer came and died on another tree, the cross of Calvary.

That's good news for you and your family. That means no matter how deeply Satan has infiltrated your home, no matter the devastation he has wrought on your marriage and in the lives of your children, because of that other tree, the Cross, you have hope in God's salvation.

Although Adam and Eve didn't get to taste the fruit of the Tree of Life because of sin, we who know Jesus Christ have savored the fruit of the tree called the Cross. If you will establish this other tree, the cross of Christ, in your home, there will be no room left for Satan's strongholds.

19

TEARING DOWN STRONGHOLDS IN YOUR CHURCH

The Bible is clear that Satan can build his strongholds in the lives of individuals and families. But he can also gain ground in the church of Jesus Christ and erect strongholds that hinder the work of God.

Bringing spiritual warfare inside the doors of the church is a key strategy of the devil. He knows if he can weaken the church internally, he can weaken its witness and impact on the world.

Let me give you some examples of what I mean. The church in America has been laboring under the stronghold of sectarian disunity for the last 250 years. During that same span of time, the church has also been weakened by the stronghold of racism. Many individual churches are being held captive by strongholds such as ongoing conflict and bitterness that in some cases have affected several generations of their members.

We can even see examples of church strongholds in the New Testament. The church at Corinth was being held hostage to blatant immorality that the people accepted as normal. As we will see later in this chapter, the church at Thyatira (Revelation 2:18–29) was under the spell of an evil woman the risen Christ called Jezebel.

I can't imagine anything worse than the church of Jesus Christ being held hostage by a satanic stronghold, in which the people of God approach life with a worldly rather than a spiritual mind-set. But strongholds have been built in many churches, and they need to come down.

Before we talk about that, let's review the definition of a stronghold. It is a mind-set that accepts as inevitable or unchangeable something that is contrary to the revealed will of God. It is a way of thinking that says, "I can't," when God says, "You can."

On the individual level, a satanic stronghold might be an addiction or a habit that seems too powerful to break. It may be a family legacy of violence or unhealthy ways of relating. Any place where we yield ground to Satan becomes a potential location for one of his strongholds.

If Satan can deceive us into thinking we worship an impotent, powerless Savior who can do nothing for us, then he can keep a church spiritually anemic. That's why it is the task of the pastor and the leadership of the church to proclaim Christ with authority, not to preach "sermonettes" for "Christianettes," as Vance Havner once said.

Far too many sermons today are like skyscrapers—one story on top of another. Messages like that have little authority and little passion. But if we serve a little God, what do we really have to say?

I once got an invitation to speak at a church and was told that the pastor normally preached for ten minutes. I'm afraid I don't have any ten-minute sermons. I can't even figure out what a person could say in a ten-minute sermon.

I'm not equating a church's spirituality with the length of the pastor's sermons. What I am saying is that if we're not careful, we can reduce God to our size and fit Him in to our convenience. When that happens, the church is held hostage to a secular way of thinking.

THE PLACE TO BEGIN

How do we tear down strongholds in the church? The place to begin is with the Lord and Head of the church and His message to the people who make up His body.

In the opening chapters of the book of Revelation we meet the risen Jesus Christ in all of His power and glory. There is no reducing this person to a safe, easy-to-manage, Milquetoast Lord who is a threat to no one.

On the contrary, the apostle John saw a vision of Jesus Christ standing among His church, wearing the robes of judge and priest. His voice sounded like "many waters" (Revelation 1:15). He was thunderous in His statements. A two-edged sword came out of His mouth (v. 16). In fact, when John saw Jesus, he "fell at His feet as a dead man" (v. 17).

When was the last time the church had such an overwhelming vision of Jesus that we fell at His feet like dead people? If we can come into the presence of the Lord of the church and never be overcome, then we don't know who we're dealing with.

The Lord whom John saw had a message concerning the future, and that is the bulk of the Revelation. But Jesus also had a message for the present, to His church. He told John, "Write in a book what you see, and send it to the seven churches" (Revelation 1:11).

In the Bible, seven is the number of perfection or

completion. So even though Jesus' message was for seven real churches in Asia Minor, it was also His complete message to all churches in this age.

The word Jesus gave to John in Revelation 2–3 tells the church how we are to function under His lordship, and it gives us insight into how to tear down the strongholds of Satan.

But before we hear the word Jesus has for us, we need to understand who is delivering this message. So Revelation opens with John's vision of Jesus. The picture John describes is so overwhelming that no artist could possibly capture it. Jesus transcends whatever image of Him people may have hanging on their living room walls. He is the King of kings and Lord of lords who speaks with final authority.

In fact, the heart of Jesus' message to the seven churches is simply this: He and He alone is the standard by which the church is to measure itself and to function. When the people of God function in accordance with this standard, then the church is the church; anything less won't do.

You will see a lot of proper Englishmen on the streets of London wearing suits and carrying watches on chains in their vest pockets. Sometimes you will see a man pull out his watch, look up, and then check his watch again and adjust it.

When you see him do that, you can figure he has looked up at the clock in the tower of the houses of Parliament. The clock in this tower, which is famous for its great bell called Big Ben, is noted for its accuracy. If a Britisher's watch doesn't match the time in the Big Ben clock tower, he may adjust it, because the clock in the Parliament tower is considered the standard.

Jesus is the standard to which the church must adjust. He wants us to adjust our programs, our plans, and our thinking to who He is. When the church obeys Jesus, we will see a church victorious over the devil rather than a church victimized by the devil.

Before we study these seven messages, I want to note something. It's a principle of spiritual warfare we have already encountered, but it needs to be restated here because it relates directly to the Scripture we are about to study. Although we are already victorious over Satan because we are seated with Jesus Christ in the heavenly places, it is possible to be defeated by Satan in the day-to-day, hand-to-hand combat of spiritual warfare.

For instance, in 1 John 5:5 the apostle John says we have already overcome the world. But Jesus tells the members of each church in Revelation that they need to overcome. This is the difference between our standing in Christ, which does not change, and our current state, which can change every day.

That is, you can be victorious by your standing but not be victorious in your state. It is possible to have a right relationship with God and never experience the power of God. You can be an overcomer in your position but not in your practice. I want us to keep this distinction in mind as we go along.

JESUS CHRIST'S MESSAGE TO THE CHURCH

So what does Jesus say to the church? How does the church live in power and victory and tear down the satanic strongholds that are hindering us? Jesus has seven distinct messages for His church.

A Message About Love

The first message is to the church at Ephesus, and it is one of love:

I know your deeds and your toil and perseverance, and that you cannot endure evil men, and you put to the test those who call themselves apostles, and they are not, and you have found them to be false; and you have perseverance and have endured for My name's sake, and have not grown weary. But I have this against you, that you have left your first love. (Revelation 2:2–4)

The first lesson of the risen Christ to His church is that if we want to see His power and authority operating in our midst, we must never let programs replace our passion for Him.

The church at Ephesus had a great program. This church believed all the right things. They had doctrinal soundness. Truth was present, but it was truth devoid of love.

It is possible for the church to have all the right answers and still fail the test. The church can be doctrinally correct and yet spiritually dead when it loses sight of Christ.

It's necessary to have correct doctrine. But correct doctrine ought to help us to love Christ more. It's right to take a stand for the truth. But the truth should make us more passionate to know Christ intimately.

If you know more now than you did last year, and yet you are enjoying your spiritual life less, your priorities are off. The Bible likens our relationship with Christ to a marriage. The partners in a marriage can be faithful to each other, yet can have a passionless marriage.

One reason for this is that most people date in order to marry, when they ought to be marrying in order to date —that is, after marriage people should continue caring about each other, spending time together, and paying attention to each other.

People who quit dating after they marry often get

bored. They wonder what happened to the fire. The fire went out because the relationship is backward. When you marry in order to date, you have a program designed to keep the passion of the relationship alive.

That's how it should be in the church's relationship with Christ. Satan can gain ground in the church when we leave our first love for Jesus Christ. The city of Ephesus was dominated by the temple and the worship of the goddess Diana, so the demonic world was very active in Ephesus.

In this pagan environment, God's people needed to keep their love for Him strong. So do we in our evil environment. This issue of first love for the Savior is so important that Christ saw its lack as a sin to be repented of. Failure to do so would mean that Christ would remove His presence from the church (Revelation 2:5).

A Message About Faithfulness

The second church Jesus addressed was the church in Smyrna. To these believers Jesus says:

> I know your tribulation and your poverty (but you are rich), and the blasphemy by those who say they are Jews and are not, but are a synagogue of Satan. Do not fear what you are about to suffer. Behold, the devil is about to cast some of you into prison, that you may be tested, and you will have tribulation ten days. Be faithful until death, and I will give you the crown of life. (Revelation 2:9–10)

This was a message concerning faithfulness. Jesus is saying to His church, "Be faithful to Me no matter what. Don't quit standing up for Me when the going gets tough. Don't be a convenience-loving church made up of convenience-loving Christians who only serve Me when they are being blessed."

The believers in Smyrna were going through hard times. Many of them were poor, and they were facing persecution by a group of people energized by Satan. It would have been easy for the church in Smyrna to throw in the towel and let Satan have the victory he sought.

A lot of people are willing to follow Jesus as long as they are getting Christmas blessings. Everybody likes a God who gives out goodies, who simply invites people to "name it and claim it." But Jesus has called us to take up our cross and follow Him (Mark 8:34).

A cross is an instrument of suffering. We can't follow Jesus only during the good times and call ourselves the church. We must be faithful to Him even when following Him involves suffering. When times are good, they are good because God is good. But even when times are bad, God is still good.

The church's job is to obey Christ faithfully, not to please everybody. Our church in Dallas gets criticized a lot because we practice things like church discipline. People will say, "What right do you have getting into other people's business?"

Well, it would be a lot easier not to practice church discipline. It would save us a lot of headaches. The only problem is the Lord has not given us that option. He commands the church to apply discipline where it is needed, and we have to obey.

The church is not on earth to win friends and influence people. If it's a choice between standing for Christ and winning popularity, there's only one choice the church can make. We are called to be faithful no matter what, and when we do that Jesus will take care of the rest.

We live in a day of quitters. People bail out on their marriages when times get tough. People leave the church when things don't go the way they like.

A little girl was looking at her grandmother's thick wedding rings. "Boy, Grandmother," she said, "they sure made wedding rings thick back when you got married."

"Yes, darling," the grandmother said. "That's because when we got married, wedding rings were made to last."

Many people today are ready to quit the minute the heat is on. But Jesus says, "If you want to know My power and spiritual authority, stand firm in trouble and I will make you an overcomer." That's the message of faithfulness.

A Message About Compromise

The third church the risen Lord sent a message to was the church in Pergamum:

> I know where you dwell, where Satan's throne is; and you hold fast My name, and did not deny My faith, even in the days of Antipas, My witness, My faithful one, who was killed among you, where Satan dwells. But I have a few things against you, because you have there some who hold the teaching of Balaam, who kept teaching Balak to put a stumbling block before the sons of Israel, to eat things sacrificed to idols, and to commit acts of immorality. Thus you also have some who in the same way hold the teaching of the Nicolaitans. (Revelation 2:13–15)

"Satan's throne" was a reference to the throne of Zeus, which was on a hill in Pergamum. Jesus called it Satan's throne because behind every idol or false god is a demon. Pergamum was another city in which Satan was having a field day in terms of spiritual warfare.

The church at Pergamum held to its witness even when one of its members was martyred for Christ. But the church was also compromising with the enemy by tolerating false teachers in its midst. This was a spiritual warfare issue because false teachers are energized by Satan.

When the church allows people to teach false doctrine, it puts a stumbling block in the path of God's people. Satan can build some mighty strongholds in a church where the people are being led by a false teacher to commit acts of immorality and defile the worship of God.

One reason we are not seeing the power of God in the church today is that there is too much compromise. We want to make everybody happy and accommodate everyone's opinions. But let me tell you something. Any politician who is popular with everybody is bad news because his popularity means he doesn't stand for anything. The same is true for the church. Watch out for the church where everybody feels comfortable all the time.

When you handle the Word correctly, some people are going to get uncomfortable. For instance, the church that takes a stand against all forms of sex outside of marriage is going to get some flak from somewhere.

Plenty of churches today are searching for ways to accommodate people of every "sexual orientation." It's not popular to take a biblical stand on issues like homosexuality, but anything short of a biblical stand is carnal compromise.

Some in Pergamum were teaching that a little immorality here and there wouldn't hurt anyone. Jesus accused them of following the "teaching of Balaam." The false prophet Balaam couldn't curse the nation of Israel because God wouldn't let him, even though Balak hired Balaam for that purpose (Numbers 22–24). So Balaam took a different approach and succeeded in enticing the people of Israel to commit immorality and bring the Lord's judgment. The direct approach failed, so Balaam came in a side door and got the job done for the devil.

A compromising church allows the enemy to come in the side door. A compromising church says, "Look, let's not get too carried away with this doctrine thing. A few Nicolaitans won't hurt." We're not sure who this group was or exactly what it taught, but whatever it was, Jesus hated it.

Don't get me wrong. The church is a hospital where spiritually sick people are welcome. But the job of a hospital is to treat illness and perform surgery when necessary, not simply to make the sick person comfortable or help him feel better about being sick.

Hospitals don't let people occupy a room simply because they happen to feel like coming to the hospital that day. They must be ready to deal with their problem.

It's the same with the church. The job of the church is to perform spiritual surgery. If a person comes to church bearing sin, that's fine. But the church must let the sinner know that what he needs is a scalpel to excise the sin, not a pat on the back or a nice bandage to make the problem look better.

The church must address compromise when it occurs, because God has called us to a higher standard. The church is to be visibly different. Believers are not to be joined in marriage or other close partnerships with unbelievers because, as Paul asks, "What fellowship has light with darkness?" (2 Corinthians 6:14). Answer: none.

The Bible calls being joined with an unbeliever

compromise. I know things like this sound radical today, but the biblical standard often seems radical when held up to the "anything goes" standards of our culture. The church's first call is not to try to be relevant. Its first call is to be biblical.

What do you tell your children when they tell you everybody else is doing something? You tell them, "Well, you're not everybody else. And in this house we don't do that." That's what Joshua meant when he declared, "As for me and my house, we will serve the Lord" (Joshua 24:15).

Joshua was saying, "No compromise." The church needs to say today, "No more compromise. It doesn't matter what the world does or what everyone else says. In this house, we are going to serve the Lord."

The church needs to confess compromise as a sin. The Lord was pictured speaking to this church with a sharp, two-edged sword coming out of His mouth. That sword is His Word, the only thing that can cut out the cancer of compromise. The church has to stop allowing for sin and calling it culturally acceptable. We have to start saying, "Compromise is sin. And by God's grace, we are going to cut it out of the body."

A Message About Holiness

The Lord's fourth message, to the church at Thyatira, gives us another side of this issue of dealing with sin in the church. This was a message about holiness:

> I know your deeds, and your love and faith and service and perseverance, and that your deeds of late are greater than at first. But I have this against you, that you tolerate the woman Jezebel, who calls herself a prophetess, and she teaches and leads My bond-servants astray, so that

they commit acts of immorality and eat things sacrificed to idols. (Revelation 2:19–20)

Like the other churches, the people at Thyatira had some good things going for them. They had grown in their faith and love and service to the Lord.

But the church had a major problem in its midst, a woman the Lord called Jezebel. That may not have been this woman's actual name, but in using the name Jezebel, Jesus was drawing on the image of Israel's wicked, conniving, domineering queen who manipulated her husband, King Ahab, and everyone else. Jezebel ran the show.

That's what this woman was doing at Thyatira. She was out of her place, because she was dominating the church, something God does not allow a woman to do (1 Timothy 2:11–12). She was rebelling against her role, and in addition she was teaching false doctrine. This woman had theologized her rebellion by giving herself the title "prophetess." But that only masked her sin.

Let me mention something here. I realize that a church, especially a large church with a lot of outreaches and ministries, cannot vouch for the theological soundness and personal holiness of every person who walks through its doors.

But that's entirely different from allowing messed-up people to go public in the church with their messed-up theology and lifestyles. The condemnation of the Thyatira church was that this woman Jezebel had gone public with her heresy and immorality, because she was teaching it to everybody else.

And what's worse, the church was tolerating her. No one was dealing with the problem; no one was speaking out against her rebellion and sin. She claimed to be spiritually gifted, and the authentic leadership of the church wasn't calling her on it.

It's pretty easy for Satan to build a stronghold in the church when the church invites his kids inside and gives them a hammer and nails. This church may have tolerated Jezebel, but God didn't tolerate her. She and her followers were under His judgment:

> I gave her time to repent; and she does not want to repent of her immorality. Behold, I will cast her upon a bed of sickness, and those who commit adultery with her into great tribulation, unless they repent of her deeds. And I will kill her children with pestilence. (Revelation 2:21–23a)

The church cannot tolerate unholiness, because God will not tolerate it. There were people in Thyatira who had remained faithful to God and had not followed Jezebel (v. 24). But when evil is tolerated in the church, it spreads and infects the whole body the way a little bit of yeast spreads through a whole loaf of bread (1 Corinthians 5:6).

God said, "Since you refuse to judge Jezebel, I will judge her for you." This stuff of being the church is serious business.

A Message About Progress

Sardis was another church with major problems. In fact, there were only a few people in the entire church who had not "soiled their garments" and were therefore worthy to "walk with [Christ] in white" (Revelation 3:4). To the rest, Jesus sent this message:

> I know your deeds, that you have a name that you are alive, but you are dead. Wake up, and strengthen the

things that remain, which were about to die; for I have not found your deeds completed in the sight of My God. Remember therefore what you have received and heard; and keep it, and repent. If therefore you will not wake up, I will come like a thief, and you will not know at what hour I will come upon you. (Revelation 3:1–3)

Jesus was addressing a sleeping church that had made no spiritual progress worth talking about. It's hard to move forward when you're asleep.

Why do some churches fail to make progress? One reason is that they are living off what God did yesterday. Watch out for a church where all the people can talk about is what God did in the good old days, how things used to be around there. The church at Sardis didn't have much left, and even the things that remained were about to go belly-up. This church was stuck.

The problem with this, of course, is that you can't stand still in the spiritual life. You are either moving forward, or you're moving backward. There is no such thing as coasting in neutral.

The Sardis believers were asleep in the pews, so Jesus told them, "Wake up! Time is passing, and you are losing ground." Sometimes Satan makes a direct, frontal assault on the church to establish his strongholds, as he did with Jezebel in Thyatira. But at other times he lulls the church to sleep so no one notices that he is gaining a foothold.

Do you have trouble waking up in the morning? Millions of people do. You may have to drag yourself out of bed in the morning and stagger around trying to regain consciousness.

But even if you have a hard time waking up, you still get up every morning. Why? Even though you don't like getting up, you know that if you don't, you will soon lose your job and starve. The fact that you showed up at work last week won't put food on your table this week.

The wonderful things the church did for God yesterday are history. They are in the past. Of course, we should celebrate them and thank God for them and build on them, but we can't relive them. We can't recapture the past.

The same goes for the mistakes the church made yesterday. We need to learn from past mistakes so we don't repeat them, but we also can't linger over them.

That's why Paul said he forgot the things that were behind him and pressed forward to the things ahead of him. He was after the prize of God's "Well done," and he didn't want the past weighing him down (Philippians 3:13–14).

Someone has said, "If I spend all my time today thinking about my failures or my successes yesterday, then I will ruin my tomorrow. When today looks at yesterday, I am borrowing from tomorrow's time."

Living in the past is like trying to drive while staring in the rearview mirror of your car. You move forward by focusing on the windshield, not the rearview mirror.

Notice how large your windshield is compared to your rearview mirror. The windshield covers a lot more territory because the object of driving is to move forward. You only need to glance back every once in a while to avoid making a mistake while you're moving forward.

Satan wants to keep the church focused on the rearview mirror of yesterday so we won't pay attention to where we're going today. Jesus says, "Wake up, open your eyes, and move on to tomorrow."

A Message About Obedience

The church at Philadelphia was the church Jesus commended so highly. He had nothing negative to say about this faithful church. And yet, Satan was there trying to gain a foothold even in the Philadelphia church:

> I know your deeds. . . . You have a little power, and have kept My word, and have not denied My name. Behold, I will cause those of the synagogue of Satan, who say that they are Jews, and are not, but lie—behold, I will make them to come and bow down at your feet, and to know that I have loved you. Because you have kept the word of My perseverance, I also will keep you from the hour of testing, that hour which is about to come upon the whole world, to test those who dwell upon the earth. (Revelation 3:8–10)

We don't need to belabor this point. We have seen again and again the importance of obedience to God in waging successful spiritual warfare. This church kept God's Word even though Satan was harassing the believers through the people in one of his "synagogues." Satan was trying to build a stronghold in the church, but the people wouldn't allow it.

Notice that the secret to this church's success wasn't its great power. "You have a little power," Jesus told them. The key was that they kept His word and did not deny His name. When the church is obedient to Christ, He will take care of Satan. But if we deny Him, He will deny us.

One reason we don't see more prayers answered in the church is that so many believers basically deny Christ by their actions all week. They don't acknowledge that they know Him, but come Sunday they are ready to hear from Him.

God says to that, "Don't play Me for a fool. I will keep you from Satan and his attacks, but you need to obey Me and keep My Word." The best preventive for Satan's work in the church is obedience to the Word of God.

A Message About Commitment

The seventh and final church the risen Lord addressed was the church of Laodicea.

Laodicea was a wealthy Roman city. The church was rich too, and the people were really with it. This was "the church of what's happening now." But it was also very sick:

> I know your deeds, that you are neither cold nor hot; I would that you were cold or hot. So because you are lukewarm, and neither hot nor cold, I will spit you out of My mouth. Because you say, "I am rich, and have become wealthy, and have need of nothing," and you do not know that you are wretched and miserable and poor and blind and naked. (Revelation 3:15–17)

This is one that really hits home for a lot of us, especially in big cities where people tend to flaunt the symbols of their material success.

There is nothing wrong with being financially successful, if your success is the result of God's blessing on your legitimate efforts. But the church at Laodicea reminds us that it's possible to become too successful. And when that happens, Satan has some good ground on which to build a stronghold.

How do you know when you've become too successful? You've become too successful when your focus on the blessings of God on your life has replaced the presence and power of God in your life. You're too successful when the blessing of God has allowed you to upgrade your lifestyle so much that you now have nothing left to give back to Him.

Someone has said there are three types of people: the haves, the have-nots, and the have-not-paid-for-what-they-haves. A lot of us fall into this last category, and God has been squeezed out of our budget and our time.

If you have more today than you have ever had before, and yet God has less of you than He has ever had before, you are a Laodicean Christian. God had a stern warning for this rich, complacent church that had let go of its commitment so it could grab the good life:

> I advise you to buy from Me gold refined by fire, that you may become rich, and white garments, that you may clothe yourself, and that the shame of your nakedness may not be revealed; and eyesalve to anoint your eyes, that you may see. Those whom I love, I reprove and discipline; be zealous therefore, and repent. (Revelation 3:18–19)

These are serious words. Laodicea was a garment-making center, so the people had fine clothes. But spiritually, they were naked. They also made an eye ointment in Laodicea, but the church there was spiritually blind.

The Laodiceans needed to make a few purchases, but not with money. They needed spiritual gold, garments of righteousness, and the eyesalve of the Holy Spirit. These are things that money just can't buy.

I hope you have learned that. Money can buy you a bed, but it can't buy you a good night's sleep. Money can buy you books, but not brains. It can buy you food, but not an appetite. Money can buy you a house, but it can't provide you a home. It can buy you medicine, but not health.

There's one more thing. Money can buy you a cru-
cifix, but not a Savior. When God's people get so
successful we say, "I am rich, and have become wealthy,
and have need of nothing," we make God vomit (Revelation 3:16). He says, "You have need of Me." That's
what Jesus was saying when He said to this church, "Behold, I stand at the door and knock; if anyone hears My
voice and opens the door, I will come in to him, and will
dine with him, and he with Me" (Revelation 3:20). Jesus was knocking on the door of His own church, trying
to get in.

Trouble was, the church of Laodicea had already
moved to a better neighborhood, and He wasn't welcome there. Satan had a stronghold built there, but the
Lord of the church was shut out. It was now up to each
member to welcome Christ.

So even if your church is not responding collective-
ly to Christ, you can still respond individually and enter
into intimate fellowship with Him.

TAKE DOWN THE SIGN?

The story is told of a newlywed couple on their way
home from their honeymoon. A tractor-trailer pulled
out in front of them, and they collided with it. The car
was sent flipping over.

The young groom was OK, but his new bride was
bleeding profusely. The desperate man looked up from
the side of the road and saw a house with a sign that said,
"Dr. Rufus Jones, Internal Medicine."

The young man gently picked up his beloved and
struggled up the hill to the doctor's house. He knocked
feverishly on the door until an old man opened it.

"Are you Dr. Jones?" the young man asked.

"Well, yes, I am," the old man said hesitantly.

"Then please save my wife! She's dying!"

But the old man replied, "I'm sorry, Son, but I can't help you. You see, I stopped practicing medicine many years ago. I don't have any instruments or anything. I just never bothered to take down the sign."

We have a world that is bleeding to death out there. And we're telling people, "Come to the church and you'll find healing for your wounds. Come to the spiritual hospital."

But if we're going to put up a sign that says CHURCH, we had better *be* the church. We don't want people dying on our doorstep because we stopped being the church years ago. Let's tear down Satan's strongholds and be the authentic church Christ intended us to be, or let's take down the sign.

20

TEARING DOWN STRONGHOLDS IN YOUR COMMUNITY

We have covered a lot of biblical ground over the last nineteen chapters, and we're ready to wrap up our study in spiritual warfare.

It's appropriate that we end this book talking about the church's impact in the community, because if our faith doesn't work out on the streets and in the neighborhoods and marketplaces where people live, work, and play, we may as well stay inside the church.

When I use the term *community* in this chapter, by the way, I don't mean just the street you or I live on. I'm using the term for everything from our neighborhoods to entire nations. The community is the world we live in.

It's spiritual warfare out there in the world, and Satan has his strongholds all over the place. If we don't tear them down, there's no one else to do it.

Whole neighborhoods, cities, states, and nations can be under the sway of Satan and his demonic hosts. That's because of the principle we have seen all the way through this book: An invisible spiritual battle in the heavenlies is responsible for the visible battle on earth.

This means that what happens in the heavenly, angelic realm can either make a mess here on earth or fix what's wrong here on earth, depending upon whose forces are carrying the day. Our own sin or our obedience can affect the battle in ways we never dreamed of.

When we talk about satanic strongholds in the community, we are talking about strongholds that could affect government, education, or the private corporate world. The Bible teaches that Satan is in control of the institutions of this world, so his influence can be seen in every sphere.

THE PROBLEM OF COMMUNITY STRONGHOLDS

Colossians 1:16 says that through Christ, God created all things, "both in the heavens and on earth, visible and invisible, whether thrones or dominions or rulers or authorities—all things have been created by Him and for Him."

We have looked at this verse several times before, but let's slow down and study it once more. Paul says the four entities he names were created both in heaven and on earth. So there are heavenly thrones, in other words, and there are earthly thrones. The same is true of dominions, rulers, and authorities.

This means that behind the thrones, dominions, rulers, and authorities we see on earth are thrones, dominions, rulers, and authorities in the heavenly realm.

If you want to tear down strongholds in any of these categories on earth, you must be able to address the problem from the standpoint of heaven. Let me define the four terms Paul uses in Colossians 1:16 because they are societal in nature. They have to do with the community, the world around us.

Four Aspects of a Community

A *throne* is a chair of authority. Kings and queens sit on thrones. America doesn't have a throne, but we have a chair of authority. It's the executive chair the president occupies in the Oval Office of the White House.

A *dominion* is the territory that is ruled by the authority on the throne. America's dominion includes the fifty states and the territories our nation rules around the world.

The third term Paul uses in Colossians 1:16 is *rulers.* A ruler is a specific person who occupies a place of authority, whether that person be the mayor, the governor, the president, the chairman of the board, the king or queen, or whatever. Rulers sit on thrones to rule their dominions.

The fourth term is *authorities.* These are the rules, the laws, the traditions or sanctions that legitimize the throne. In the case of America, our authority is the Constitution. It is the governing document by which the throne rules.

Created for Good

These are the four areas or categories by which life here on earth is organized. What we need to understand is that these entities were created by God, but since government was instituted after the Fall, it is subject to the same spiritual disorders as the rest of creation.

When sin entered the world, it corrupted not only human individuals but also human institutions. Therefore, Satan has his minions operating behind every human institution because we live in a fallen, sinful world.

When you hear of evil people doing evil things through human institutions, those people are being manipulated like puppets on a string by a power outside themselves.

And when good people do good things through human institutions, they reflect the fact that Satan does not control every person in every position of authority. On the contrary, God is still in control and has His people at every level of human government, education, and business. He can and does use fallen people, and even Satan, to accomplish His purposes.

Evil people are still responsible for the evil they do, but what I want us to see is that institutional, structural evil is not just accidental or random. There's a plan operating behind the throne.

Bringing Heaven to Bear on Earth

Therefore, if there is a problem with government or any other sphere of life, ranting and raving and fussing about the people we are up against is not the first thing we need to do. The first thing to do is to get heaven acting on our behalf.

Let me give you an example of what I mean. In the 1960s, there were two basic attempts to change the oppressive laws of the land that propagated segregation in America. One method was the use of violence, of guns and bullets, illustrated by groups like the Black Panthers.

The other method was a movement born in the church and led predominately by the church with Dr. Martin Luther King Jr. at the head. What was impressive about that movement is that it was generated and energized by activism bathed in prayer.

Every time you looked up, whether it was a march or some other event, you saw people getting down on their knees to pray. This was the correct understanding of the situation, because in prayer the people addressed heaven about the mess on earth. They were asking God to do something about the spiritual power that was behind the earthly throne and authority.

Some years ago, a young woman from our church came to my office distraught because her boss was intentionally making her life miserable. He was resisting her even though she was fulfilling her responsibility under God on that job.

Her boss had told her, "I'm going to make sure you don't get a promotion. I don't like you. I don't like your Christianity. I don't like your morals. I'm going to make sure you go nowhere in this company."

She came to me and said, "Pastor, would you pray for me that God would intervene in this situation?" We prayed for about a week.

At the end of that time she came in to see me all excited. I said, "What's going on? Did you find a new job?"

She said, "Let me tell you what Jesus did. When I went in to work yesterday, my boss's office was cleaned out. *His* boss was dissatisfied with his work and fired him. And I was promoted to his job."

That was something I'll never forget. This young woman could have gone to war using the weapons of the flesh. She could have gotten ugly or become vindictive. But instead, she went to war in the heavenlies and there was a change in the power structure on earth.

Unless you believe the world works like this, you won't operate this way. If all you see is the earthly conflict, you'll want to roll up your sleeves and fight. But when you understand the warfare in the heavenlies, it changes your approach.

Satan seeks to control a community through its institutions. Therefore, human institutions have a spiritual dimension to them. This is why there can be structural evil, systemic evil, corporate evil, as well as individual evil.

And yet, as we saw earlier, the Bible says that Jesus Christ created these entities. This means that business, government, and education as created by God are good. It's the intrusion of sin into the structures of this world as well as the people of this world that causes what God meant for good to be used for evil. Satan builds his strongholds in a community through people and institutions that are influenced by the Evil One.

That's why the church must attack institutional and structural evil, just as it attacks other forms of evil, if it wants to have maximum impact in our communities.

A Biblical Example of Strongholds

When it comes to the issue of community strongholds, we have an interesting parallel in the slavery of the Israelites in Egypt. Here was a people enslaved by the institutions of Egypt, by a ruler called Pharaoh who occupied an unrighteous throne.

Demons controlled Pharaoh through the idols of Egypt, its false gods. He had an unrighteous regime with unrighteous laws. For Israel, Egypt was an unjust, oppressive environment.

Exodus 1:6–14 explains how the Israelites' bondage in Egypt came about. Joseph and all of his generation died, yet the people stayed in the land of Egypt. And the people began to multiply—to such an extent that the new Pharaoh, who did not remember Joseph, got worried (vv. 6–9).

Pharaoh saw all those Hebrew boys and could only see one thing: an army of future soldiers who might someday join with Egypt's enemies to fight against him. So Pharaoh devised a plan to subjugate the Israelites:

> "Come, let us deal wisely with them, lest they multiply and in the event of war, they also join themselves to those who hate us, and fight against us, and depart from the land." So they appointed taskmasters over them to afflict them with hard labor. And they built for Pharaoh storage cities, Pithom and Raamses. (Exodus 1:10–11)

Pharaoh rendered the Israelites powerless by subjecting them to slavery, even though they were "more and mightier" than the Egyptians (v. 9). Then he put them to work building storage places for him.

This is exactly what the devil wants to do with the church. He wants to convince us that we are powerless and helpless so we will wind up being satisfied to be slaves. We'll be satisfied to have no victory in our lives, and before long we will be helping Satan out, building storage cities for Pharaoh.

A Theology of Powerlessness

Unfortunately, the church has helped Satan out here by what I call a "theology of powerlessness." This is a theology that says the best we can hope to do is just get by. One reason so many believers are victimized by the theology of powerlessness is that they can't distinguish what is from God and what is from Satan. They wind up resigning themselves to the wrong thing.

The Bible says we are to give thanks in everything (1 Thessalonians 5:18). That does not say we have to give thanks *for* everything. For instance, if your loved one is dying, you don't say, "Thank You, God, that my loved one is dying." You say, "God, I thank You that You are in control of our circumstances, and that You have promised to sustain us with Your love and grace no matter what happens."

You don't have to give thanks for death because death is part of the curse. It's an enemy, a result of sin. We wouldn't know death if it were not for Satan and his rebellion. Death is his weapon.

So in a hard circumstance like the death of a loved one, we have to distinguish between what is of God—grace, peace, strength, and comfort—and what is of the devil—death and decay and the ruin of sin.

If we don't make this distinction, we may wind up passively accepting things from Satan that we should be fighting against with our spiritual weapons. In other words, we accept as unchangeable that which is contrary to the revealed will of God. That is a satanic stronghold.

See, God's intent in any given situation is to build you up and strengthen you and make you more like Christ. Satan's intent in the same situation is to hurt you and tear you down and ultimately to destroy you.

This is like the difference between a doctor cutting you in surgery and a mugger cutting you on the streets. Each one has a knife. Each one makes you bleed. But are they cutting you with the same intent? Not at all.

The doctor wants to heal you. The mugger wants to hurt you. The doctor's intent in surgery is to fix something that's wrong so as to make you stronger. The mugger's intent in cutting you is to disable you and make you weaker.

So although you readily submit to the knife of the doctor in surgery, you don't want to face the knife of the mugger who is trying to cut you on the street.

If you're operating under a theology of powerlessness, when the mugger called Satan comes to hurt you,

you simply say, "Oh well, I can't do anything about this. I'll just have to let Satan carve up my life."

No, you don't have to let Satan carve you up. You have been given powerful weapons to resist him and tear down his strongholds.

Breaking the Enemy's Power

Let me show you how this principle of being able to distinguish between what is of God and what is of the devil works in a community setting. For this we need to go back to Exodus 1.

When Pharaoh saw that putting Israel under slavery wasn't keeping the nation from growing, he ordered the Hebrew midwives to kill all the male Hebrew babies while sparing the female babies.

A messed-up Israelite who felt powerless in the face of the oppressor might say, "Well, this order to kill all the boys is horrible, but there's nothing we can do about it. At least we get to keep our girl babies." That kind of thinking would have allowed Satan to build a stronghold among the Israelites and destroy the nation.

But the Hebrew midwives refused to accept Pharaoh's order as unchangeable. They knew what the will of God was in that situation, so they saved the male babies, and the nation got a liberator in Moses.

The Israelites allowed Pharaoh to enslave them as the enemy had a field day with the nation. But after a while, the people became weary enough of their bondage that they did the right thing. They took their community stronghold problem on earth to heaven:

> Now it came about in the course of those many days that the king of Egypt died. And the sons of Israel sighed because of the bondage, and they cried out; and their cry

for help because of their bondage rose up to God. So God heard their groaning; and God remembered His covenant with Abraham, Isaac, and Jacob. And God saw the sons of Israel, and God took notice of them. (Exodus 2:23–25)

When Israel had had enough of their Egyptian bondage, its people made contact with heaven. And God said, "Let Me come down and do something about this."

The story of Israel's deliverance from Egypt did not begin until the people got tired of their powerlessness and cried out to God. Satan's stronghold over the nation wasn't broken until the people brought the resources of heaven to bear on the institutional structures of Egypt. The Israelites were duped into giving up until they remembered God.

When it comes to our communities, too many times the church is a relief agency and not an army. We just want to patch people up and send them back out to get wounded and enslaved again, instead of setting them free.

God wants to set people free, not just patch them up. He wants them to be fully alive, not just exist. But our neighborhoods, cities, states, and even our nation show the effects of too much patchwork. We don't see God's authentic freedom at work because we are not attacking Satan's strongholds in our communities.

JESUS' POWER OVER COMMUNITY STRONGHOLDS

The power to tear down strongholds on an institutional level is the same power we draw on to tear down personal, family, and church strongholds. It's the power of Jesus Christ.

Colossians 2:14–15 says that through His death on

the cross, Jesus Christ disarmed and triumphed over "the rulers and authorities" that Satan controls and seeks to bring against us to defeat us.

Disarming Satanic Forces

Therefore, by virtue of Jesus' victory, the thrones, dominions, rulers, and authorities mentioned in Colossians 1:16 no longer have the final say. Jesus has overcome them and rendered them powerless.

Remember, we're not saying that human institutions are totally evil. Romans 13:1 says the powers that exist are ordained by God. But the Bible clearly teaches that the systems of this unregenerate world are under Satan's power. "The whole world lies in the power of the evil one" (1 John 5:19).

In fact, instead of writing off our community structures as hopeless, we need to put committed Christians in places of authority where they can bring the righteous rule of Jesus Christ to bear on these institutions. If Christ has conquered the thrones and dominions of this world, we ought to see His victory being reflected in the way our communities function.

Accepting the Church's Assignment

Someone may ask, "Since Christ has already defeated Satan, why doesn't He just go ahead and wipe out all the evil and set up His rule on earth? Why do we have to put up with all this mess?"

Someday, Jesus is going to come back physically and establish His worldwide rule. But until then, He wants us to wrestle against the principalities and powers. Why? The church is the vehicle through which God has chosen to demonstrate His authority in this age.

In other words, the Head of the church has done His

part. He has disarmed Satan and given us all the power and spiritual authority we need. Now He wants His body to do its part, which is to take His victory into every sphere of human life and demonstrate His authority over it.

This is why Paul prayed that we would know "the surpassing greatness of His power toward us who believe" (Ephesians 1:19). Paul went on to explain that power:

> [This is the power] which He brought about in Christ, when He raised Him from the dead, and seated Him at His right hand in the heavenly places, far above all rule and authority and power and dominion, and every name that is named, not only in this age, but also in the one to come. And He put all things in subjection under His feet, and gave Him as head over all things to the church, which is His body, the fulness of Him who fills all in all. (vv. 20–23)

There it is again, just as Paul said in Colossians 2. Christ has been raised and exalted far above all powers, whether earthly or demonic. And because we are seated with Christ in the heavenly places, all of Christ's power and authority are placed at our disposal. We are God's delivery service, taking God's solution to a sick society.

Obeying Our Head

This ought to raise a question in our minds. Since the church is armed with God's authority, and since Satan and his forces have been disarmed and humiliated, why aren't we seeing Christ's victory being reproduced on earth? Why aren't the thrones and rulers and dominions of this earth recognizing the authority of Christ?

There can be only one answer. The church is not doing its job. The body of Christ is not obeying its Head.

Our assignment is to carry out what has been accomplished by Christ on the cross by comprehensively applying all of God's truth to all of life.

If our communities are going over to the enemy, it's because the church is spending too much time within its own walls and not infiltrating society. Such passivity is often made possible by a defeatist theology that uses the imminent return of Christ as an excuse for not seeking cultural transformation. We must seek to disciple the nations while simultaneously looking for the return of Christ.

We have not taken the kingdom of God beyond the four walls of the church. We are only discipling those already in the church, when we have been commanded to disciple the nations (Matthew 28:19–20). We are not out in the world, demonstrating to the powers of this age that Jesus Christ is Lord.

Instead, we have allowed Satan to infiltrate the community and build his strongholds at every level of community life. He now has his way in every institution in society because the church operates under a theology of defeat.

You might think the way to fix this problem is simply to attack Satan's community strongholds through Christian political and social activism—mobilizing believers to get out on the streets and march, to get Christian candidates elected, to get bad laws overturned, and so on.

I want you to understand me clearly. It is good for Christians to be involved in all of these activities. As I write this chapter, a member of our church in Dallas has just been elected chairman of the school board in this city. He is a godly man who has been bringing God's kingdom agenda to bear in the public sphere for a long time. I applaud that.

But the place to start penetrating society and tearing down the institutional and structural strongholds of the enemy is through *prayer*, so that our activism has power and divine direction. Let me remind you of three outstanding examples of what I mean.

THE INCREDIBLE POWER OF PRAYER

God moved the heart of the most powerful king on earth, Artaxerxes of Persia, rebuilt the holy city of Jerusalem, and restored His people through a man named Nehemiah. All of this came about because Nehemiah went on his face before God in prayer (Nehemiah 1:8–11).

Esther was used of God to save the Jews from the institutionalized evil of Haman. But her victory was not achieved until she decided to pray and fast about her course of action. God used her position as the queen to save a nation (Esther 4).

And our old friend Daniel changed the face of the most powerful pagan empire of his day when he went on his face before God in prayer (Daniel 9–10). Without prayer, everything else is a waste of time.

All of these godly leaders were skillful in their work, yet they understood that hard work and socio-political involvement by itself would not be enough to overcome the evil in their societies. Their activities had to be bathed in prayer.

Manifesting Jesus' Victory

Our job as the church is explained in Ephesians 3:10. Paul writes, "That the manifold wisdom of God might now be made known through the church to the rulers and the authorities in the heavenly places."

The church's job is to advertise, to manifest, to work out the victory of Jesus Christ here on earth. That means we must want to make a difference in this satanically controlled, sinful world. It means we don't want our communities held hostage by evil people. It means we want to see the righteousness of Jesus Christ permeate every area of life.

Paul tells us where to begin in demonstrating Jesus' victory on earth. "*First of all,* then, I urge that entreaties and prayers, petitions and thanksgivings, be made on behalf of all men, for kings and all who are in authority" (1 Timothy 2:1–2a, italics added).

Prayer First of All

Paul tells Timothy, "First of all, pray." If we could get believers to respond to calls for prayer the way they respond to other Christian events and programs, the church would be way too much for Satan to handle.

Why? Prayer engages the heavenlies. Paul understood that if you really want to see things change, the first Person you have to talk to is God. If we want to see Satan's strongholds in the community come down, first of all the church needs to go to prayer "for kings and all who are in authority."

The reason is given in the second half of 1 Timothy 2:2: "In order that we may lead a tranquil and quiet life in all godliness and dignity."

Do you want a more peaceful neighborhood? Do you want an environment of peace and tranquillity in which the church is able to maximize its ministry unhindered by hostile authorities? The first thing you need to do is not petition the city council or try to get your party elected into power.

The first thing to do, Paul says, is to carry those public officials to the throne of grace in prayer. We must pray for them because it is the people in authority who can influence and shape the quality of life for those in their domain. We want to influence the influencers, because every earthly throne has a counterpart in the spiritual realm, and what happens in that realm controls what happens in the earthly realm.

But we are also to pray that those in authority might be saved. "[Prayer for those in authority] is good and acceptable in the sight of God our Savior, who desires all men to be saved and to come to the knowledge of the truth" (1 Timothy 2:3–4).

We should pray for the redemption of earthly authorities. And even if they do not come to Christ, we are urged to pray that God might still influence them for good so that we will live tranquil lives.

In other words, the church's prayer life should be so powerful that it helps to shape society. Could it be that we are not seeing more of God's movement in society because rather than praying first, the church is praying as a last resort?

To be sure, our prayers must be married to righteous activism that seeks to tear down the evil in community structures. Without action there is no evidence that we are praying in faith (James 2:17). However, the most dedicated activity in the world won't go very far unless it is rooted in prayer.

Paul also says back in 1 Timothy 2:1 that we should pray for "all men." Our prayers are not limited to those in power. We need to pray that all people will be saved. Everybody has some kind of impact on society.

If you want to pray with power for unsaved people, ask them if they have any needs you can pray for. Let me tell you, when you pray for the needs of unbelievers in order to help them, and help lead them to Christ, God is inclined to act because He desires all people to be saved.

Jesus in Our Midst

I want to leave you with one more passage of Scripture to keep in mind as we close our study on community strongholds and finish the subject of spiritual warfare.

Jesus said in Matthew 18, "If two of you agree on earth about anything that they may ask, it shall be done for them by My Father who is in heaven. For where two or three have gathered together in My name, there I am in their midst" (vv. 19–20).

The issue here is not the number of people praying, because all of us have had occasions where we prayed for something as a group, but God chose not to answer it. The key is our agreement with each other and our agreement with Christ.

Believers must be in unity to see answered prayer. If we are going to be successful in tearing down the powerful satanic strongholds that plague our society, the hands we lift to God in prayer must be "holy hands, without wrath and dissension" (1 Timothy 2:8).

This is even true on the personal and family level. God says the prayers of a husband who does not honor his wife will be hindered (1 Peter 3:7). There must be agreement of heart before there can be agreement in prayer.

That's why the Bible tells the church to be diligent to "preserve the unity of the Spirit in the bond of peace" (Ephesians 4:3). We don't create unity; we just preserve it. God creates unity. Our job is not to let Satan steal it.

So we come together in agreement, praying about the needs in our communities. We agree in asking God to help us storm the strongholds of Satan and bring them down in God's strength.

Notice that we must also come together in Jesus' name (Matthew 18:20). This does not mean just closing our prayers ". . . in Jesus' name. Amen."

Jesus is not our errand boy. His name represents His authority. He must agree with what we are asking for in prayer. This is what prevents people from just asking for whatever they want and expecting Jesus to OK it.

In other words, it doesn't do believers any good to agree on something that Jesus has no intention of doing. That's why the church is not getting more of its prayers answered. We are trying to get Jesus to agree with us and do for us what we want Him to do. Meanwhile, Jesus is trying to get us to agree with *Him*.

If we are in agreement, and Jesus is agreed to what we are asking for, we can pray with power because Jesus has promised to be in our midst when we pray like this.

Let me explain that phrase "in their midst" (v. 20). When you and I gather in a room, Jesus comes in with us because He indwells us. But Jesus can be in you and in me and yet still not be in our midst.

Being in our midst means that Jesus is in the center of the circle. All eyes are focused on Him. He's the object of our attention, and He alone.

We often want Jesus to be the circle and ourselves to be in the center. We say, "Jesus, this is what I want You to do for me today."

Jesus says, "No, you form a prayer circle and put Me in your midst. Put Me in the center of the circle, focus on Me, and find out what I want to do." When we find out what Jesus wants and we pray for that, He can assure us that His Father will answer that prayer, because the Father has never refused the Son.

A Biblical Prayer Formula

So here is a biblical formula for the kind of spiritual warfare praying that brings down satanic strongholds. There must be agreement and unity, we must come together in Jesus' name, and we need to focus on Him, bringing Him into the midst of our prayer circle.

When we do that, and then act in light of God's comprehensive revealed Word, including the application of the revelatory aspects of the Old Testament law, we'll see prayers answered. We'll have power to affect the community that we never thought possible. When Jesus is in our midst, He brings His limitless power along as well.

But unless the church makes Jesus its focus, this world won't get the help it needs. Jesus must be in the middle, all eyes and hearts focused on Him. When we call on His name, then God will shake this world order, until He returns for His millennial rule where He will personally reign as King of kings and Lord of lords!

EPILOGUE

The story is told of a chess champion who was on vacation in Europe. One day, while visiting an art gallery, he came to a particular painting that mesmerized him.

The painting was of a chess game, which deeply interested this chess champion. But this painting depicted a chess game like no other this man had ever seen. On one side of the chessboard was the devil, laughing, full of gaiety and even frivolity. He had his hand on the board getting ready to make a move.

On the other side of the chessboard was a young man who was shaking and trembling all over. His knees were knocking, sweat was coming down his forehead, tears were coming from his eyes, and he was biting his fingernails.

The chess champion came to understand the meaning of the portrait when he saw the title: "Checkmate." The devil was about to make the final move to win this young man's soul. The devil was laughing, while the young man was terrified because he knew he couldn't do anything about it.

The chess champion was so taken by this portrait that he studied it for several hours. Then he broke out into a smile and went to look for the proprietor of the art gallery. "Sir, would you happen to have a chessboard here?"

The staff scurried around and found an old chessboard. The champion put the chessboard at the base of the painting and set it up to duplicate exactly the arrangement of the chess pieces on the board in the portrait.

After he had done this, the man looked at the portrait, then looked down at the chessboard. He did this several times, looking back and forth between the painting and the board. Then he turned the chessboard to the young man's side of the painting and said, "Young man, I wish you could hear me right now, because if you could, you could stop trembling and wipe the tears from your eyes. I have good news for you.

"I'm a chess champion, and I know this game backward and forward. You are trembling for no reason at all. It only looks like the devil has the final move. He has tricked you, but there is still one more move left on the board. Your life can be transformed. The devil doesn't get to make the last move."

The human race is in the same position as the young man in the painting. It looks like the devil has won the chess game of history, and people are trembling in fear.

But we have a Champion who will make the last move on the devil! God made the first move in this cosmic contest when He created the world, which included all the angelic host. Satan countered that move by rebelling and taking a third of the angels with him in his rebellion.

God countered that move by creating Adam, who would be His new representative to rule over earth. Then Satan tempted Adam and Eve to rebel against the authority of God. God then provided redemption for Adam and Eve so they could be brought back into fellowship with God.

Satan tried to counter that move by getting Cain to kill his brother Abel in order to cut off the godly line. However, God reintroduced the godly line through the birth of Seth. Not to be outdone, Satan's countermove was to lead the entire world into rebellion against God.

Oh, but God had another countermove to make. He found a righteous man named Noah and commanded him to build a boat, providing salvation for a family and wiping out the rest of the world.

So Satan found his own man, Nimrod, and tempted him and his friends to build a kingdom in an attempt to be independent of God, a move that led to the judgment of the Tower of Babel.

That's when God made a brilliant countermove, going to Ur of the Chaldeans to call a man named Abraham and send him to Canaan to become the father of a righteous nation.

Satan countered God's move by causing Israel to become enslaved in Egypt. God sent Moses to Egypt to tell Pharaoh, "Let My people go." Satan tried to pin Israel against the Red Sea so they would be destroyed by the Egyptian army. But God countered Satan's move by opening and closing the Red Sea at the right time.

That's the way it was throughout the Old Testament, God and Satan countermoving in a cosmic struggle. Of course, the ultimate outcome was never in doubt, because Satan has never been a match for God. As the Old Testament closes, there is a period of four hundred silent years when Israel receives no word from God. But when God's time is right (Galatians 4:4), the New Testament opens with His greatest move of all. He sends His Son to enter history as the virgin-born Son of Mary and to die on the cross and rise again.

The coming of Jesus Christ was God's greatest move in this spiritual "chess game" called spiritual warfare. Jesus decisively defeated Satan for all of time and eternity and stripped the devil of his power. Then He called out a people for Himself, the church which is His body, and invested us with all the spiritual authority necessary to carry out the victory Christ won on Calvary.

Through Jesus Christ, our victory over Satan has already been secured. Satan has no countermove that can thwart what Jesus has done. Our task now is to announce and to manifest God's victory over Satan by the way we live in our personal, family, church, and community lives.

INDEX OF SCRIPTURE

INDEX OF SUBJECTS